William Ferguson Beatson Laurie

Ashé Pyee, the Superior Country or the Great Attractions of Burma to British Enterprise and Commerce

William Ferguson Beatson Laurie

Ashé Pyee, the Superior Country or the Great Attractions of Burma to British Enterprise and Commerce

ISBN/EAN: 9783337230180

Printed in Europe, USA, Canada, Australia, Japan

Cover: Foto ©Suzi / pixelio.de

More available books at **www.hansebooks.com**

ASHE PYEE,

THE SUPERIOR COUNTRY;

OR,

The Great Attractions of Burma to British Enterprise and Commerce.

BY

COLONEL W. F. B. LAURIE,

AUTHOR OF "OUR BURMESE WARS AND RELATIONS WITH BURMA," ETC.

"Look here upon this picture, and on this."
HAMLET, *Act* 3, *Scene* 4.

It is evident that the country and the people have before them a great future."
SIR ARTHUR PHAYRE, *at the Society of Arts, May* 1881.

LONDON:
W. H. ALLEN & CO., 13 WATERLOO PLACE,
PALL MALL, S.W.

1882.

PREFACE.

READER, this is a peaceful book. Unlike its far larger and more ambitious predecessor, it does not deal with war. Peace, national security, and commercial prosperity are its watch-words; and if these three can be perpetuated and extended in the "superior country" here under consideration, without war and without annexation, the greater will be the triumph of British statesmanship. Lord Ripon, wishing to carry out the spirit of Lord Canning's proclamation of 1858, last year declared that the continuation of Native States was an advantage to such states, and to Great Britain. Of course, there must be exceptions to such a wise, general rule. Great Britain, unfortunately, too often finds herself, while endeavouring to civilise mankind, in the position of the Psalmist, who was for peace while his enemies sought for war. Peace on earth is still very far distant. Nowhere seems she to find "rest with men." The Burmese Question, in the humble opinion of the writer, should now occupy the large share of public attention which has been given throughout the past year or more to Afghanistan; and when the Viceroy has so forcibly remarked that peace and rest are the real wants of India, in order that the country might "devote itself to the improvement of its agriculture and commerce"—our late military successes and upholding of British prestige in the former region affording suitable opportunity for such a remark—turning from Afghanistan to Burma at this time would seem to be a natural and prudent step. It is just one from financial ruin to financial prosperity, with Commerce beckoning to her enterprising supporters to come on. As a practical subject of the first importance, the Burmese comes far nearer to us than many other questions; for in its settlement a lasting good is sure to follow; while as regards the solution of other weighty national problems, it must candidly be said, at present—

> "The dawn is overcast, the morning lours,
> And heavily in clouds brings in the day."

Is it not pleasing, then, to turn from such gloomy prospects, and give attention to where Hope, on practical grounds, pictures the dawn of a prosperous and tranquil day breaking out in all Burma; a land in these fast times of education and so-called national enlightenment shamefully unknown to the intelligent classes of Great Britain. However tribes may be warring against tribes in the East at the present time—however wily European diplomatists may be looking out for the decline of Albion's influence in Asia—let us be placed on sound and profitable as well as peaceful relations with the people of our next-door neighbour, Upper Burma. With the lower portion of the country under our control, paying for years past a surplus revenue of some millions sterling to the Indian Imperial Treasury, surely the upper portion demands far more attention than it has yet received; for, as hereafter will be urged, the real interests of the two are inseparable. But, look on the two pictures—on British and Independent Burma; what a difference in local progress, happiness, and prosperity! And what a tremendous difference between the results of the last Afghan and the Second Burmese Wars. There is something terribly monotonous about many of the political questions of the day. "Fresh woods and pastures new" are urgently required by politicians as well as by the public. In the spirit of what Grattan said of Ireland, when he gave her a free trade by opening all her harbours, we may yet hope to see the land of the Golden Foot "rise from her bed and get nearer to the sun." It may hereafter form the subject of grand debates in Parliament. When the great governing intellects now grappling with a most serious and distressing question at home shall have conquered every difficulty, they may, perhaps, devote some of the working of their comprehensive and practical minds to long-neglected Burma and the Burmese Question, which is simply—"Can we establish sound political and commercial relations with Upper Burma?" Although written or compiled with much peaceful intent, this little book may be deemed a fitting companion to *Our Burmese Wars and Relations with Burma*; and in a brief space the writer has endeavoured to entertain as well as instruct. With a special view to this end, the last three or four chapters are submitted to public notice.

To the London Press the Author is very thankful for the kind, judicious, and frequently elaborate critiques his former work had the honour to receive from those competent to form an opinion; while to other would-be censors who were not competent—lacking, as they did, the chief requisites for a critic, information and impartiality—he is also obliged, as such amiable *littérateurs*, taking up a somewhat novel and important Eastern subject, may eventually be led, through careful study, to become kinder or wiser men, and better critics.

The Author cannot conclude this Preface without remarking on the strange contrast between the state of affairs at the end of the last and close of the preceding year. In 1879, all was uncertainty and "toil and trouble" in Afghanistan. Fighting before Cabul; attacks on General Roberts; warning to Ayub Khan, as to his holding Herat; with numerous Russian intrigues in Central and Western Asia; while in Eastern, the Chinese seemed to be going ahead in their usual way. And, also, at the close of 1879, although there appeared to be little chance of our being launched into a serious war with Upper Burma, there was a great dispute between the Chief of Karennee and King Theebau, which might have led to blows. At the end of 1880, things became more settled. A political enchanter seemed to be at work; success after disaster cheered us on in Afghanistan; and although a British Resident was sadly wanted at Mandalay, the Burmese capital, to supervise the Golden Foot, and procure valuable information, the spirit of affairs was changed, as if by magic. True enough, China appeared to be more resolute than ever to defy

Russia in her long course of hereditary aggression; while the brave and energetic Skobeleff was engaged among the fierce Turkomans. Then China was ordering Austrian ordnance rifles, in preference to the German, thereby showing independent action and practical knowledge in the selection of arms. On the whole, things were in a far better condition throughout Eastern Asia, than they had been for some time but, during the first half of 1881, affairs again, in certain quarters, became somewhat shrouded in mystery. Upper Burma—too long silent for any good—appeared to be resuming, through its capricious and monopolising King, the old ways of error; while China was about to conclude a remarkable treaty with Russia—a treaty of the cession of Kuldja (or Ili on the part of the Russians, to be immediately followed up by the opportune annexation of the great Trans-Caspian region of the Turkomans—all giving the vast Northern Power, in Central Asia (and, of course, in other parts) an amount of political influence in the East unexampled in our time. If Russia is ever to be predominant in Central Asia, it would, of course, be suicidal to our Eastern Empire not to keep her clear of approach towards India, S.W. China, and Burma. No doubt, with our usual pluck, we shall always be able to do this, but we must look more to Eastern

Asia ; and if only sufficient attention were now paid to Upper Burma, we might check various ambitious designs, while a change for the better might be effected by us in that "superior country"—so valuable and yet so little known at home to the enlightened English statesman and the keen British merchant—which attention would certainly, ere long, bring us in both wealth and honour.

W. F. B. L.

LONDON, *July* 1881.

P.S.—It was intended to publish this little work about the middle of the year; but deserted London, and the three grand Questions on the tapis—the Egyptian, the Transvaal, and the Irish—would have precluded many readers from looking into the condition and prospects of Burma. Advantage has been taken of the delay to continue a miscellaneous record of events, with remarks thereon, from July to October, which, as for the previous months, the writer trusts will add to the utility and interest of his volume—probably the conclusion of his pleasant labours on the subject of Ashé Pyee, the Superior Country.

October, 1881.

CONTENTS.

CHAPTER V.

CHAPTER VI.

CHAPTER VII.

CHAPTER VIII.

CHAPTER IX.

SUPPLEMENTARY CHAPTER.

MISCELLANEOUS RECORD.

ADDENDA TO CHAPTER IV.

ASHÉ PYEE,

THE SUPERIOR COUNTRY.

CHAPTER I.

THE BURMESE QUESTION.—I.

TOWARDS the end of 1879, the writer concluded his volume on *Our Burmese Wars and Relations with Burma*, with a brief account of events before and after the British Resident's departure from Mandalay.* The Envoy having "stalked away," the Burmese Nero and his advisers at the capital were left to the dictates of their own sweet will. Massacres, burying alive, and every other iniquity associated with the cruel "dark places of the earth" might be perpetrated, and humane and generous Great Britain not be one whit the wiser; for, although the Resident was never told one half of the deeds of dreadful note committed in the Palace, still, while he remained at Mandalay, there was always some information forthcoming to freeze the blood, or make our hairs stand on end "like quills upon the fretful porcupine."

Speedily an important opinion was entertained at Rangoon that, in the event of a campaign, it would be rendered

* Page 466.

easier if, on the declaration of hostilities, Nyoung-Yan (or Nyoungyan) were publicly recognised as the British nominee, and received with royal honours, while a proclamation was issued placing him on the Burmese throne. This was considered by some to be preferable to the "violent act" of annexation, while others were firmly convinced that we must in some fashion or other—to secure the peace and advance the prosperity of British Burma—reign supreme at Mandalay.*

Early in December, a Burmese Embassy, which had been for some time detained at Thayetmyo, awaiting permission from the Indian authorities to proceed, received a communication from the Viceroy, through the Chief Commissioner (Mr. Aitchison), recording the Viceroy's serious dissatisfaction with "the position and treatment of our Resident lately at the Burmese Court." The Embassy had "not come with authority to propose anything likely to be acceptable." A reference to the Court for further instructions was advised; otherwise the Ambassador could not be received.† The Embassy remained at Thayetmyo awaiting instructions from Mandalay. And so the author concluded a somewhat "eventful history," at a most uncertain stage of our relations with Burma. Time went on, and with the disappearance of our Resident from the Burmese Court, the "merry," but cruel and inexperienced monarch, Theebau, and the really valuable land of the Golden Foot, lost much of their interest. Attention in the East was now almost wholly concentred on the wild bleak mountains

* Page 47 † Page 476.

and hills, the extensive tracts of waste land, and here and there the fertile plains and valleys of Afghanistan, destined to cost England so much blood and so many millions which might have been useful elsewhere.

Early in the New Year (1880) it was expected that papers regarding Theebau and our relations with Burma were to be asked for in the House of Commons. But it was evidently not a convenient season to grant them, for none were forthcoming. The present writer had gladly hoped that the production of such documents would draw attention to the subject of Burmese affairs. In a despairing mood he wrote to the coming Premier, who was soon to commence his second brilliant campaign in Midlothian, even from one who with a rare method finds time for everything, hardly expecting an answer. But an answer did come, and very soon; and the *musmûn* (purport) of it, as we say in Hindustani, was an ardent wish "to understand the painful question raised in Burma, on which but little light seems to have been thrown by discussions in the public press."* And again, with a generous solicitude regarding an Anglo-Indian author's work:—"It cannot be otherwise than a work of great interest and value at the present moment"; also, it would not prove "insensibility to the importance of the subject if he did not find an early opportunity of examining it."† Recently, like some far less great, yet able and energetic financiers, having been at war with deficits in Indian and other budgets, of course the Chancellor of the Exchequer could have found

* February 6th, 1880. † February 25th, 1880.

but little time for the study of Burmese affairs; but it may be hoped that if more deficits are to be discovered, and relief sought for, British economists and calculators will turn their serious attention to the undeveloped resources of Upper, and our own possession of British Burma, where, in proportion to the population, the trade is more than ten times greater than that of magnificent and populous India!

The eastern country, "superior to all others," could expect little attention during the unsettled state of Afghanistan. The elections naturally made the subject less than a secondary consideration; and there can be no doubt that the English people are always touched most by what is nearest to them, or, according to Dr. Johnson, we secure the mind's attention to "domestic rather than Imperial tragedies."

It is passing strange, but nevertheless a fact, that, towards the close of the nineteenth century, when education has done so much for our country, there are millions of intelligent people who, for the time, would look with greater concern on the destruction of the Crystal Palace or the Alhambra than they would exhibit if we lost India or British Burma! It will be long before Great Britain really begins to appreciate the vast political and commercial importance of her splendid Eastern Empire.

As time advanced, occasional great events were reported from Mandalay. The King had long surrendered himself to the Nâts (spirits), and was more superstitious than ever. Intelligence of Nât propitiation, cruel massacres, burying alive, small-pox, and so forth, came from Rangoon. The steady, wise old Woons (ministers) about the Court had changed the King's warlike intentions towards the British. It was necessary, therefore, to find some other kind of excitement at the capital; for lotteries, general gambling, drinking, and the reported currency of lead for copper, had done their work. April and May (1880) were probably contemplative months at Mandalay; but at the end of the latter month, action in the shape of a rebellion began to ring through the Burmese land.

Should the reader have the writer's last volume beside him, at page 387 he will find it recorded that (in February 1879) the Nyoungyan and Nyoungoke Princes, brothers, had found it expedient to flee with their families from the Palace of Mandalay. They first took refuge in the British Residency, but were, after a time, sent down to Rangoon, and thence to Calcutta. The Nyoungyan Prince was the favourite in the succession, and King Mengdon, Theebau's father, had desired his election. However, young Theebau got the throne, and became, with apparent ease, Lord of all the White Elephants, of Golden Umbrellas, and of Earth and Air. The chief hope of the brothers, it may be presumed, was now that Theebau's reign might be a short and a merry one, which, judging from the chapter on the Royal Progress,* seemed a contingency not far distant. Nyoungoke at length proved himself to be more impatient and ambitious than his elder brother, Nyoungyan. With a small force of "raiders" (May 24, 1880) he suddenly appeared near the British frontier, cut the telegraph

* See Paper VI., "A Sketch of King Theebau's Progress," in *Our Burmese Wars and Relations with Burma*, page 374.

between our boundary and Mandalay; and so began what seemed like a bold and determined endeavour to stir up a rebellion against King Theebau. The insurgents, at first successful, were repulsed at Minhla, some sixty miles from the frontier, defended by Royal troops, guns, and a fort. The Burmese local authorities became speedily alarmed at the insurrection, and the Woon (governor) of Sillaymyo* had (25th) seized the *Yunan*, British steamer, bound from Mandalay to Rangoon. It was said that the silly Woon pretended to believe that the English had invaded his country. However that may be, the steamer was detained for thirty-six hours.

A few days after this detention—in some respects as great an insult as that which brought on the second Burmese War—it was announced from Thayetmyo that the insurgents were encamped near the boundary pillar, and the Burmese Government had addressed a communication to the British Government, through the Burmese Commissioners, who were still at Thayetmyo, to the effect that the insurrection was only a sort of dacoit outbreak,† and had "no political significance." No notice, it was asserted, had been taken of this despatch, because "all friendly intercourse and show of courtesy" had ceased between the representatives of the two Governments. With reference to the Burmese Embassy—which seemed to be a political or diplomatic fixture—by the middle of May the Chief Commissioner had written to the Ambassadors

* A village on the banks of the Irawadi, about twenty-five miles above Minhla.

† One of plunderers.

at Thayetmyo that it was "necessary to postpone their business for the present." The Embassy was requested to return to Mandalay, at a time when the telegraph to that station was interrupted. It was further announced from Rangoon that the evidence was complete that certain contemplated April sacrifices had been begun, and "were only stopped on the representation of the Ambassadors that the British Government would intervene." There was constant quarrelling and intriguing among the Ministers at Mandalay; and, "in spite of Mr. Aitchison's letter," the Embassy still remained at Thayetmyo * The Embassy had positively done nothing to improve our relations with Theebau and Upper Burma; but "a variety of obviously inadmissible and grotesquely incongruous propositions and pretensions were put forward by the Burmese Government," and the various points already at issue between the two Governments were steadily ignored The Envoy was told that if he was not likely soon to have something more satisfactory to suggest he should return "as speedily as convenient." He could not be got to specify the questions which he was empowered to discuss; and, after requesting leave to move forward to Rangoon, he had been "reminded that, according to all diplomatic usages, a substantial basis and the definite points for the negotiation must be settled before a personal discussion can begin."† But it would be easier to square the circle than obtain such desirable hypotheses; and not even a Talleyrand or a Lord Palmerston could have advantageously extracted a substantial

* *Daily News.* † *Times* Correspondent.

basis or a definite point from a wily Burmese diplomatist. The Burmese idea of diplomacy in Mandalay at the present time is a brief but comprehensive one. It simply amounts to this: "Restore Pegu, with all her fine ports, to the Golden Foot, and we will trade with you as much as you like; but there are certain time-honoured monopolies which the King *must* have; Free Trade must leave these alone," concluding in the style of the old Burmese State papers—*This is Burman custom!* And so the unchangeable rulers of the Burman race, in an age of progress, strive to obstruct the mighty advancing tide of human thought and civilisation.

By the middle of June, it was thought that the rebellion in Upper Burma had entirely collapsed; but this was a mistake, as followers of the adventurous Prince were springing up in several directions. There can be little doubt, if Nyoungoke had played his cards well, and with some military genius, he might have paid King Theebau a visit at Mandalay during the month of June; and it was said, probably with some truth, that had Nyoungyan appeared on the scene, he "would have commanded a much larger following than his brother." But he wisely remained in Calcutta—like Abdul Rahman for Afghanistan—the "coming man" for Burma. The Burmese Envoy at Thayetmyo had at last left. Strong hints, and, it was said, threatened stoppage of allowances—the best hint of all—at length sent him back to Mandalay, where, doubtless, he was not received in a very gracious manner by his Sovereign. It was again well said that the future position of the British Resident at Mandalay appeared to be "one essential preliminary point for determination before the question of diplomatic relations could be effectively entered upon, and on that point he had no satisfactory proposals to make."

After some fruitless efforts on the part of the Prince, the King's troops, headed by the only available Bandoola, the Mingoon Woon, arrived on the frontier by steamer, entirely defeated the insurgents, and gained a practically "bloodless" victory. Prince Nyoungoke's was a rather inglorious end; he was captured by our police, lodged in the Circuit house of Thayetmyo, and strongly guarded, previous to his being sent back to Calcutta.

By the end of June, the rebellion had completely collapsed. Nyoungoke was considered to have "abused the asylum afforded to him by us, in that he made our frontier the base for his attack on Burma." He was sent back under arrest to Calcutta, where he arrived early in July. King Theebau was apparently becoming conciliatory, and had been drilling very small bodies of troops at Mandalay.

It was telegraphed from Calcutta* that Mr. Bernard had taken over the Chief Commissionership from Mr. Aitchison, who had proceeded to Simla to take his seat in Council. At a dinner given by the Rangoon community on the occasion, in his speech Mr. Barnard gave no indication as to the policy which would be pursued by the British Government regarding Burma; but it would not be one of annexation. "To be, or not to be," with reference to Upper

* *Times* Correspondent, July 11th.

Burma's independence, then,—or, more directly, in the case of King Theebau, the French translator's rendering *Vivre ou mourir*,*—was not yet "the question." And it was highly necessary that "Afghan complications" should pass quite away before the necessary amount of public interest could be concentrated on Burmese affairs.

As to the present Golden Foot, it has been remarked to the writer, by a learned and zealous Member of Parliament, that he may not be so black as he has been painted; but at this stage, the remarks of an able and acute military officer, who knows Upper and Lower Burma very well, may be usefully cited:—"Until Upper Burma is blessed with a ruler who will not consider it his only duty to sit in his palace, and listen to accounts of his country, which are only framed with a view to tickle his ear and flatter his vanity, the country will never improve; and a policy of interference may be forced upon us, however reluctant we may be to enter upon it, for the protection of our trading interests."

Thus, the Burmese is, in many respects, essentially a commercial question, as, in fact, nearly all the questions of lasting importance which come forth on Eastern Asia, must invariably be. Of "a very fine country," the highly-intelligent officer already quoted gives a most flourishing description. To use the language of Richard Cobden, in an essay written by him in 1836, upon Russia, Turkey, and England, Upper Burma may be described with regard to its present backward condition commercially, as follows:—

* Être, ou pas être ?

"Nothing but a tyrannical despotism, at once sanguinary and lawless, could have had the effect of repelling commerce from its noble water highways; but, alas! the thousands of merchants who might have been tempted to embark in profitable commercial speculations, would have sought in vain for the rich freights of silk, cotton, wool, cutch, earth-oil, and precious stones, which ought to have awaited their advent. Such is the character of its rulers, that no native capitalists even have been emboldened to accumulate a store of merchandise to tempt the rapacity of a dissolute set of kings."

Regarding the Burmese Embassy, King Theebau and the British Government, the British public are much indebted to a London Correspondent* at Rangoon, who was most zealous in furnishing interesting information. Before the departure of Naingangya Woondouk (in this case a diplomatic Secretary of State), the chief of the Embassy, from Thayetmyo, it appeared that the Deputy Commissioner (Colonel Davies) had informed that high functionary, by order of the Viceroy, of Lord Lytton's wish to leave his successor perfectly free to take up the subject of a treaty with the King of Burma, or leave it alone. During the settlement of the difficulty in Afghanistan—unless in a case of actual invasion—it was not easy to find leisure for the discussion of Burmese affairs; and as there did not seem to be any intention on the part of the Embassy to come to a settlement, as had been suggested six months before, nothing could be more reasonable than the request, by letter, to leave for Mandalay. The letter to

* *Daily News*, July 9th, 1880.

the Woondouk, wrote the above Correspondent towards the middle of June, "is all the more unexpected, because the general idea among the Burmans was that, with Mr. Gladstone in power, they would be able to conclude a treaty immediately, and get all they asked for. The *Mandalay Gazette* exulted over the return of the Liberals to power, and said, 'The new Premier, as a Knight of the Tsalwé, will be reasonable, and not persist in the foolish and presumptuous course of his predecessor.'" To have been reasonable where no reason existed, would have puzzled even a cleverer and more shrewd statesman than the late Premier. The Correspondent proceeds to give us some interesting particulars regarding "the boast of heraldry, the pomp of power," in Burma, to which I shall add a note, also new: "It may probably be news to most people in England, that Mr. Gladstone is a Knight of the most elephantine and ancient Burmese Order of Knighthood; but it is a fact nevertheless. The late King, Mengdon Meng, sent him by the Kinwoon Mingyee the collar of the fifteen strings, the second in rank under that of the princes of the blood, who have twenty-one strings. The King himself has twenty-four. The knights of premier rank glory in eighteen." This badge of the order of nobility among the Burmese consist of six classes.† From the highest authority, I shall now state as follows:—Some Orientalists and others appear to entertain the idea that there is an order styled "The Golden Sun of Burma"; but there is no such order. However, the King of Burma claims descent from

* For an account of the order of the Tsalwé (or Tsalway), see General Fytche's *Burma Past and Present*, vol i. p. 232 (*note*).

the Kshatrya Rajas of India of the "solar race," and confers titles, adopting the recipients into the "race of the sun." Perhaps this is what is alluded to by those who bring forward the "Golden Sun of Burma" to enlighten the public.

After this brief digression, it may be well to return to the Rangoon Correspondent, who reported at the end of June that King Theebau was "making a great show of being civil to us," giving some interesting particulars regarding the Naingangya Woondouk. From these we may learn the wholesome lesson how great men in the East in office sometimes escape punishment, just as they do occasionally in Russia, Turkey, and other European countries. Such a vast amount of material for future history is now furnished by Correspondents of the London press, that it is folly to neglect what is thus presented to us even in our own time. We have yet to learn that there is more in a Woon or a Woondouk than "is dreamt of in our philosophy." The Naingangya "on his way up in the ambassadorial steamer, took on board the Woon of Sillaymyo, the official who so unceremoniously detained the mail steamer *Yunan*. No doubt with a lively sense of what might very possibly be soon his own fate, the Woondouk had the over-energetic governor put in irons, and, on his arrival in Mandalay, forthwith handed him over to the Illot, with a vivid description of the wrath of the British Government at the prisoner's proceedings." The Woondouk hoped that his own diplomatic failure might possibly be overlooked. "The Sillaymyo Woon's case occupied all the attention of the Ministers. He was thrown into prison, there to await trial by the Illot Dau, the Supreme Court." It was then thought that the Sillaymyo Woon would lie a few weeks or days in confinement, escape, hang about Man dalay for a few months, and finally get "a richer province than that he lately governed."* Such, it was believed, had been hitherto the way of punishing offenders against the British Government; but on this occasion it was the Irawadi Flotilla Company—doubtless, for their own advantage—they earnestly wished to conciliate; and so it was arranged that the captains should not be summoned on shore, but be visited by the governors (with a very small unarmed escort) if thought necessary. Thus was the Court of Mandalay beginning to assume the virtue of civility towards the British, though, as yet, in reality they had it not; and such behaviour—not of yesterday's date—tends to render the solution of the Burmese question by no means easy.

At present, then, the question is hardly one of annexation. It has become—and, perhaps, very properly—a question of conciliation. If anything can be given better than annexation, if any *permanent* plan can be brought forward to avoid it, let us have it by all means; and the present writer fearlessly produces the following arguments against the violent and distasteful measure, unless it be strongly forced upon us. "Many men not conversant with Burmese and Chinese frontier affairs have advocated the annexation of Upper Burma, more, perhaps, from a commercial standpoint than from sound policy; but annexation from any point of view must be condemned." "All that is required in Upper Burma is a friendly and capable

* *Daily News*, July 26th, 1880.

Government. Annexation is out of the question" "We have got quite as much as we want of Indo-Chinese soil." In answer to the sentiments of a "commercial friend," one of the warlike element (who considers annexation "impossible") thus remarks:—"I think Mr. Aitchison (the Chief Commissioner), than whom there is not an abler nor an honester servant of the Empress at present in her Eastern dominions, has 'no voice or stomach' for annexation, but he would desire to see 'good government' introduced into the King's dominions, peaceably if possible; if not, then by means of guns, sniders, and British soldiers to use them." The mercantile gentleman—a gentleman to the backbone—remarks: "The country is full of wealth which only requires the commonest form of just government to tap and draw off. Now that all the mischief that can be done to trade has been done, and troops are on the spot, it is to be hoped that Government will make such arrangements—be they in the form of annexation or of a definite treaty with suitable guarantee for fulfilment—as will put trade on a secure basis, and prevent the recurrence of a similar commercial crisis." The stern and able representative of the "warlike element" replies: "Although, my merchant friend, trade is not *everything*, there appeared to be no necessity to bring over those troops,* which, as you say, have caused a paralysis of trade. No; it would have been wiser and more economical to have got them

* The present writer does not agree on this point; he considers that it was absolutely necessary to send over reinforcements at the time (1879). See *Our Burmese Wars and Relations with Burma*, pp. 389, 393.

ready as for employment elsewhere, and if King Thibo (Theebau) showed any desire to fight with a view of recovering lost territory, we might have allowed the 'Golden Foot' to be caught in the trap. But where divided counsels prevail, then, my friend, many other things besides commerce become submerged." No wonder that our relations with the King of Burma have recently been the subject of much comment, both in the English and Indian press; and, in the words of the mercantile friend, "much has been written to which the word misrepresentation might truthfully be applied." He is also of opinion that, "it is difficult in a few words to take up the subject of the political situation, which, speaking from a commercial point of view, is a very grave one at present." This writer—a member of the Chamber of Commerce at Rangoon, who, in May 1879, sent an article on the "State of Affairs in Burma" to the *Glasgow Herald*, from which the foregoing extracts are taken—is further of opinion that, "even now, the only causes of depression of trade in the King's territory and Mandalay are imported from British territory, where rumours of annexation are daily promulgated by those whose interests lie in that direction; and with the exception of merchants who have large stakes outstanding in the country, directly and indirectly nearly everybody is included in this category." Again, the shrewd merchant makes the following very pithy remark, which, beyond all question, has considerable truth in it:—"Upper Burma occupies pretty much the relation to British Burma that a lunatic asylum does to a contiguous private residence. It is a constant object of dread to the merchant, and from a political point of view, it is a standing menace to British power and prestige in the East." With reference to "rumours of annexation," and the apparent desire of the mercantile community at Rangoon for war, I can bring forward as an undeniable fact, that, when at Rangoon in 1864, I found the feeling to exist in a remarkable degree. And knowing this, when about to re-publish my third paper on Burma, on the progress of trade, and the prospects of Pegu,* I should have considered that the "Brief Review" bore on the face of it proof that the information had been culled from, if not all written by, one of the "Merchant Kings" of Rangoon, who, it was said, strove their best to bring on a war in order to "settle their accounts"; *i.e.* balance their books as to goods sent on credit to Mandalay and not paid for. Then such sentences in the paper as "Rangoon is behindhand in facilities for repairing vessels," true in 1864, has not been so for some years past; yet I left the remark without any corrective note.

But we must not leave our gifted friend of the "warlike element" without deriving some more benefit from his company, which, it is to be hoped, will cause the British public —above all, rising politicians and statesmen who would seek a new and splendid ground for debate—to take more interest than ever in the Burmese question.

This "military man," then, who, in his useful career, resided for some little time under most favourable circumstances at Mandalay, under two very different Residents, is evidently a man of very decided views. For instance, he

* *Our Burmese Wars, &c.*, p. 346.

considers annexation as being "worse than the futile attempts on that detestable Afghan frontier of Northern India in this direction have hitherto proved to be." After describing the magnificent valley of the Irawadi, he arrives at the northern boundary line separating this valley or Pegu, from the territory of Upper Burma. It is marked by a line of stone pillars; and standing on one of these, not far from Meeaday, on the left bank of the river, the great Pro-Consul, Lord Dalhousie, "the father of British Burma," in 1853, declared, before a small yet brilliant assembly of sunburnt men, "that Pegu had passed into the possession of Queen Victoria and her heirs, and he added:—

> "I have heard some of my friends, whom I see around me, say, we now want but roads, canals, and railways, to make this a wealthy, flourishing, populous, and prosperous province; but I say, gentlemen, for many years to come, no other highways will be required than those already provided by bountiful Nature, to this province, viz. her magnificent water highways, including this noble river, the Irawadi, on whose banks we are now standing."*

There is perhaps no picture in British Eastern history so strikingly grand, so prophetic of the prosperity of a newly-conquered country, as this. When, in some future day, instead of Lower Burma, after defraying the cost of every branch, furnishing only a million or two to the Indian Imperial Exchequer, Burma shall furnish her ten or more millions, the figure of Lord Dalhousie on the boundary pillar, near Meeaday, as he reaches the spot, will pass before the intelligent and inquiring traveller. The Burmese question, long resolved into a prosperous settle-

* See also *Our Burmese Wars, &c.*, p. 309.

ment, will then, like other important questions, in all probability be forgotten. "This line of pillars," says our military friend, "leaves the Arakan hills at a point called 'the ever visible peak,' and running east, passes the Irawadi at fifty miles distant from its commencement, and thence on, still eastwards, forty-three miles, to the Pegu Yoma range of hills; thirty-three miles further on, it crosses the Sittang, and finally the pillars lose themselves in a desert of mountains thirteen miles further east." And now, with the same apparent hatred of extension of frontier as he displays towards Afghanistan, he says, *This is that misty easterly frontier which may lead us we know not where, unless great caution is exercised.*

Again, "Telegraph lines extend over the Pegu province, and it only remains to complete the line of the Irawadi Railway eventually to Mandalay, and perhaps on to Bhamo, when we have a reasonable being on the throne of Upper Burma to deal with."

Truly, the "steady increase in the prosperity and progress of British Burma, since it came under our rule, can hardly be equalled, and certainly not surpassed, by any other province or portion of the Empire, in the East." And from Burma British Indian financiers may take an instructive lesson, that "Had India been less extravagantly dealt with, perhaps it might have been financially sound."

The comparison of Upper with Lower Burma is very striking in every respect, and should be studied by all who are anxious to understand the Burmese question. In the former we have poverty, starvation, and barbarous oppression by the rulers, where the people are taught "that gambling is a virtue, and life and property of no particular value"; in the latter, there is safety for all under a beneficent Government—"peace, contentment, and happiness, and such a steady and ever-increasing development of the resources of the country as might make any wise ruler anxious to imitate a system which has produced such marvellous results."

Perhaps the most sanguine friends of British rule throughout the world might do well to take a lesson from the generally peaceful and contented state of Pegu, Lord Dalhousie's pet annexation, over which the British flag should wave as long as the sun shone in the heavens.* In the middle of an eventful year, it was pleasant to read that the subject of Burma was at length brought before the House of Commons. Perilous, profitless Afghanistan, with its "terrible war," to use the words of the Premier, and ever-disturbing Ireland, appeared to have shut out all chance of getting in a word edgeways regarding the Land of the Golden Foot. It was not so always. Twenty-eight years before, Burma had been considered a theme of no small importance. The ablest statesman of both Houses gave attention to the Burmese question. The Earl of Derby, the "Rupert of Debate," and Lord Lansdowne, thought it not unworthy of their eloquence in the House of Lords; and the greatest soldier of the age—or rather who, like Shakespeare, lived not for an age, but for all time—wrote his last great State paper on the Second Burmese War.†

* *Our Burmese Wars, &c.*, p. 322. † *Ibid.* p. 462.

On the 1st of July 1880—

"Mr. Bryce asked the Secretary of State, for India what was the present state of diplomatic relations between the Government of India and the King of Burma; and whether having regard to the conciliatory disposition evinced for some months past by the King of Burma, Her Majesty's Government would consider the propriety of directing the British Envoy to return to Mandalay.

"The Marquis of Hartington was understood to say that, in consequence of the attitude of the Government of Burma to the British residents, and other causes, the relations of the Indian Government to the Government of Burma last year were extremely strained, our representative was recalled, and Colonel H. Browne was immediately despatched to succeed him. But, in consequence of the difficulty of transacting business, that gentleman was also recalled, and an assistant-resident appointed in his place. The latter found his position at Mandalay so precarious that it was impossible for him to remain any longer without danger to his own life and that of his assistants, and he also was directed to leave. Demands for redress had been addressed to the Government of Burma, but the result was not yet known. The Indian Government would consider the propriety of appointing a British resident as soon as certain stipulations, which it was considered right and necessary to insist upon, with regard to the treatment of the mission should be accepted. A special mission had been sent by the King of Burma to the frontier; but, although it was said to have full powers, it appeared that the Envoy had not power, or had not been able to assent to the preliminary conditions which the Indian Government considered indispensable to the establishment of a British mission at Mandalay. The whole question of our relations with Burma was now under the consideration of the Government of India, and no doubt the Viceroy would be greatly assisted by the advice of a gentleman who had lately been appointed a provisional member of the Council of the Governor-General."

So, then, when we are done with Afghanistan, there is a good chance of Burma's becoming an exciting and, as it must ever be, an interesting theme; the more so, in the event of a war between Russia and China, should the Russian bear be successful against the "heathen Chinee," and take it into his head some day that, as no one seems to care very much about developing the resources of Western China—particularly south-west Chinese Yunnan and Sze Chuen—he may as well fulfil a portion of the great Peter's universal object, and occupy these most valuable lands. Of course, such a consummation is far from devoutly to be wished; but should, by any chance, Russian territory ever border on Upper Burma, the Golden Foot, whoever he may be, if we have not honourably secured either him or his country before, will certainly have good cause to shake in his shoes.

This forces from the writer another question: Should China be eventually successful over all her enemies, were Russia to fall back, would the Flowery Land become a dangerous rival to British supremacy in India? Material for a tolerable army could be found out of a population of three or four hundred millions. Meanwhile, let us think only of the Burmese question, and the prospects of trade with south-western China. For the speedy settlement of the former, let us now introduce some real friend of Burma who has drawn up some questions on the subject, and wishes the best answers given to them, and in the directest and shortest manner procurable. The most important of them may be the following:—

Question. The loss of the sea-ports being so sorely felt by the Golden Foot, is there no way of our extending the benefit of these ports to the King; he, on his part, binding himself to assist us in securing a free right-of-way to western China, and to do all in his power to further the progress of commerce between Upper Burma and Pegu? And what monopolies of his own could he best give up for such benefits? Could he not be liberal to us in the way of petroleum, teak, precious stones, &c.?

Answer. When we give up the monopoly of opium, perhaps the King of Burma may give up petroleum, teak, and precious stones.

Teak! why *we* make a monopoly of teak.* For the rest, see our existing treaties. Again, what has puzzled many British statesman more than any other aspect of the position:—

Question. The *Shoe Question* being held of such paramount importance by the high Burmese officials, &c., could no middle course be taken to satisfy Burmese regal or courtly vanity?

Answer. There is no middle course.

In the Shoe Question† we at least have a show of reason in the Burman, who, after all, in such matters, is not so very much unlike ourselves; and to the Golden Foot Pope might, perhaps, have applied his famous line—

"In pride, in reasoning pride, the error lies."

As to our giving up the opium monopoly in India, such has been ably proved, in the present crippled state of Indian finance, to be utterly impossible; and so, in the present state of Burmese civilisation, for a king or his ministers to give in on the Shoe Question, appears to be equally impossible. Thus difficulty after difficulty enters into the question of our relations with Upper Burma. If there is to be a new treaty, and a Resident again at Mandalay, much of the difficulty will disappear if we strictly

* See Note I., "Royal Monopolies."

† *Our Burmese Wars, &c.*, pp. 395, 406.

observe the rule of honesty in all our dealings. And we must never for a moment allow the value of our *prestige* to go down in British and Upper Burma, but keep up our dignity—even if we cannot settle the Shoe Question—in every possible way. As to keeping up our dignity in the capital, there is a good story told of that highly eminent political officer, the present Sir Arthur Phayre. In Burma eight golden umbrellas are carried over the royal or king's letter; and when the Burmese authorities would not permit the umbrella to be carried over the Governor-General's letter, according to custom, Major Phayre, our Envoy to Burma in 1855, insisted upon the Union Jack being waved over it on its way from the Residency to the Palace.* Even used in such a novel fashion, the glorious old rag had more dignity about it than a whole kingdom of golden and white umbrellas. It may here be stated that white umbrellas are the emblems of royalty in Upper Burma, and none but royal personages can have these carried before them. Thus, in East and West alike, are kings and grandees to be found, "pleased with a rattle, tickled with a straw!" Monopoly and vanity, then, may be considered leading features in a Burman monarch's character; and with regard to the former, but chiefly with reference to our "Concurrent Commercial Interests,"

* See a very pleasing *Note of the Day*, on "Burmese Umbrellas," in the *Globe*, June 18th, 1880. Eight days later, appeared another amusing article on "Tipsy Kings of Burma." It should have been remarked in this paper, at the time, that when Prince Nyoungoke came over, King Theebau, it was reported, commenced a heavy drinking bout in the palace; this love of the "liquid ruby," or the white spirit, adding difficulties to the Burmese Question.

I shall now cite a few valuable remarks as bearing in no small degree on a satisfactory settlement of the Burmese question.

The difficulties placed in the path of traders from China through Burma to the sea by the late King, Mengdon Meng, in the shape of ruinous duties, were no doubt of a serious character. "He probably acted thus through feelings of jealousy and dislike of the English and other 'Kulla' settlers in his own territory, but more especially to those of British Burma, by means of whom his country had been deprived of many of its ablest-bodied sons, who resorted in considerable numbers to British territory. . . . His policy was a very ruinous one, as is proved by the present impoverished state of his country, and this he eventually well knew before the Angel of Death ran him in. General Sir A. Phayre, when Chief Commissioner of British Burma in 1863, wrote on this subject of ruinous duties and the King's monopolies in trade, as follows:—'This system is no doubt very pernicious, but foreign interference may do more harm than good. We must trust in time to let the King learn the advantage of giving the industry of the people free scope.' Time, however, passed away, and on the 4th October 1878, when Mengdon Meng was officially reported to have passed into the Buddhist future state called Nirbana" (Neibban or Nirvâna is the "eternal city"), "this pernicious system was in as full swing as it was in April 1863. There is really no other exit for the Chinese trade from Sze-Chuen and Yunnan than by the route going through Bhamo, past Mandalay, and so on down to Rangoon, and the countries beyond the Indian Ocean. By the stoppage of this route, Bhamo has become a place of but little importance as regards trade, and it is a miserable sight to see those five steamers of the Irawadi Flotilla Company, running to and fro between Rangoon, Mandalay, and Bhamo, almost empty. The trade may yet, however, ere long revive, under happier auspices, and Bhamo (in an extensive wild and beautiful province, governed by a Woon, *lit.* civil governor) may become, what it undoubtedly can become, a wealthy and prosperous centre of trade." And when we consider that Rangoon, as I have frequently styled it, *the future Liverpool or Glasgow of Chin-India,* has been brought within about fifty-six hours of Calcutta by steam, and quite next door to it by telegraph, the British merchant—should he honour the latter portion of the following sketch with a perusal—will doubtless appreciate the vast importance of opening up trade with south-western or it may be other parts of China. Unless this be well and amply provided for, there can be no satisfactory solution of the Burmese question. South-western China penetrates into every cranny of it; and whoever states to the contrary is ignorant of the real facts of the case. We have deprived the Golden Foot of the prosperous tail (the ports);* so of course he is naturally more than ever bent on keeping the undeveloped head. If this part of the question be well managed, its entire solution will not be far distant; if neglected, it will be impossible.

In his humble efforts to publish commercial as well as

* See also *Our Burmese Wars, &c.*, pp. 386, 391.

military information concerning Burma, the writer, in addition to the kind and encouraging remarks of the London press, has been honoured with some observations by a zealous and learned Member of the House of Commons, which may not be out of place here, as they represent a large section of public opinion on the subject: "So far as I can judge with my limited knowledge, the capabilities of Burma are all that you say, though I am not sure that I can follow you if you desire it (Upper Burma) to be annexed to our already almost too vast Indian dominion. With what you put so clearly and forcibly regarding the desirability of opening up trade with China, I entirely agree; understanding that you desire to see this effected by peaceful means. What I hear privately regarding the present King of Burma leads me to believe that he is not so black as he has been painted by some of the newspaper correspondents at Rangoon." Strange enough, the latter opinion concerning King Theebau is similar to that entertained by the gallant and able member of the "warlike element," to whom the present writer is so much indebted for his valuable "Notes" on Upper and Lower Burma. At Mandalay (June 1879), this graphic writer was joined by a German gentleman, who was making a tour of the world, and was very anxious to see King Thibo (Theebau). An order was procured for an interview through the Kinwoon Mengyee, or Prime Minister; and the "amusing" traveller's curiosity was fully gratified. "One thing observed by my friend was that the young King did not present the slightest appearance of having indulged in the debasing habit of intoxication, with which he has been so freely credited. If this was true, surely a youth, who certainly never in his father's lifetime tasted a drop of any intoxicating liquor, suddenly embarking on such a course, drinking as some said nearly a bottle of gin at a sitting, would have shown some signs of its effects. My friend positively asserted that no such signs could be noticed, that he seemed a quiet and rather timid youth, not yet quite accustomed to his exalted position. Mr. Archibald Forbes in February last (1879), said the same thing about Theebau as this travelling German gentleman." Again, "It is of course impossible to say with any certainty whether or not this young king is a drunkard, and is responsible for the cruel deaths of his relatives." Let us, then, be kind and liberal, in a liberal age, under a Liberal Government, and give the Golden Foot, King Theebau, the full benefit of the doubt, on the fair understanding that he gives his powerful aid in settling for Great Britain and Burma this what otherwise promises to be an eternal Burmese question.

London, August 2, 1880.

CHAPTER II.

THE BURMESE QUESTION.—II.

UPWARDS of three months had elapsed since the writer penned the foregoing remarks, and the idea became forced on him that this is what may be styled an Interrogative Age, as well as an Age of Various Local Interest. Questions and Situations have been so rapidly succeeding each other, even in a quarter of a year, that one is sometimes disposed to doubt if any comparison can be made between the famous ages of the ancient Hindus and Greeks, and those through which we have passed, till, sending the Golden, Silver (the Brazen must be allowed to remain), and Iron ages adrift, we seem to cling, like the former remarkable people, to a present "Evil Age," waiting for reform everywhere, to be brought about by some Liberal Vishnu *in esse*, who, as the ninth incarnation (Kalki), seated on his white horse, with a drawn scimitar in his hand, is yet to come and renovate creation with an era of purity. Question so rapidly succeeds question, that it is difficult to conceive where this looked-for universal reformer is likely to appear first; whether in Afghanistan or Burma in Asia, or in Turkey, England, or Ireland in Europe. He will have to be a greater than even Burke, Fox, Earl Russell, or Mr. Gladstone. The numerous questions and situations which have been thrust on our governing statesmen and the public during the last three or four months have been perfectly overwhelming, the larger swallowing up the minor—or rather what only seem to be the larger taking the chief place in public interest—till at length we seem to long for the present "Evil Age" (Kali Yúg) to be swept away, to be succeeded by one far happier and better. That many dark places of the earth are almost as full of cruelty as ever is hardly to be denied by close observers of the world's progress; and, perhaps, there is no corner of the earth where this is more apparent than in the shattered independent kingdom of Upper Burma, to which far too little attention has recently been given, although in commercial and military strategic importance—especially in the case of our Eastern Empire—it far transcends many of those regions which, in the shape of questions, have been so lavishly thrust on our notice. It is not enough to simply call attention to the undisputed fact that Burma is a great self-producing country for Great Britain—"a country destined ere long to be more important than any other in Asia"—Ashé Pyee, the Eastern country, or that "superior to all others"; * but strong and various argument should be used to teach every true-born Briton what a valuable possession he has in British Burma, and

* *Our Burmese Wars, &c.*, p. 17.

how that value may be increased by forsaking useless and profitless regions, where more blood and treasure have recently been lost, and turning a larger share of attention to one of the fairest and productive regions on earth.

Various Governments—especially the direct Governments of India—are by experienced judges considered in some measure to blame for the present wretched state of Upper Burma, and much of the anxiety and restlessness in Lower or British adjacent territory.

A liberal remedy is now sought; and this makes the Burmese—although there is much of a seeming inertia hovering around it—not less politically important, and intrinsically far more so, than the Turkish, the Greek, the Montenegrin, the Afghan, or the Persian question. What shall we do for Afghanistan?—the war in which country Lord Northbrook, in his recent masterly and interesting address on India,* trusted was at an end; and where, in the more recent words of our ever-eloquent Premier, "a more hopeful condition has been restored," †—is now bound to give way to the mighty, sensible, and practical question, What shall we do for our valuable Chin-Indian next-door neighbour, Upper Burma? At length it has been well and emphatically said of Afghanistan: "We have had enough of it; the British nation is sick of the name of that turbulent country." And no wonder. To say nothing of the treachery and bloodshed our ever-brave troops have borne witness to, the late wars in that region have cost us a few millions more than the terribly expen-

* October 29th, as President of the Midland Institute, Birmingham.

† Banquet Speech, Lord Mayor's Day, 9th November, 1880.

sive First and the moderately expensive Second Burmese Wars put together.* And what have we gained? Nothing. Positively worse than nothing; except further proof of the well-known fact that our forces in the East, European and Native, can beat, if properly commanded, any number of disciplined or undisciplined troops, under any circumstances, in any part of Asia.

What Mr. Gladstone has styled "the great Indian Empire of the Queen, that large, important, indispensable part of the obligations of the Imperial Government," demands from Great Britain the most earnest and speedy attention to Burma, locally, financially, and commercially, which no other British possession at present has the same right to claim.

Musing over the Burmese question in its various bearings, my attention was turned to a remarkable pamphlet written in January 1826, a month before the conclusion of the First Burmese War, and the treaty of peace at Yandaboo. The author is Colonel Stewart, formerly Aide-de-Camp to Earl Minto and Marquis of Hastings, Governors-General of India. The title is *Some Considerations on the Policy of the Government of India, more especially with reference to the Invasion of Burmah*; and the well-chosen motto for those who write or debate on Indian affairs, from Tacitus: "Non tamen sine usu fuerit introspicere illa primo aspectu levia, ex quis magnarum sæpe rerum motus oriuntur." Alluding to the "monstrous incongruities" united in the government of our East India

* See *Our Burmese Wars, &c.*, pp. 79, 80, 288, and 464. See also Note V. "Relative Cost of the Afghan and Burmese Wars."

provinces, the writer answers the question *how* they are united :—"by the only means by which such a union was possible—by the influence of an army of a hundred and sixty thousand men." And these incongruities extended not only through the government, but through the whole frame of society. The difficulty—though not impossibility—of effecting a direct and strong union between British and Upper Burma, and say also the Shan States, is almost foreshadowed by Warren Hastings in his famous memoir relative to the state of India. "I fear," says Mr. Hastings, "I fear, I say, that the sovereignty will be found a burden instead of a benefit, a heavy clog rather than a precious gem, to its present possessors. I mean, unless the whole territory in that quarter be rounded and made a uniform compact body by one grand and systematic arrangement, such an arrangement as will do away with all the mischiefs, doubts and inconveniences, both to the governor and to the governed, arising from . . . the informality and invalidity of all engagements in so divided and unsettled a state of society, and from the unavoidable anarchy and confusion of different laws, religions, and prejudices, civil and political, all jumbled together in one unnatural and discordant mass." So far as India is concerned, vast strides of improvement have undoubtedly been made in these and similar matters since the first Governor-General wrote, or during the last century of our rule; but with every conquest we make they re-commence in all their pristine strength, as would be found if we had such turbulent countries as Afghanistan and Upper Burma (with he adjacent territory) entirely at our feet to-morrow. No nation has been a victim to "the force of circumstances," since the world began, like our own.

We have launched a strong political school in the East, and it would appear that we must ever go on teaching if we would hope to hold our position. As it might be said, England is the universal schoolmaster, ever ploughing and sowing as she goes or plods along, with the old motto, "Vires acquirit eundo." But during our progress, it is consolatory to know that we are frequently vested with the power of selection. Afghanistan has been weighed in the balances, and sadly found wanting. The Afghan question should be made at once to give way to the far easier and infinitely more valuable one of the Burman, or, What should we now do for Northern or Upper Burma? And whatever mode of action may take place—

"If 'twere done,
Then 'twere well it were done quickly."

Standing firmly on the defensive, and dismissing the Russian bugbear for ever, England can very well afford to drop Afghanistan with all the glory it has won us, and the losses and the tears it has caused, and leave the Afghans to make peace among themselves; and at any time it is possible, to use the words of an able and humorous military writer, "the drama of the Kilkenny cats may have begun in Cabul"; but it is very different with Upper Burma. We cannot in any way afford to leave it quite alone. We have cut the apple in half, keeping by far the best half for ourselves; and now the other half seems destined to come into our hands.

Colonel Stewart remarks, on the subject of the first

invasion of Burma: "The only event that can be quoted, with any appearance of similarity, as a precedent, is the invasion of Nepaul, during the administration of the Marquis of Hastings. The cases were the same, in so far as little additional revenue was to be loked for from cessions of territory; but in all other respects, the contrast between the circumstances is remarkable." The writer compares the two countries with respect to India, but such a comparison would not hold good at the present time; for what good as a barrier Nepaul was then, and is now, may be equalled, if not surpassed, by the splendid barrier and strategic base of operations afforded by Lower, and which would be mightily increased if we possessed, or had supreme influence over, Upper Burma.

When the Government of India was forced into a war with Nepaul, as we might any day be with the present arrogant and cruel Golden Foot—a plan that promised and deserved complete success was presented; and here were "wise and legitimate objects to look to as the fruit of victory." It was never the intention of Lord Hastings to destroy the independence of Nepaul as a separate kingdom. He would not remove such a valuable barrier interposed between the British possessions and the dependencies of China; but sufficient was done to cut the claws of Nepaul, and prevent much future trouble during our great march on the road to Empire. Colonel Stewart writes of the narrow strip of Nepaul, hemmed in along with us by the same impassable rampart, with an immense frontier in its front, and no depth; and of Burma as a country lying beyond the natural limits of India, touching on our possessions but for a small portion of its length, and that on a strong natural frontier, and opening behind with vast regions; "with great rivers, presenting so many successive lines of defence, and connecting itself, by neighbourhood, with many powerful kingdoms" When the shrewd and gallant Colonel wrote we did not even possess Arakan and Tenasserim—although we had conquered them—far less Pegu, our present "princess among the provinces," which Sir Arthur Phayre created and left on the sure road to progress and wealth, after, wizard-like, turning the swamps of Arakan into the granary of the Bay.* Stewart protested against the process of aggrandisement—yet acquiring power that we may be safe—strongly advocating the fixed principles held by many able statesmen of the present day, against firing a shot beyond the confines of India, except in the pursuit of an aggressor. Surely the story of our whole Eastern Empire is a strange one; and we still continue to forget that we are creatures of circumstances. We were obliged to fire "a shot," and a good many, when the terrible Sikh invasion of British India took place (1845–46); the annexation of the Punjab (1849) eventually ensued; and he who, through the Punjab, became the "Saviour of India" during the mutiny (1857)† really founded the policy, now again (November 1880) to be adopted—to think not of conquest, but defence only, and, with the great Indian chiefs, concentrate all attention on "internal progress." At the commencement of his

* See the Author's *Pegu*, p. 146.

† The annexation of Pegu was also of great use during the Mutiny. See *Our Burmese Wars, &c.*, Preface.

reign, the Marquis of Ripon has declared his intention of "resuming the policy of Lord Lawrence." More *rounding off*, however, will yet have to take place before this wise policy can be adopted *in extenso*. We are not yet even near "the beginning of the end!" And yet the fact is undeniable, that there is wherewithal in India to satisfy the highest ambition. But there is a secret impelling power which defies such prudence.

Upper Burma, then,—and there may be some other "undiscovered country"—is in a strait betwixt two modes of action on our part: one to invade and annex, which is quite repugnant to the new policy; the other to rectify, aid the right, and check the wrong, which we shall ever find it difficult to do, especially in some portions of Chin-India. What Colonel Stewart wrote at the beginning of 1826 is as true now as then; and in an age when military glory is almost considered of secondary importance to financial considerations, it may be well to cite his remark:—"It seems to be admitted on all sides that accessions of territory in that direction" (Burma) "will be unproductive of any proportionate revenue, and they will most infallibly entail expense." And yet fifty years later we find British Burma—to say nothing of revenue furnished to the Imperial Exchequer—with exports and imports amounting to 13½ millions sterling, more than four times the population, which proportion, if it existed in India, would make the commerce of our greatest and most splendid dependency ten times greater than it is.* The

* See *Our Burmese Wars, &c.*, pp. 352–353.

dismemberment hitherto of the fairest portion of the old Burmese Empire, it must be candidly confessed, we have managed admirably. In fact commerce in Burma, even now, looking to a bright future, wears her "rostral crown" rejoicing.

A peculiarity surrounds the Burmese question which makes it differ entirely from most European and Oriental questions. In its solution England is almost alone interested. As what may be styled an isolated question, therefore, and also possessing a greater right to deal with it than any other powers—from the simple fact of our already possessing the better half of the golden apple—no power is able to compete with us in the variety of arguments elicited by—what shall we do for Upper Burma? We need not at present fear China. Russia will keep her employed in watching that aggressive yet wonderful power for years to come. Strange enough it was recently stated by high authority that the "new peril for India" was China, aided by Nepaul, and not Russia, which would, therefore, in her turn, cause the great northern power to keep strict watch over the erratic doings of China! What a strange and unexpected event it would be for the future historian to record that the Chinese had threatened English supremacy in India! The old Russian bugbear of Afghanistan will then, perhaps, like Islam, have "withered away"; King Theebau will have been long gathered to his fathers; Upper Burma will be entirely ours; and what was a sad wilderness under his rule will, under ours, rejoice and blossom like the noble *Amherstia* * and the Rose. It may

* See *Our Burmese Wars, &c.*. p. 309.

also be predicted that, unlike barren and turbulent Afghanistan, should we leave it to its fate, it will, from our strategical position of Pegu, cause us far less anxiety, and always afford the hope of profit, honour and advantage, more than any other Eastern country not actually our own.

It may now be well to record briefly, as materials for future history, the principal events which occurred in Upper Burma during a period of three or four months, after the discomfiture of Prince Nyoungoke, who headed the rebellion, about the middle of the year, against King Theebau, which events may tend to throw some light on the present aspect of the Burmese question. In truth, such events form a strange medley, affording sufficient food for a sensation drama, to which we have too long passively been spectators. There could be no doubt whatever that things had nearly come to the worst in Upper Burma. Our sage, Bacon, almost seemed to have the present state of the land of the Golden Foot in his eye when he wrote: "Time is the greatest innovator; and if time of course alters things to the worst, and wisdom and counsel shall not alter them to the better, what shall be the end?" * While Lord Hartington was giving his countrymen "an important and satisfactory statement (August 9th) about the evacuation of Cabul," some interesting items of information, from "Our Correspondent at Rangoon," † were published in London. What would England do without the services of such intelligent and ubiquitous Correspondents? Strange, there have been so many new orders of knighthood in late years, and not one to the Knights of the

* *Essays.* † *Daily News*, August 10th, 1880.

Press! Only a journalistic K.P. would run the risk of being mistaken for a Knight of St. Patrick! Anyway, there should be an Order of Merit especially for them, admitting all who have been distinguished by graphic description and daring adventure.* At Rangoon, the political atmosphere had cleared again, and the ardent Rangoon annexationists were contented to bide their time. Nyoungoke had been defeated; and there were no more signs of opposition to Theebau. When the rebellion broke out, the King was becoming more and more unpopular,—a most dangerous state for a Burmese monarch,—and everything seemed in Prince Nyoungoke's favour, except that he "did not bear a good name among the Upper Burmans. They said he hated his brother—a very grave sign among the Buddhists; they said he loved money—a very common failing all the world over; finally, they declared they did not believe he would be any better than Theebau—about as crushing an accusation as could be brought against anybody; but all the time they allowed that he was brave; in fact, they said that was the only good quality the Prince had." But what use is bravery in a Burman or any other military commander, without the knack of looking ahead and knowing something at least of strategy? It only makes matters worse; and in intrinsic value, without the above qualifications, is nearly as bad as running away—which the Prince certainly did from the Royal troops. There seemed little chance of Nyoungoke raising another rebellion.

The same Correspondent at Rangoon further wrote, about

* The far-famed Correspondent at Merv should be among the first to receive the order. (September 1881.)

this time, regarding the English church at Mandalay, alluded to in my larger work,* that King Theebau had caused it to be published that since the English priests were afraid to resume charge of their church in Mandalay, he meditated presenting it to "the Baptists, or the Roman Catholics, or whatever sect would take it." Perhaps it entered the writer's mind that such a vacant church would form a fitting temple for the Ritualistic ones who came under the wrath of the Court of Arches; and at Mandalay they might carry out the ceremonies of their ornate religion unmolested, with the chance of a reformed Theebau—after studying "Churchism," and thinking how little of genuine Christianity was in it all—becoming one of the congregation! It should be mentioned that it was not probable that either the Baptists or the Romanists would accept His Majesty's offer; so the church is likely to remain vacant till we, or the Shans, take Mandalay, or till the appearance of a new British Resident there.

Numerous promotions of "intelligent and progressive men," had now taken place at the capital of Upper Burma, owing to the rebel defeat. The concluding report on the operations of the Nága Field Force (by General Nation), had also been published; so we now had, about the same time (middle of July), praise distributed by our Government to the officers and troops engaged against the unruly Nágas, and promotions by King Theebau for the repulse of the adventurous Nyoungoke.

August 1880, will ever be an important epoch in Burmese annals, especially to Burmese astrologers, for during this

* *Our Burmese Wars, &c.*, p. 471.

month took place a serious revolt of the Shan States, and a daring attempt on the life of King Theebau. From what has been said elsewhere, of course such striking events were to be expected at any time; and had success crowned both endeavours, there is no saying what might have happened in Upper Burma. A glorious future for a fine yet undeveloped country would probably have now begun, and the reign of uncertainty and terror would have been closed for ever. In the united (if such be possible) action of the Shan States, lies an important key to the whole Burmese question. And this is a fact that Indian statesmen would do well to bear in mind. With the numerous Shan tribes well disposed towards us, and say the Nyoungyan Prince as our steady ally on the throne of the Golden Foot, what a splendid barrier we could have to our possessions in Eastern Asia! But it would be useless to maintain a good monarch on the throne, or even to annex, if we did not conciliate the Shans. They are, I repeat, the *sine quâ non* of our policy in Chin-India. I have frequently referred to this remarkable people in my other work, and too much attention cannot be paid to their doings and progress. They may yet form the nucleus of a mighty commerce, which will make the English merchant's heart rejoice, and all of us to wonder how we had so long and foolishly neglected them.*

Were thorough rebellion at any time to break out in Upper Burma, we could not "shunt" the Shan question. They must be either for us or against us; and two or three

* See *Our Burmese Wars, &c.*, pp. 364, 366, 394,—Tribes, Shan Producing Countries, &c. Also Lord Dalhousie on the Shans and Hill People, pp. 289–290.

millions of such a brave people might give us some trouble, especially—which in these days is too likely—if our hands were tied in other quarters. It is the tribes inhabiting in and around the old Burman Empire which make the Burmese question a difficult problem to solve to the satisfaction of all parties.

Some of the Shan tribes, then, rose against King Theebau nearly two months after Prince Nyoungoke's failure. It was reported in Rangoon, and, of course, fully believed in the bazaar, that the Shans had surrounded and besieged Mandalay, and that Theebau's last days had come. But three only of the Tsawbwas (as the chiefs are called), had risen—two of them, the heads of the Theinnee and Thonhsay clans, the most powerful of all.

The Shan chiefs, as was to be expected, acted quite independently of each other. They seem in the present case to have simply raised their standards, and commenced marching on Mandalay, burning and slaughtering all along their route. The King's troops missed them at first, and, falling upon the Thonhsay chief's village, sacked and burned it. "The enraged Tsawbwa, however, exacted summary vengeance. Within a day or two he fell upon the Royalists, cut them up at the first onslaught, and spent the rest of the day hunting them down. The hot-tempered old Tswabwa of Theinnee, whose daughter was married to one of the princes, and massacred along with her husband last year," * now also fully enjoyed the intense sweetness of revenge.

* Correspondent of the *Daily News*. See also *Our Burmese Wars, &c.* pp. 397–398, "King Theebau's Progress."

But, after all, there was no actual beleaguering of Mandalay. If, however, the town outside the walls had been taken, Theebau would almost certainly have been put to death. The able correspondent remarks significantly on this occasion :—" The Burmese have an ancient custom that way with their Sovereigns, and it will not be difficult to find plenty of men ready to put an end to the blood-stained life." At the end of August 1880, it was communicated from Rangoon that there might be more political meaning in the revolt of the Shans than was at first supposed. The Shan Tsawbwa — probably the old and naturally irate Theinnee—with some knowledge of the art of war, had come to the conclusion that it was better *not yet* to attack the royal city ; " for they forthwith spread themselves all over the country to the north of Mandalay, burning and plundering wherever they came upon a village."

But the daring achievement of attempting the King's life was now on the cards, and was about to be put into effect. A man, dressed as a Phongyee, by some means or other got into King Theebau's private apartments in the palace. On being questioned as to his business he became flustered, was seized and searched. A dhâ (Burmese sword) was found " beneath his koyone, the yellow upper-garment of the monk " ; and his Order being forbidden to carry arms of any kind, there was strong evidence against the intruder. The actor of " the Ascetic," might have been killed on the spot, * had it not been suggested that he might have

* It is death for anyone to bear arms inside the Palace.

accomplices. After inquiry, it was found that "the intended regicide had come from the Shan camp with ten followers, who were immediately seized. The leader and one of the ten—said to be his nephew—were "tortured to death forthwith"; and the remaining nine were thrown into prison. It was said that the palace authorities did their best to keep the attempt on King Theebau's life a secret; and it has not yet transpired who the would-be regicide really was. It will henceforth be difficult for strangers of any kind to enter the palace; probably no one—not even the British Resident *in esse*—will be allowed to enter without being searched. The lively Correspondent at Rangoon then concludes:—"The young monster Theebau, therefore, continues to be fortunate. If, however, the would-be assassin was really a Shan, the incident is much more significant than a mere independent attempt on the King's life would be." It is highly probable that, in addition to the Shans' hatred, Theebau's subjects are tired of him already; and, were the former successful at any time, others in and around Upper Burma would at once join in.

It is most desirable that we should steadily bear in mind the fact of the Shans, as it has been well expressed, surrounding Burma "like a fringe, and without gaining a footing anywhere, forming an important and respected, or detested, part of the population everywhere round the kingdom." Again, with reference to the revolt of the Shans, the same authority, writing from Rangoon, at the end of August, forcibly remarks, after speculating on the chance the badly-armed yet brave and sturdy Shans would have in a war against the comparatively well-armed "vaunted invincibles" of Theebau:—"If, however, the Kinwoon Mengyee (the former Prime Minister) were to see in the present a favourable opportunity for wiping out his disgrace" (these Burmese Woons—especially the Prime and War Ministers—are ever getting into and getting out of disgrace!), "and rising again to supreme power, the matter would be very different, and the Shan rebellion might be the salvation of Burma. . . . The sudden end of Theebau might prove rather awkward to us. There is no legitimate heir anywhere near Mandalay. Claimants would immediately spring up in Rangoon and Calcutta, and possibly even in Upper Burma; but what the Burmese Ministers might do in the interval no one knows—probably they themselves least of all."

With regard to heirs apparent in the Burmese Royal Family, it may alleviate the Englishman's surprise when he hears of the murder of a prince, or even of a batch of princes—their extinction "at one fell swoop"—if I remark that there are no rules in favour of primogeniture among the Burmese. The King may appoint whom he pleases as his successor; and murders of the Royal Family are considered—especially by King Theebau and his advisers—like revolutions, as belonging to the national stock of Burmese customs.*

It was recently announced that the Hindus at Benares—the city of Siva, the Destroyer—were led to believe that the British Government proposed to make human sacrifices

* See also General Albert Fytche's *Burma, Past and Present*, vol. i. pp. 211, 234.

on the opening of a railway bridge across the Ganges. It is to be hoped they did not take the idea from King Theebau's real or projected sacrificial antics of some months ago, thinking that the British, like the Golden Foot, might thus abjure or propitiate misfortune, and court prosperity. The Brahmans must now be convinced that the splendid march from Cabul to Candahar by our victorious General, has placed Afghanistan in a fair way of being settled—at least so far as we are concerned—while the Lord of the White Elephant is still surrounded by the implacable Shans, waiting their opportunity.

Later accounts of the attempt on the King's life, made it appear extraordinary that he should have escaped. The so-called Phongyee was seized when within "easy striking distance," and there seemed to be no doubt that he belonged to "one of the bands of Shans plundering about the capital." We have material for a good tragedy in the fact of the old Theinnee Tsawbwa having sworn to revenge the murder of his daughter by Theebau. There may be fresh attempts "to kill a King"; but the process hereafter will be far more difficult, on account of the guards being threatened with death should a stranger be found within the inner court of the palace.

In September, it was announced at Rangoon that the "Hpoung Woon, destined to take the place of the Kinwoongyee, had returned to Mandalay, laden with treasure, screwed out of the unfortunate river township, for which he had been created a Mingyee, the highest titular rank under that of the blood-royal."* It was now supposed that if

* Rangoon Correspondent in *Daily News*, October 1st, 1880.

this important Burmese official got into power, that all hope of an amicable arrangement between Theebau and our Government would be at an end. But another Woon might at any time appear on the scene, and quickly drive out the ambitious Hpoung. And so runs the world away at head-quarters in Upper Burma.

There is a distinguished actor, mentioned at the commencement of the first portion of this paper, whom I have neglected on account of the interest attached to the Shan revolt: and that is our old friend the Naingangya Woondouk. It had been affirmed early in August that he was poisoned by the King's orders. Be this true or not, it is tolerably certain that the unfortunate Burmese diplomatist, who could not come to terms with us, has not since appeared in the Burmese drama at Mandalay. It is just possible he may have gone off to the Shans, or may appear some day as a "pretender," which would produce a new phase of the Burmese question. No one could tell what had become of Oo Myeh, the Secretary to the Embassy.

It was now said that Theebau, having got rid of the outward signs of his so-called rebuff by us, and having got news of our latest disaster in Afghanistan, was inclined to "bluster." It was also hinted that the King would not have "a new treaty with us, even if we were to come and beg for it."

It may aid the future historian to record that, about this time, the *Mandalay Government Gazette* gave—

"a list of all the chief civil officials of Burma, including two or three new and important appointments. The four principal grades of civil authority are:—(1) Menggyi or Chief Minister, (2) Atwengwung or Minister of the Interior, (3) Myo-wun or City Magistrate, (4) Wundauk or Sub-Minister. The highest military office is that of 'Weng-do-hmu,' or Commander of the Palace Guard, who ranks next to a Chief Minister. Ordinarily there are four Meng-gyis, four Atweng-wuns, two Myo-wuns, four Wundauks, and three Weng-do-hmus, viz. those of the Right, the Left, the Eastern, and Western quarters. The prescribed number of chief ministers, city magistrates, and commanders is rarely, if ever, exceeded; the other two grades are filled with more irregularity. During the reign of the last King there were five Atweng-wuns, one being stationed as a special revenue superintendent at Bhamo, and no fewer than seven sub-ministers. A brief summary is given of the services of each of the new functionaries. The Taung Khweng, chief minister, has passed through the grades of herald, governor, sub-minister, and minister of the interior. The Pauk Myaing Atweng-wun has been envoy to the courts of France, Italy, and England, and has acted as herald and sub-minister. The achievements of the Hletheng Atweng-wun are given more in detail. He has been in the palace employ from a very early age, and during the late monarch's reign was promoted successively, through the ranks of slipper-bearer, tea-server, and betel-box-holder, to that of the Governor of the Royal Barges. For his loyalty and energy (which signifies the active share he took in the late massacres), the present Lord of Existence created him city magistrate, and has now exalted him to the dignity of minister of interior. His special charge, till recently, was the supervision of the Shan country and the middle territory. A notification in the same *Gazette* now appoints him Supreme Governor of all the lower fluviatile provinces. He is placed in command of a large military force, and is to take immediate measures to prevent disturbances in the skirts of the country, and the access of robbers and bad characters, who are causing terror and insecurity to the traders and cultivators of the Golden Kingdom."

We must not here leave the Shans and their country without thinking well over the very important part the Shans may be destined to play in any present or future Burmese political military drama. Here there is a people, as before remarked, two or three millions of them, with vast trading capabilities, and inhabiting some of the fairest and most producitve countries of the earth, apparently seeking to wheel into the ranks of civilisation if we only gave the word of command. I persist in the assertion, and defy contradiction, that the tide in their affairs has almost come; and when it does come will surely lead us and them on to fortune if we take prudent advantage of it. The picture must be kept before our eye till something is done for the people—that of the rather Chinese-looking Shan, with his fair wife and still fairer daughter, in their picturesque broad-brimmed straw hats and pleasing costume, the rare Shan ruby setting off their charms; the Shan pony, with merchandise on his back, and the Shan children in rear of their four-footed friend,—all marching onward through the rugged defile as if bent on a nearer approach to civilisation.

The same mail which brought to London detailed news of the Shan revolt, brought also some important intelligence from China. First, Chung-How (famous in the Kuldja question) had been released; Russia was said to have announced her intention to send a high officer to Pekin to settle the differences between the two countries; and, most important of all, Colonel Gordon, who had quitted Lord Ripon's Staff towards the middle of the year for the flowery land, had just left China. He had not been able to do much for the Chinese; but his advice should be written in letters of gold on the walls of Pekin and Canton. He had told them that the Russians could take the coast ports all of a heap, and Pekin, within six weeks if they so desired; he had told them it would be simple madness for China to go to war with such a power as Russia. He had suggested the capital of the Empire being removed "from Pekin to the centre of the country." Still, everything seemed decidedly warlike in China. It was said that the elder Empress and Prince Ch'un had thoroughly determined upon war. And Russia now appeared determined to bring one on if she possibly could. The result of the questions pending between the Russian and Chinese Governments seemed to have ended in an irritating demand of a heavy indemnity from the Chinese, which they certainly would refuse to pay, as they conceived there should have been no naval demonstration in their waters; and so, through the winter, China and Russia, with swords drawn, would be longing to attack each other, like the famous Sir Richard Strachan and Earl of Chatham.

Of course, Burma all this time was watching the aggressive policy of Russia towards her old master, China. Some of the old Woons probably thought that Russia was going too far. It would be useless to enforce on King Theebau Colonel Gordon's advice to the Celestials, not to think of going to war with a superior power; but, doubtless, it came to the Golden Ears, bringing a wholesome lesson and probably dread of British power. But Theebau, like most of his predecessors, is a thoroughly impracticable monarch. He knows we have all his ports already; but he never seems aware of our long-suffering or patience, and that "doing the thing" at any moment would be as easy as lying. Being young, there is yet time for him to become "every inch" a useful king, identifying the true interests of his country with ours. We do not wish to fetter him at all if it can possibly be avoided. What shall be done, then, to give life and prosperity to an unfortunate country so highly blessed by Nature? On England depends entirely the answer to this question. Resuming very briefly the thread of this sketch; news at length arrived from Mandalay that Theebau's queen (one of the four head) had presented the Golden Foot with a son and heir; and the circumstance, it was thought, could "simplify matters very much" if the King were assassinated. There would be some one to rally round in case of rebellion. But the report soon after was announced to be false, for the expected "son and heir" turned out to be a daughter, after all!

It was now reported from Upper India that Prince Mingoondeing Mintha was dead.

He and his brother, the Mingoon Prince, were the leaders in the Rebellion of 1866 *; and, after various misdemeanours, they were eventually exiled to Benares. With reference to Mingoon's claim to the throne, it was well remarked:—"If we interfere to put anyone on the Burmese throne, it should most certainly be the Nyoungyan, who is the eldest living prince of the pure blood royal, is popular with the Burmese, and, moreover, is a pious and kindly man; while the best we know of the Mingoon Mintha is, that he tried to kill his father, and to burn the people who saved his life."† Truly, we have hard material to deal with in some princes of the royal blood of Burma.

* See *Our Burmese Wars and Relations with Burma*, pp. 380–381. "These princes actually concocted a plot to sack and burn Rangoon."

† *Daily News* Correspondent at Rangoon.

While at home we were speculating on the probability of another era of commercial prosperity being before us, provided that Turkey, Afghanistan, South Africa, Burma, and even Ireland, did not lead us into "extraordinary and ruinous expenditure," and while affairs were dull, and tranquillity seemed to prevail, for the time, in Upper Burma, the British station of Thayetmyo, on the Irawadi, suddenly assumed a warlike aspect. For some time little news had been received from Mandalay, and it was supposed that, "although diplomatic relations had not been resumed," things were likely to continue in a state of *inertia.*

But now the most exaggerated rumours flew about everywhere, and the ever busy and watchful Special Correspondent flashed by telegraph to London,* that the King, rendered arrogant by the easy suppression of Prince Nyoungoke's rebellion, was preparing for war with us. Two detachments of the King's regular troops, it was said, had arrived at the frontier, and taken up their posts on the banks of the river, facing each other. They were one thousand strong, and their tone was "insolent and arrogant in the extreme." They gave out that they were about to attack our territory, "in retaliation for Prince Nyoungoke's attempt to incite insurrection in Burma." They were in daily expectation of reinforcements under a General, with instructions from the King to demand from the British Government an indemnity "for the losses suffered by Burmese subjects from the expedition of Prince

* *Standard*, October 12th, 1880.

Nyoungoke," and that, failing to obtain the indemnity, they would at once cross our frontier and attack us. It was also said that the Burmese intended to blockade the channel of the river, to prevent the upward passage of our gun-boats.

This is all so very like the stereotyped fashion of "coming events" from Upper Burma, that we have now got quite accustomed to it, and so the only way is to be always prepared for it. The very frequency of its repetition may lull us into a dangerous security, and, therefore, I have thought it necessary to refer to it before concluding my remarks on the Burmese question

It was actually thought, by fair judges, that we should now have trouble with "the tyrant of Burma," and that the long-expected crisis was at hand, which would have brought about an easy solution of the Question. But neither the time had yet come, nor the man! Telegrams, of the 13th and 17th October, from the Viceroy, were published by the India Office, that it had been announced by the Chief Commissioner, Rangoon :—

"In case exaggerated accounts reach you, I beg to report as follows:

"On Sunday, the 10th, Deputy-Commissioner Thayetmyo reported that Upper Burmans were collecting on frontier and intended to attack British territory. On Wednesday he arranged with commanding officer for increasing the Allanmyo * garrison by one company of Native Infantry. Yesterday (Monday) Deputy-Commissioner telegraphed that possibly native informants had been misled, and there was no cause for alarm now. The cause for dissatisfaction was said to be our refusal to pay indemnity for losses caused by Nyoungoke Prince's incursion last May. I do not anticipate trouble, but have directed Deputy-Commissioner to take steps

* Allanmyo, on the left bank of the Irawadi, nearly opposite Thayetmyo, which is about 250 miles up the Irawadi from Rangoon.

to improve his sources of information, as alarms of this kind harass the troops and disturb the public; such rumours will have effect on trade; and already Flotilla Company's agent Thayetmyo has telegraphed alarming rumour to his Rangoon principal. Latest news from Mandalay gave no sign of probable troubles."

Again, the Chief Commissioner telegraphed to the Viceroy from Moulmein *:—

"Nothing has occurred on the Thayetmyo frontier, and no fresh rumours are reported thence. Origin of previous rumours not ascertained. I have no grounds for anticipating unusual events on frontier."

Anxiety, however, prevailed at Rangoon and up the river (Irawadi); and two companies of Native Infantry were ordered up to protect the villages which might be exposed to attack, and support the detachment at Allanmyo. And now came the rumour that the Nyoungyan Prince had escaped from Calcutta, and the crown of Theebau was about to pass away for ever. The transition from Nyoungoke to Nyoungyan was simple and natural; so Englishmen, as well as Burmese, believed the story of the escape in Rangoon; and no wonder it was believed in London. But there was really no cause for alarm. Nyoungyan—wisely biding his time—had only absented himself for a night or so from his house in or near Calcutta; and as nothing could be done without the "King" *in esse*, and intelligence was received from Mandalay that there was no probability of a disturbance on our frontier, all things flew into their places again very speedily; of course, just to wait till the next time. The assembly of royal troops on the frontier was also ascribed

* Moulmein (Maulmain) is about ninety or 100 miles nearly east from Rangoon, across the Gulf of Martaban.

to the number of dacoities (robberies) in the adjacent districts; but, of course, this was as absurd as the reported escape of Nyoungyan—or rather the departure of the favourite Prince for Ashé Pyee—as King Theebau was quite shrewd enough to know that his troops, unless under a very superior and *honest* General, were very likely, according to Peachum's view of a lawyer, to "encourage rogues" that they might "live by them!"

The whole play was thought to be got up by the King, as part of the political game which has been so long played at Mandalay, to see if we were on our guard; what effect false rumours of would be great events might have on the people of Burma; or to give the idea of ubiquity and readiness for service being attributes of the Ava soldiery. Theebau had this time missed his mark, and done something to facilitate the solution of the Burmese question. Each irritating movement made by the Golden Foot compels the Government of India to ask "how long this kind of thing is to be permitted to last? how long are British subjects to be subjected to periodical fits of excitement? how long is their trade to be upset and injured?"*

The same writer continues:—"However averse the English public may be to a policy of annexation, each successful demonstration made by men like Theebau inevitably forces upon the Government of India the consideration whether it would not be better for all parties in

* See a capital article in *Allen's Indian Mail*, October 14th, 1880—"The Mandalay Menace."

Burma, if the British frontier line were extended to Mandalay, or even to Bhamo."

And again, "A great deal has been said and done about the rectification of the frontier on the north-west of India; but there are politicians who are of opinion that a little rectification of the north-eastern frontier would not do any harm."

The political and commercial advantages of annexation, he says, "are obvious. The produce of the fairly rich country lying between Assam and the Irawadi would find a natural outlet in the emporium of Bhamo, whence it could be sent to China or to Rangoon, as happened to suit the interests of the merchant." Free trade on the Irawadi, from Bhamo to the sea—the noble river bearing on its ample bosom the wealth and produce of Upper Burma and south-western China—would create the grandest commercial revolution in Eastern Asia ever known by man!

It is impossible for any one who knows Burma not to agree in some measure with the following remarks, which the present writer found much in accordance with his own:—"At present the commerce of Upper Burma finds a precarious market just as the ruler of Mandalay or his officials may choose to interfere with it; but under British Government rich argosies would be borne along in one constant stream on the bosom of the great river, instead of the sparse and precarious fleet of boats which is at present the result of misrule at Mandalay. The advantages of annexation would be as great to the people as to trade. The Shans, who are in a perpetual state of rebellion against the Government of Independent Burma, would be brought into the ways of peace and industry." Pegu and Arakan would be rid of dacoits from Upper Burma, who can enter through well-known passes, and "the resources of a splendid country would have a fair chance of proper development." Such probable advantages as these (and a hundred others) surely cannot be ignored. These are the ends to be brought about; and if they can be consummated without annexation, so much the better for the thorough non-annexation argument. The question, then, comes to be, as matters at present exist, Is it possible to break up all the old worthless pieces, and to crystallize the mineral anew, without the political chemist, Great Britain, taking entire charge? If such be possible with Upper Burma, then farewell to annexation for ever: it will never more be required in our Eastern Empire. Anyway, as annexation is far from the policy of a wise and Liberal Government, the apparently more conciliatory mode will be sure to have a fair trial. The question then comes to be, Has not Upper Burma had a fair trial already? When Dr. Johnson said to his toady friend, Boswell, "You do not see your way through the question, Sir!" he remarked what might be applied to far greater men at the present day than the eminent biographer—to statesmen and others who take a one-sided view of a question, and are as difficult to move as the heavy siege-trains in a campaign of bygone days. It is a species of political creed which makes no progress whatever; and it too often proceeds—as is very probable in the present—from sheer ignorance of the position or the question at issue. Then we have those who halt between two opinions, who are not able to come boldly forth and say, "It would be utter madness to think of annexing useless and barren Afghanistan; it would be an act of wisdom and humanity to annex fertile and wealthy Upper Burma." "But it is useless to hamper our already overgrown Eastern Empire with countries that won't pay!" Is *pay*, then, to be made the grand sole criterion of success in our onward march of civilisation? Would it pay? It is sad to think that many well-educated men are incapable, when arguing on political and other subjects, of asking any better question. It might not pay all at once; but, as Pegu has done, it would eventually, and then greatly assist the impoverished finances of India. If nothing decided should be done now, it is quite possible that the inhabitants of Upper Burma, aided by the Shans and other tribes, may come forward at no distant date—yes, come boldly forward to the Viceroy, and declare, "We shall no longer have a Golden Foot to reign over us. Our country has, from bad government, become ruined and desolate, which once was flourishing and 'full of people.' As you have taken care of Pegu, so take care of us." This would, in fact, be making all Burma ONE, which, in every sense, it seems destined to be. Even Afghanistan may soon come forward and offer herself up to us, when the brave Afghans (so lately eulogised by the gallant and energetic Sir F. Roberts) find their country going from bad to worse; may come forward with "the keys of the Khyber" in their pocket, and, perhaps, with wild and chaotic Heratees, "the key of India" round their chief's neck; and it may be, also, various wild tribes in that quarter may come, all asking us to open up the lock of peace and prosperity which has so long been closed to them. They must be quite aware of what advantages the Punjab has gained by our rule, in the same manner as the people, even "the disaffected," of Upper Burma must often turn a longing eye towards Pegu and the beneficence of our local government.

The difference, of course, in the two cases is simply that we require either possession of, or strict control over, the one country, to make an harmonious whole; but we do not at all, at present, require the other. We can wait for Afghanistan, if it is ever to be ours, meanwhile fortifying ourselves against all chance of attack; but we cannot wait for something to be done with Upper Burma without damaging Lower or British Burma. The old and profitless *régime* has gone on too long in Chin-India; so, in public interest, for years to come, if we would be wise in time, it should be BURMA *versus* Afghanistan! And, by chief control or possession in Chin-India, what a checkmate we give to Russia in Eastern Asia! Strange it is that the "bugbear" should so long have excited a sensation in the West, and that the East should have been almost ignored. Even after the first disastrous Afghan war, or after forty years,* it is surely time to look more eastward,

* Look on this picture of eighty-two years ago, and compare with the present time:—India in a far from settled and comfortable state. Zemaun Shah, the King of the Afghans, and the remaining head of the Mahomedan power in the East, was with a powerful army at Lahore, hanging over our frontier. Among various well-known salient-points is then mentioned "a general ferment in the minds of the Mussulman princes and nobles, many of whom had been very recently deprived of power. 'When one looks back,' says a very distinguished Indian governor, 'on those times, one can hardly believe in the panic (Afghanistan) lately felt in India, which led to so

especially as troubles may be on the card between Russia and China. How Russia first got in the wedge—in south-west China at least—will be briefly told hereafter. But here, with a Russian fleet in the Pacific, or in Chinese waters, it may be well to remark, with reference to Professor Marten's brochure, *Le Conflit entre la Russie et la Chine*: "In regard to the question actually pending between Russia and China, the restitution of Kuldja, the Professor assumes that China wants war, and justifies Russia's detention of territory on the supposition that the return of the Celestials would be followed by a general massacre of the inhabitants." And when the flame spread, the power of England in Burma would chime in well with the steady "conciliatory attitude of China," displayed while resisting "the ever increasing demands of her antagonist."*

Although the recent apparent "Menace" from Mandalay came to nothing, still it educed certain points which seemed to put fresh difficulties in the way of solving the Burmese question. At any moment it might now be believed by the Burmese that Nyoungyan had escaped from Calcutta, and gone off to the Shan States to organize an insurrection against King Theebau; while the Royal troops continued their usual boasting, that they will double-up, crush, or crucify any English or Burmese troops who may support

many real dangers and evils!'"—"Vizier Ali Khan; or, the Massacre at Benares. A chapter in British Indian History." By Sir John Davis (1844).

* See Special Correspondent (St. Petersburg) of *Standard*, November 17th, 1880.

Nyoungyan's claim. Again, there is not so much fear on the frontier line as at Rangoon. The place was said to swarm with Theebau's subjects, those who for months past had been spreading sedition throughout the district in the smaller towns.

Of course, there are still Burmans who talk about "the glories of the old days," the triumphs of the Peacock flag, and "the fear of the Burman name extending far into India and China." So there is a certain amount of natural national vanity to be dealt with in considering the question. It is here worthy of remark that the excitement on the frontier and at the commercial capital having occurred during the Buddhist Lent (the end), it was wonderful how well the peace was kept at Rangoon—a result which would be greatly in our favour should any similar and more important "panic" or "scare" ever occur. The alarm, then, wore off, and Theebau became in "a quiet mood." He even sent down one of his steamers for merchandise to Rangoon. The captain announced his readiness to take goods back with him; but he did not get any. Some Chinese and other merchants, however, had offered to pay the King a subsidy for the use of his steamers. Regarding these vessels, it was remarked at the end of October:—

"If they were properly worked, and kept decent time, they might make large profits; but under the present management no traders will have anything to do with them."*

It is presumed that some idea will now have been formed,

* Rangoon Correspondent of *Daily News*, October 29th.

especially by those hitherto unacquainted with the subject, of the complicated nature of the Burmese question. It stands forth, like Satan, "proudly eminent," in apparently inextricable confusion, above all other Oriental questions. It seems like a question with a mysterious beginning and a doubtful end. Here, in Burma, for the greater part of two years, the next-door neighbour of our flourishing Province has been on his trial, continually letting, so far as we are concerned, "I dare not, wait upon I would"; neglecting our advice, laughing at our treaties, and wondering at our magnanimity and forbearance; ruining the concurrent commercial interests which must ever naturally exist between British and Upper Burma, and keeping Pegu locally, politically, and commercially in a continual state of anxiety. What is to be done with King Theebau? Is there any chance of amendment? It has before been remarked that this pertinacious Golden Foot may not be so black as he is painted; but still, taking the most charitable view, so far as we are interested, black enough in all conscience, as if a throne had been given by the evil genii to designed "obstructive" to progress and civilisation in Chin-India. What is to be done with him? On the answer would appear to rest at present the solution of the entire Burmese question.

While remarking elsewhere* on "Annexation and Non-Annexation," I endeavoured briefly to enumerate a few of the difficulties we labour under in our endeavours to reform Upper Burma, and make this grand region a worthy

* *Our Burmese Wars and Relations with Burma*, p. 416.

brother to his prosperous sister, Pegu. It is just possible that some strange mental revolution for the better may yet take place in King Theebau; but all will admit that is a long time in coming. As the King is said to be very well disposed towards the Liberals, he surely should make a fair start in the game of reform during the Liberal Government. This would, at least, prevent his crown from being taken away from him and given to another; the probable result, failing annexation, if he continues in the error of his ways.

It was lately rumoured that an English Commission was inquiring "into the legitimacy of the Mingoon (before alluded to) being Theebau's successor"; but to the writer, the Nyoungyan Prince being alive, the story seemed incredible. Any way, however, Theebau's crown, without the desired reformation, is "a crown of tinsel."*

Mr. Bryce, lately discoursing with his usual earnestness on Eastern affairs, declared that it was not a new question "whether the grievances of oppressed populations made it worth while to interfere with the Government of Turkey. . . . . But things had got beyond the point when the alternations of movement and rest were before us. The existing condition of Turkey could not be maintained. There was nothing solid to preserve."

For "Turkey" let us read the Kingdom of Ava, or Upper Burma, and state, as is the case with the former, that there, under the present rule, all things seem in a

* Lord Dalhousie. See *Our Burmese Wars, &c.*, p. 289. "Touching on Afghanistan, and the uselessness of making a treaty with the Golden Foot," see also pp. 287, 291.

state of "hopeless confusion"; and it is only a question of time, or "how soon the inevitable collapse will come." And, again, by carrying out the principle of leaving things alone too far, we simply invite a war!

The true greatness of a once famous kingdom depends on our early treatment of the Burmese question. Peace, commercial prosperity, the development of hidden resources, and how to make, like Themistocles, "a small town a great city," have been the author's watchwords in writing these few remarks. The misfortune with Theebau is that, unlike the great Athenian, he can "fiddle," but he cannot do anything for his kingdom. There is at present absolutely nothing going on in Upper Burma "to the weal and advancement of the State." To take the very mildest view of the whole matter, especially of one whose strange progress occupied some space in his larger work, perhaps the writer is warranted in supposing there may be "counsellors and governors" around Theebau, "which may be held sufficient, *negotiis pares*, able to manage affairs, and to keep them from precipices and manifest inconveniences; which, nevertheless, are far from the ability to raise and amplify an estate"—like Lord Lawrence or Sir Arthur Phayre—"in power, means, and fortune";* by doing which, if Orientals would only emerge from their selfishness and seclusion, and learn the easy lesson, there must ever be mutual benefit in sharing these inestimable blessings with others. When this reciprocal philosophy is fairly understood in the East, European and Indian states-

* Bacon's *Essays*.

men will no longer have to puzzle their brains with intricate, tedious Oriental questions. Then the political millenial day will be ushered in, the joy-bells ringing forth "Peace on earth—good-will towards men!"

December, 1880.

CHAPTER III.

BRITISH AND UPPER BURMA, AND WESTERN CHINA: THEIR CONCURRENT COMMERCIAL INTERESTS.

"Commerce wore a rostral-crown upon her head, and kept her eyes fixed upon a compass."—TATLER.

[To the June (1880) number of the *Journal of the Society of Arts*, p. 644, the present writer contributed the greater portion of the following paper. In the same number of the journal will also be found some interesting statistics on the "Opium Trade in India," the production and sale of opium being a Government monopoly (casually alluded to in "The Burmese Question"), yielding eight and a half to nine millions sterling. The writer had then nothing to say about the consumption of opium in British Burma. Mr. Pease, in the House of Commons on the 8th of July, asked the Secretary of State for India whether he had received a copy of a memorandum forwarded in the spring of the year (1880) by Mr. Aitchison, Chief Commissioner, on the subject. The Marquis of Hartington replied that the paper in question had not been received by the India Office. It is difficult to see, in the opinion of not a few observers, why Great Britain should interfere with the opium eaters of China, Burma, and India. Like alcohol in England, the moderate use of the valuable drug has many virtues and great healing power, especially in Eastern countries; and the Oriental has therefore as much right to his opium as the Englishman has to his pipe, beer, and spirits, which, if used, and not abused, solace him after his daily toil. We have much to do in the East before interfering with the time-honoured custom of opium-eating. There it is everywhere a case of "Local Option." What gin, whisky, and ale are to the Briton, opium is to the Oriental, with this difference, that if the Asiatic can enjoy "an elysium on earth" with a small piece of opium in his cheek, he can easily forego the spirit which so much more speedily renders a man useless, or "drunk and incapable." Commerce being essentially a sober game, perhaps this view of the question may be kept in mind in any future discussion of Concurrent Commercial Interests in the East.]

The concurrent or mutual commercial interests of foreign countries must ever engage the attention of the merchant and the politician: of the merchant, because the very life and soul of his calling depend on them; and of the politician, because it will be invariably found—especially in the East—that commerce is the secret or unseen guiding star of all political conduct.

Politically speaking, British and Upper Burma should be one, to make matters entirely safe in Eastern Asia. Commercially speaking, the unity of these two countries, in the vast interests of a comparatively new and rapidly rising commerce, as well as of civilisation, cannot be too much insisted on. It is simply a natural state of things—a sort of holy alliance designed by a far greater than Indra, and brought about chiefly by the mighty Irawadi—the grand artery or highway of Burma—which it were idle not to recognize. Ireland is not more necessary to the power and prosperity of England than Upper Burma is to Pegu. Alompra, the hunter, founder of the present dynasty, knew well the value of what I have styled elsewhere a "Princess among the Provinces"; and it did not require any very great genius to know that a kingdom, such as Upper Burma, entirely cut off from all communication with the sea, or from the advantages of many fine ports, was sheer mockery—a crown of tinsel, as Lord Dalhousie remarked; and this was the cause, in the Treaty of 1855, of the late King of Burma's persistently yet naturally refusing to sign away Pegu, the glorious conquest and inheritance of his ancestor, notwithstanding the well-arranged existence of "friendly relations" between us.* Without any desire to advocate annexation, I believe there is a deeply felt yearning for British rule or British protection throughout Upper Burma; for the people of the lower country are a thousand times safer and happier than ever before, as would be immediately seen by treading "the long extent of backward time" in the histories of Pegu and the former kingdom of Ava.†

* *Our Burmese Wars, &c.*, pp. 379–380. See also pp. 418–419.

† Some slight idea of former Burmese and Peguese misery, under a cruel despotism, will be gained by the perusal of a paper on "Sparseness of Population," commencing at p. 328, especially of pp. 335–336, *Our Burmese Wars*, &c.

In some way or other, Humanity, and Civilisation, and Commerce all cry aloud for our assistance in the present crisis; and shall we deny it to one of the fairest and most productive countries of God's earth?

For the sake of those who have not been able to give much time or attention to Burma, before turning to commercial matter, I shall beg leave to state very briefly that Pegu, Arakan, and the long line of sea-coast named Tenasserim—the three maritime provinces of Chin-India or India beyond the Ganges—were united under one administration in January 1862, and called British Burma. Arakan and Tenasserim were acquired by treaty after the first Burmese war of 1824–25–26; and Pegu was occupied and retained consequent on the second war of 1852–53. The entire length of the country is upwards of 900 miles, and the area about 90,000 square miles,* or half the size of Spain. The country lies between 20° 50′ on the north, and on the south in about 10° 50′ north latitude. British Burma is bounded on the west by the Bay of Bengal; Arakan on the north by Chittagong, and some independent states, and on the east by the Yoma mountains; Pegu is separated from Upper Burma on the north by a line corresponding to the 19° 30′ parallel of north latitude, and is bounded on the east by the Salween river; Tenasserim is bounded on the east by a long line of mountains separating it from Siam, and varying from 3,000 to 5,000 feet above the sea. The physical aspect of the country is thus described:—Arakan is separated from

* Arakan contains 18,000; Pegu, 34,000; and Tenasserim, 38,000 square miles.

Pegu and Upper Burma on the east by a range of mountains, which attains at its greatest elevation a height of 7,000 feet. The range runs nearly parallel with the line of sea-coast, and gradually lowers towards the south. The northern portion of the country has a large extent of alluvial soil. In the lower course of the river Kuladan (which rises in the mountains to the east of Arakan) and its numerous affluents, the breadth of the land from the shore to the water-shed mountains is from 80 to 90 miles. The water-shed range separating Arakan from Pegu extends southerly, and between that range and the sea-shore for a length of nearly 200 miles, as far as a point near Cape Negrais, the country is a mere narrow strip of land. Pegu and Martaban lie in the valleys of the Irawadi and Sittang rivers. These valleys, bounded east and west by mountain ranges, are narrow in their upper portions, but expand at the delta of the Irawadi into "a magnificent alluvial region, penetrated by a vast number of tidal creeks, and extending over 10,000 square miles."* Unlike India, drought is unknown in Burma, and, consequently, famine, that occasional scourge of our Imperial dependency, is there quite unknown.

To give a more general idea of the country, I shall cite a few extracts from a valuable work † which has recently appeared at Rangoon, the capital of British Burma. Rangoon is described as "a district in the Pegu division,

* See George Duncan's *Geography of India, &c.*, pp. 59-60.

† *The British Burma Gazetteer*, in two volumes. Vol. II., compiled by authority. Rangoon: Printed at the Government Press, 1879. Of course, these extracts were omitted in the paper for the *Society of Arts'* journal.

occupying the sea-board from the mouth of the Tsit-Toung westward to that mouth of the great Irawadi river which is generally known as the China Bakir, but is more correctly called the To, and extending inland up the valleys of the Irawadi and the Tsit-Toung rivers to the Henzada and Tharawadi districts on the west of the Pegu Roma, and to the Shwé-gyeen district of Tenasserim on the east."

"*The general aspect of the district* is that of a vast plain extending along the sea-coast, and, slowly rising, stretching north for some twenty-five miles, when, in about the centre, it is met and, as it were, checked by the lower slopes of the Pegu Roma, and, struggling up amongst these mountains in the valleys of the Poo-zwon-doung (Puzen-doun) and the Pegu, it folds round them east and west, and rolls on, forming portions of the valleys of the Tsit-toung and of the Hlaing. South of the Pegu and in the greater part of the valley of the Hlaing or Rangoon, for some distance above the latitude of the town of the same name, the country is everywhere highly intersected by tidal creeks; the water, a few feet below the surface, is brackish and undrinkable and wells are useless, but further north are streams tidal for some distance and fresh higher up."

"The only MOUNTAINS in the district are the Pegu Roma, which enter in the extreme north, where they attain an estimated height of 2,000 feet, the highest elevation of the range, and a few miles lower down fork out into two main branches with several subsidiary spurs. The western branch (which has a general S.S.W. direction) and its offshoots divide the valleys of the Hlaing and Puzendoun rivers, and, after rising once more in the irregularly shaped lime-stone hill called Toung-gnyo, a little to the south of the seventeenth parallel, terminate as a hilly range some thirty miles north of Rangoon. The range is continued as an elevated ridge past that town, where it appears in the laterite hills round the great pagoda and, beyond the Pegu river, in the Syriam Koondan, finally disappearing beneath the alluvial plains of the delta, being last seen in the rocks which crop up in the Hmaw-won stream. The southern portion of this ridge lying between the Pegu river and the Hmaw-won runs in a direction nearly parallel to and about three miles east of the Rangoon river, and, nowhere more than five miles broad, is locally known as the Thaulyeng (Syriam) Koondan or 'rising ground.' The eastern branch continues from the point of bifurcation towards the S.S.E. and, intersected by the Pegu valley, sinks near the town of Pegu, and finally disappears south of the Pegu river, where it is represented by an undulating wooded tract of no great extent. The sides of the main range are, as a rule, steep, and the valleys sharply excavated, but the upper portion of the Pegu valley has more the character of a table-land with a hilly surface, intersected by deep ravines." "The principal *river* is the Hlaing, which rises near Prome as the Zay, and entering this district in about 17° 30′, flows S.S.E., at first through high sandy banks, past Rangoon, falling into the sea in about 16° 30′ as the Rangoon river. It is navigable by the largest sea-going vessels as far as Rangoon at all seasons, and during spring tides ships of considerable burden can ascend for thirty miles further; but just below Rangoon the Hastings shoal stretches across the river, and bars the approach of ships of heavy draught except at springs. During the north-west monsoon river steamers can ascend to beyond the northern boundary of the district, and boats of from 200 to 300 baskets burden can navigate the upper portion at all seasons. The tide is felt beyond the northern boundary, and the water is brackish and undrinkable as high as the village of Kywai-Koo, about twenty miles below Hlaing." "The Puzendoun rises in the eastern slopes of the southern spurs of the Pegu Roma, and falls into the Pegu river at its mouth at the town of Rangoon, after a south-easterly course of some fifty-three miles through a valley at first narrow but suddenly widening out eastwards. At its mouth it is 440 yards broad, and large ships could formerly ascend for a short distance to the numerous rice-cleaning mills erected in the Puzendoun quarter of Rangoon and on the opposite bank. It is now silting up, owing to the vast quantities of rice husk discharged from the mills. Small boats can, during the rains, go to within twenty miles of its source, where the water is sweet and the banks and bed rocky. The valley through which this river flows is rich in valuable timber in the north, and in the south is well cultivated with rice. The Pegu river rises in the eastern slopes of the Pegu Roma, and falls into the Rangoon, or Hlaing river, at Rangoon. For some distance from its source it traverses a narrow rocky valley, and is fed by numerous mountain torrents; but below the old town of Pegu it enters a flat and fertile country, well cultivated with rice. During the rains it is navigable by river steamers and by the largest boats as far as Pegu, but during the cold and hot seasons large boats can ascend that distance during spring-tides only. At all seasons sea-going vessels can pass up for a few miles. . . . A new locked canal forms a portion of the eastern boundary of the district. West of the Hlaing the whole country is divided and sub-divided by tidal creeks, many navigable by large boats, which unite the Hlaing and the numerous mouths of the Irawadi."

"The FORESTS include tracts of all classes."

"The LOCAL ACCOUNTS and the Telugoo and Tamil traditions seem to show that, probably some thousand years B.C., the inhabitants of Tulingana visited and colonised the coast of Burma, finding there a Mon population. . . . and the country of the colonists appears in the word *Talaing*, known to surrounding nations and to Europeans. The palm-leaf histories allude to a city called Aramana, on the site of *the present Rangoon*, and assert that during the lifetime of Gautama, that is before 543 B C., the Shwé Dagon Pagoda in Rangoon was founded by two brothers, Poo (*dove*) and Ta-paw (*plenty*), sons of the King of Ook-ka-la-ba, west of Rangoon, and near the modern Twan-te, who had visited India, and had met and conversed with Gautama, from whom they had received several of his hairs; but *the first notice of the country* which can be considered as historical is given in the Sinhalese Mahawanso, which speaks of the mission of Sono and Uttaro, sent by the third Buddhist Council (held in 241 B C.) to Savarna-bhoo-mee to spread the Buddhist faith in its purity. It seems clear that the delta of the Irawadi was not exempt from the almost 'religious war' which prevailed between the followers of the Brahmanic and Buddhistic faiths, the victory eventually passing to the one body in India and to the other in Burma. Here the differences lasted for several hundreds of years, until about the end of the eighth century, the Buddhists being recruited in the meanwhile by the arrival of their co-religionists expelled from India. One of the results of these religious differences was *the foundation of the city* of Pegu in 573 A.D. by Tha-ma-la and Nee-ma-la, sons of the King of Tha-htoon by *a mother* of Nága descent, who were excluded from the throne of their father." It is said that Martaban was now founded. "The country was unsuccessfully invaded in 590 A.D. by the King of Bij-ja-na-ga-ran (*Vizianagram?*). Thirteen kings followed between this period and 746 A.D., and by this time the kingdom had been much extended (from the Arakan mountains on the west to the Salween on the east)." "The Buddhist religion was not generally accepted in the country, and the tenth King of Pegu, Poon-na-ree-ka (Brahman heart), and more especially his son and successor Tek-tha, appears to have been at least inclined towards Hindu traditions." There is a great hiatus in the history of Pegu between the death of Tek-tha and the year 1050 A.D., "when Anaw-ra-hta, the King of Pagan, conquered the country, and it remained subject to the Burmans for some two centuries." For more information regarding early Pegu, the readers of the new *British Burma Gazetteer* are referred to that highly distinguished and "learned and patient investigator," Sir Arthur Phayre, whose history of

Pegu, published in the *Journal of the Bengal Asiatic Society*, is considered "by far the most trustworthy work on the subject."* It is curious to think that in British Burma's first Chief Commissioner, a greater than any of the early Pegu kings should arise in our time—one of our own countrymen, destined to create the Pegu province; or, we may say, when all its parts were scattered by disorder and anarchy and tyranny of the direst kind, to bring all together again into an harmonious whole by crystallizing the mineral anew, and consolidating British Burma.†

Rangoon (as has already been said), the capital of the Pegu Province, and consequently of British Burma, some twenty or twenty-five miles from the sea—the future Liverpool or Glasgow of Chin-India—before uttering a word about its commerce, may be considered worthy of brief mention as to the origin of the name. In the early Talaing histories it has the name of Dagon, originally that of the Shwé Dagon Pagoda, erected on the summit of the laterite formation before mentioned after the burial therein, by Poo and Ta-paw, of "some of Gautama's hairs from the Buddha himself." Afterwards, we read, in the wars which took place between the kings of Pegu and of Burma, Dagon often changed hands; and when at last, in 1763, "the Burman Aloung-bhoora (Alompra) drove out the Talaing garrison of Ava, then the Burman capital, and eventually conquered the Talaing kingdom, he came down to Dagon, repaired—and thus, to a certain extent, to Peguan feelings desecrated—the great Shwé Dagon

* *British Burma Gazetteer*, pp. 537–538 (*note*).

† *Our Burmese Wars, &c.*, p. 351.

Pagoda, almost refounded the town, and re-named it Ran-Koon ('the end of the war,' from *Ran* war, and *Koon* or *Goon*, 'finished, exhausted') or Rangoon, the name it has ever since borne, and made it the seat of the Viceroyalty which he established." In the last decade of the eighteenth century, the English obtained leave to establish a factory in Rangoon, surrounding it by a brick wall, and hoisting the British colours.

Next, the etymology of *Dagon*, which word we read is derived from the Talaing "Takoon," which signifies "a tree or log lying athwart"—alluded to in a legend connected with the foundation—" and which has been corrupted into Dagon,* or Dagun in Burmese. The word 'Shwé,' or 'golden,' is a Burmese translation of the original Talaing word prefixed to Takoon. It is now used generally as a term indicative of excellence." It is especially used with all connected with the Golden Foot, or Majesty of Ava, as I have explained elsewhere.

From this point we may pass on to the Irawadi the grand artery of Burma, and the constant feeder of Rangoon with the commerce and wealth of the upper country, south-west China, and the various States around and to the northward of Mandalay, the Burman capital, now so well-known to the British merchants of Rangoon, and made famous by deeds of dreadful note. With such a magnificent highway as the Irawadi, with its many mouths, aided by the other main rivers, the Hlaing or Rangoon, the Pegu, the Sittang, and the Beling, it may be said that there is no limit to the progress of commerce

* The place was called in the Moon (or Mon) language "Dagon."

in Burma. The Irawadi flows for about 800 miles before reaching the British possessions, through which it runs for 240 miles more. "It is navigable for river steamers as far as Bhamo, 600 miles beyond the British frontier." The velocity of its waters, when the river is full, is said to be five miles an hour. General Fytche informs us that "Colonel Yule, from facts collected by him, assumes that the Irawadi takes its rise in the lofty Langtam range of the Himalayas, whose peaks, covered with perpetual snow, separate the valleys inhabited by the Shan race of Khamtis from the head waters of the sacred Brahmaputra."* But the sources of this principal river in Upper and British Burma, which traverses the Pegu division from north to south, have never been explored, though several praiseworthy attempts have been made. The most reliable information I have seen on the subject is with reference to the attempt made in 1827 by Lieutenants Wilcox and Burlton, and more recent explorers, that it has been shown, "as conclusively as can be shown, until the river is traced to its source, that it rises in the southern slopes of the Pat Koi mountains, one branch in 28° N. latitude, and 97° 30′ E. longitude, and another in the same mountains a few days journey further eastward; the two, that to the west called by the Burmese Myit-gyee, or 'Large river,' and that to the east Myit-nge or 'Small river,' uniting to form the Irawadi in about 26° N. latitude."†

* *Burma, Past and Present*, vol. i. p. 268.

† Captain Hannay fixed the junction in 26°. See also *British Burma Gazetteer*, p. 207, vol. ii.

It is interesting to note, with reference to Henzada, a large district in the Pegu division, covering an area of upwards of 4,000 square miles, "in the valley of the Irawadi, at the head of the delta, and lying on both banks of that river," that nearly all the large towns are on the right bank of the Irawadi, though many important places are in Tharawadi, that is the country east of the river. Here, however, "the great extent of the annual inundations and the smaller extent of country fitted for the cultivation of rice, the great staple produce of the province, though perhaps favourable to the existence of numerous small villages, retard the formation of the large trading towns, and nearly all large towns in this district owe their magnitude, if not their very existence, to the trade in the products of the surrounding country." Again, "the large number of the Henzada villages and hamlets are along the banks of the Irawadi, and on the banks of the tributary streams to the west of that river. It may safely be asserted that the embankments along the Irawadi, which protect such an extensive tract of fertile rice country from the inundations to which it was annually subject, will not only produce a steady increase in the size of villages now existing and occupied by cultivators of the neighbouring plains, but will cause the establishment of many new ones in spots hitherto waste, and waiting only for relief from the superabundant waters of the river, and for labour to become valuable and fruitful fields" The breadth of the Irawadi varies from one to two, three, and even four or five miles; and of this noble river, which intersects the Burman dominions, it has been well said—"Like the Nile and the Ganges, inundating the plains, it dispenses fertility and abundance, while it affords an extensive inland navigation quite through the country to the border of China."*

Surely it is worth while knowing the etymology of such a river as the Irawadi. On this point nothing whatever was attempted regarding it in *Our Burmese Wars and Relations with Burma*, although the Arabic *wádí*†—a river or stream—was cited, to show what seemed the more correct spelling, or with one *d* only. A learned critic, however, was down upon me for want of etymological knowledge, informing the public at the same time, in the most praiseworthy manner, that the author, in his "want of philological training," had "evidently no suspicion that the whole word is a slight corruption of the Sanskrit *Airâvatî*, the feminine of the god Indra's elephant." He was also kind enough to inform me of *vati* meaning "like"; and that in the Punjab, the Ravee is also a corruption of *aira* (moisture) *vati*—the *t* omitted for the soft *v*. The critic, I found, was perfectly right. It is the name given to Indra's elephant, and signifies "great moisture" or water. Indra, in fact, answers to Zeus (Jupiter), the heaven or sky, including the atmosphere, the immediate source of rain; hence appropriate for a river. As to Zeus, a distinguished Orientalist believes that the original Greek word really referred to the material sky, including the atmosphere; and Indra, in the Hindu mythology, occupied the same position. Hindu etymology

* *Account of the Burmese Empire.*

† *Our Burmese Wars, &c.*, p. 17.

in a Buddhist country is easily explained, as, in addition to facts already mentioned, the Buddhists and Hindus, of course, had "the same original national beginning," and the same mythology, just as Catholics and Protestants equally acknowledge the Apostles and early Fathers of the Church.

So much, then, for the name of Burma's noble river, and for Indra, the Indian god of the "invisible heavens," who dwells in his celestial city, Amaravati, and who is considered also the "governor of the Eastern portion of the world."*

* The character of Indra in itself is a wonderful mythological study; and strange it is that students in England give it so little attention. In their great Indian Empire they have a mythology quite equal to the Greek—in fact, the parent of nearly all others—in which, as said elsewhere, are embedded "the fossilized skeletons of the faith." Brahma and Sarasvati (like Abraham and Sara); Vishnu, Lakshmi (the Apollo and Venus); Siva and Parvati (or *Kali*) Pluto and Proserpine—present a field in themselves for the most i teresting analogical investigation. And when their researches are fini hed in the land of the Veda, they can step with advantage int uore "silent land" of Buddha—in China or Burma.

CHAPTER IV.

BRITISH AND UPPER BURMA AND WESTERN CHINA.

(*Continued.*)

LET us now return to Rangoon, the grand emporium of commerce in British Burma, where "the quick pulse of gain" is ever on the alert, and where fortunes have been made and lost—and doubtless are still—with amazing rapidity.

Rice being the grand export of the Pegu province, it may first be of interest to note the remarkable increase of rice land under cultivation from 1868 to 1876, in spite of occasional excessive inundation (very frequent before the increase of embankments in 1862), in the Henzada district, the township of which is on the right bank of the Irawadi. In 1868 the cultivated area was 204,495 acres, and in 1876, 320,300 acres; or since the annexation of Pegu (1853), there has been an increase in the total cultivated area of nearly 250,000 acres, "greater than the most sanguine could have hoped for." It may also be remarked that the cotton grown in this (Henzada) district is inferior to that grown in the north, the produce being locally consumed.

But rice, as already stated, is the chief commodity of the Henzada district, which, situated at the head of the delta of the Irawadi, and containing much fertile land for the cultivation of this most useful grain, affords a ready market for Rangoon and Bassein, "communication with both being easy from the numerous creeks which intersect the country."

In a country like Pegu, where there is a great sparseness of population (accounted for elsewhere),* but which has risen from a little more than a million, in a quarter of a century, to about 3,000,000, it may be noted that, out of the total (176,404) males in the Rangoon district in 1872 (the paucity of the Talaings being especially noticeable), there were nearly 4,000 Christians, 600 Hindus, 300 Mahomedans, and 171,500 Buddhists. In 1878, the capital had 91,500 inhabitants. The population of the town of Rangoon for variety is, perhaps, unsurpassed in the world—Burmans, Talaings (the *Mon* race), Karens, Shans, Arakanese, Hindus, Mahomedans, Chinese, Europeans, Eurasians, Americans, and others—in the census year of 1872 giving a total of 98,700. The population is now (1880) over 100,000; for, like the river traffic between Mandalay and Rangoon, since 1862, it may be said to have gone on steadily increasing till 1878–79.

The principal articles manufactured in the Rangoon district are salt, pottery, fish-paste (nga-pee), mats, and silk, and cotton cloths; all for local consumption, except the pottery and nga-pee, which are exported, the latter to

* See *Our Burmese Wars, &c.*, p. 332.

Upper Burma. The salt is made during the hot weather, along the sea-coast, and elsewhere by solar evaporation, or by "boiling in iron or earthen pots, the iron yielding the greater out-turn."

It is interesting to look back on the state of commerce with the British settlements in India from 1802 to 1806. Then the exportation of rice and of the precious metals was strictly prohibited, and the total imports exceeded the total exports by Rs. 1,856,638. The imported articles in the year of Trafalgar (1805), were tin, wine, woollens, piece-goods, opium, grain, rum, tin and plated ware, iron-mongery, canvas, &c., giving a total value, including treasure (Rs. 19,579), of Rs. 245,232. The articles of export were timber, pepper, orpiment, coir-rope, ponies, cardamoms, stick-lac, wax, sundries, and treasure.

From 1813–14 to 1820–21, the returns of trade between Rangoon and Calcutta give the principal imports as piece-goods, raw silk, cotton, indigo, saltpetre, sugar, rice, pepper, and opium. At the close of the first war (1826), Arakan became a rice-granary of immense importance, in a great measure obviating the import of rice from Calcutta. After the second Burmese war (1852–53), Pegu became British territory. From 1826 to 1852, among the annual number of arrivals and departures, there were only twenty English vessels from 100 to 1,000 tons. In 1855, the total tonnage of all vessels, import and export, amounted to upwards of 270,000 tons, which in nine years (1863–64), became doubled,* and has been increasing in an astonishing propor-

* See *Our Burmese Wars, &c.*, p. 346.—In 1875–76, vessels cleared at the ports of the province amounted to 2,551, of 1,164,616 tons burthen.

tion ever since. No wonder it has been said that "when Pegu passed to the English trade began to improve, and has proceeded with vast strides." When we come to consider that the value of the export and import trade, excluding treasure, in 1877–78 amounted to Rs. 81,920,257, as compared with Rs. 21,310,561 in 1858–59,* we must unhesitatingly declare that such a steady prosperity as this is unparalled in the history of British connection with the East. These facts alone are well worthy of attention from the lords of British Commerce, and show what might be done were there no monopolizing obstructiveness of a Burmese Golden-Footed monarch to be encountered. If Free Trade, wandering up and down the world, should ever seek a fitting temple to dwell in, perhaps avoiding her "mutual friend" Reciprocity, and attended by the honoured shade of Richard Cobden—all regal obstructives being swept aside—she will not be able to do better, while waiting for the golden edifice, than to pitch her tent in Chin-India Upper Burma would afford her triumphs which she could not gain elsewhere, and certainly in no other portion of our Eastern Empire.

The commerce of British Burma is carried on chiefly with Great Britain, the three Presidencies of India, the Straits, Ceylon, and the Nicobars. The ports are Rangoon, Maulmain, Akyab, Tavoy, Mergui, Bassein, Kyook Phyoo, and Cheduba,—certainly no want of fine harbours for trade. The articles of import and export before the Burmese wars, have already been mentioned. The

* In 1868–69, the figures were:—Imports, Rs. 23,464,602; and exports Rs. 19,540,551, giving a total of Rs. 43,005,153.

former, after the second war, consisted chiefly of cotton goods, hardware, machinery, coal, books, provisions, woollen goods, silks, canvas, wines, drugs, dyes, spices, fruits, sugar, arms, and carriages. The exports have principally been rice, timber, petroleum, hides, ivory, cotton, grain, and ponies. To this may be added jewellery and precious stones, also a goodly list of useful sundries. In trade with Burma, as a rule, the imports have generally exceeded the exports, although such was very far from being the case in 1877–78,* and in a few other years. In a year of famine in India, or elsewhere, the exports from Rangoon would probably exceed the imports. General Fytche, in his *Burma Past and Present*, remarks, after the astonishing but truthful statement that "if the commerce of India bore the same proportion to population" (as British Burma) "it would be ten times greater than it is—that is to say, it would be about nine hundred and fifty millions, instead of ninety-five," that British Burma also contrasts favourably with India, in the value of the imports being much nearer to that of the exports.† It is useful to bear in mind that, some fifteen years ago, the annual value of the imports was rather more than £2,000,000, and of the exports than £3,000,000. In 1875–76, the value of the sea-borne and inland exports was £7,208,896, and imports £6,159,925, with a population a little over three millions, and a gross revenue over two millions sterling.

On Pegu passing to the English, the whole Burmese

* In this year the imports were Rs. 37,777,242; and the exports 44,143,015; and in 1864–65, the annual value of the exports was £3,000,000, against only £2,000,000 of imports.

† Vol. i. pp. 320-21.

customs system changed, and restrictions on importation and exportation were removed, and the interior of the country gradually developed. Rangoon soon became the third port in India. "Cotton piece-goods, salt, and various other articles have poured in, whilst rice has more than taken the place of timber, and cutch, hides, horns, and petroleum have added to the export trade."

It may also be remarked, with reference to the various imports and exports, that some of the articles merely "pass through the country; candles, cotton-twist, cotton piece-goods, earthenware and porcelain, glass, glass-ware, &c., find their way direct into Upper Burma, whilst caoutchouc, raw cotton, gums and resins, hides, horn, ivory, lac, mineral oils, spices, tobacco, and wood, are partly, and jade is entirely, drawn from that country." The duty levied, of course, depends upon the tariff.*

A great season in Rangoon—perhaps the greatest—is the rice season, which commences in January and ends in May; but there are sales all the year round. The "prices of rice in the husk at the mills in Rangoon" during seven years, varied, per 100 baskets, from 1872 to 1878, from January to October, from 55 to 100 and 200 rupees; and if any of us should think of doing a rice business at Rangoon, it may be stated that "each firm has its one or more brokers, and several buyers; the former, as a rule, residing on the mill premises† In its strictest

* For King Theebau's Tariff, see *Our Burmese Wars, &c.*, p. 414.

† In the present year (1880) the Burma rice trade is in a most flourishing state. In August the exports exceeded over a lakh (£10,000) those of 1879. Akyab, Bassein, and Rangoon, supply large quantities of rice to foreign countries.

sense, *Nunquam Dormio* may be considered a most appropriate motto for Rangoon, destined, as I have already said, to be the Liverpool or Glasgow of Chin-India.

I shall now make a few remarks on the trade *in esse* with south-western China, which I shall preface with a few words on the treaties we concluded with Upper Burma in 1862 and in 1867. By the treaty of 1862, concluded by Sir Arthur (then Colonel) Phayre, trade *in* and *through* Upper Burma was "freely thrown open to British enterprise;" and again, the Bhamo trade route (to Yunnan, in south-western China), was to be explored, "under the treaty of 1862.' * The King of Burma would not consent to a "joint mission," as desired by the Indian Government. Perhaps the vassal, Golden-Foot,—although "Lord of Earth and Air,"—thought he might offend his Chinese Lord, the "Vicegerent of all under Heaven," by so doing; but if any man could have obtained the wishes of our Government at this time, beyond all question that man was the First Chief Commissioner of British Burma. And this leads me to remark that I committed an error, or rather inadvertence, in my review of Dr. Anderson's interesting work, *From Mandalay to Momien*,† where I say that "there was evidently something wrong in the framing of the treaty of 1862." I should have written that there was evidently considerable difficulty about the "joint mission," as regarding trade with south-western China, through Upper Burma, in the endeavour to bring the treaty of 1862 to the successful issue desired by the Indian Government.

* See Dr. Anderson's *From Mandalay to Momien*, p. 6.

† *Our Burmese Wars, &c.*, p. 357.

As has been remarked, then, the treaty of 1862 paved the way for the well-known mission or expedition under Major Sladen, at the commencement of 1868, to explore the trade-routes to China *viâ* Bhamo, (consequent on the treaty, under General Fytche, of 1867), which, notwithstanding the credit attached to the officers concerned, led to no useful or practical results. "Possibly," it has been said, "King Mengdon was not displeased at our want of success;" but, strange enough, provoking and frequently petty obstructions have in some way or other surrounded British exertions with regard to commerce in Upper Burma, ever since 1868; and, when Mengdon died, towards the end of 1878, his eccentric son Theebau's dissipated and murderous career began, as if to make the chance of sound friendly relations with the British, in the interests of commerce and civilisation, more distant than ever.* And, in my humble opinion, after the withdrawal of our Resident from Mandalay, to make a treaty—commercial or otherwise—with such a modern Nero, would be highly impolitic, or the very worst thing we could do. Lord Dalhousie, in reviewing his administration, in the famous Minute of 28th February 1856, writes: "When the Honourable Court recalls to mind that from the very first, in 1852, I deprecated the reconstruction of any treaty relations with the Court of Ava at all, it will not be surprised to find me add, that I still consider peace with Ava as even more likely to be maintained in the absence of all commercial or friendly treaties, than if those conventions had been renewed as

* See article on the "Critical State of Burmese Affairs."—*Allen's Indian Mail*, February 26th, 1880, p. 180.

before." * Notwithstanding such prudent advice from a master-mind, we have since made treaties with Burma; and, for the sake of history, to be just and impartial, it must be said, and I grieve to write it, that in these matters our policy towards the Golden Foot has not always been in the right direction. For instance, in the treaty of 1867, we first ratified it, saying not a word about the "arms," and then repudiated the arrangement! (*See* Note I.) In future, then, very great care should be taken in making treaties with Oriental potentates. Let us rather have no treaties at all with them; it is impossible for the Oriental mind to thoroughly understand the solemn nature of a treaty.

Seven or eight years ago, while writing on the subject of trade with south-western China, I remarked:—"Russia is evidently busy, and anxious to conclude other commercial treaties besides those with the chiefs of Khokand, Bokhara, and Yarkand, and to become the aggressor elsewhere than in Khiva, to which all eyes are at present turned. It has been well said, that if Russia be baffled this year (1873), she will succeed at last as surely as in

* The first portion of the paragraph containing the above remarkable extract is also well worthy of notice at the present time:—"Although the mission which lately proceeded to the Court of Ava (in 1855, under Sir Arthur Phayre), with the primary object of reciprocating the friendly feeling which the King of Ava had previously shown, by voluntarily despatching an embassy to the Governor-General of India, has brought back with it no treaty of alliance or of commerce, I nevertheless regard the continuance of peace between the States as being not less secure than the most formal instrument could have made it." See also *Our Burmese Wars, &c.*, pp. 322–24, and 379.

Circassia. . . . The persevering Russians are hardly in favour at present in China. Russian merchants who had advanced have been ordered back to Mongolia; and the Chinese export trade is almost entirely in English hands. . . . It is pleasing to read that English Agents have been in China, persuading the Chinese Government of the special importance of its western provinces, which, if the information be correct, augurs well for any attempt by Great Britain to open trade through Burma, or from Assam, with south-western China. There we are free from troubles, while China continues suspicious of the designs of Russia, and we determine that the great aggressive power shall not come to the southward."*

In February 1880, we read of the Russian Government (with reference to a treaty in which Russia engaged to provision Chinese troops while operating against Kashgar rebels) having prohibited commercial caravans from crossing the Siberian frontier into Chinese Mongolia. A recent treaty concluded by the Chinese Ambassador at St. Petersburg was "too one-sided a document" to be approved at Pekin. The Chinese refusal to ratify the draft was answered by the discontinuance of commercial relations on the confines of the two empires. Russia had now forbidden her subjects to sell provender to the Chinese commanders; and so a diplomatic and commercial estrangement was thought to be complete.† This

* See the author's *Notes on Opening Trade with South-Western China*, 1873.

† See Berlin Correspondent of the *Standard*, February 12th, 1880

was probably considered, on the whole, good news for British commercial interests in Eastern Asia, as China might now turn, with more confidence than ever, to Great Britain, especially after our diplomatic victory over her wily adversary at Cabul; and the rising young Chinese monarch might just think of turning his attention to British prosperity and influence in Burma, with the view of such being extended to south-west China. And so would Russia be checkmated in nearly every corner of the East.

As I have remarked elsewhere, at Bhamo, where Burmese and Chinese influences commingle, we hope yet to see—and the Chambers of Commerce fully indulge in such a hope, notwithstanding the obstacles which have gone before—an exchange-mart for the silk, copper, gold, drugs, and textile fabrics of western China, and for British and Burmese staples.

A "peripatetic" writer in the *Times of India*, some nine years ago, remarked with great force: "The road to China for us is through Upper Burma or Burma Proper. Through Bhamo the richest side of China can be tapped. The most romantic dreams of the most sanguine have never come up to the reality which may reasonably be expected, as soon as there is a clear passage for trade from Yunnan or Hunan to Rangoon." Rangoon will become the Bombay of the Chinese and Burman empires, and something more."

The local advantages of Upper Burma in reference to trade with western China, were forcibly brought forward during the visit of the Burmese Embassy to England in 1872. The Council of the ever-zealous Halifax Chamber of Commerce gave the Envoy an extraordinary welcome, stating in their address to His Excellency that the

"Council, having always considered the rich products and the fertile lands of Burma as affording great inducements to the spread of commerce and agriculture, have from time to time carefully considered the many projected trade routes through the possessions of His Majesty the King, to open up a commercial highway to the unlimited resources of western China." In his reply, "the Envoy Extraordinary and Minister Plenipotentiary from His Majesty the King of Burma" said, with a degree of common-sense not always found in Orientals: "In reference to the question of trade routes through Burma to western China, I need merely repeat what I have said in other places, that His Majesty the King of Burma is most anxious to promote, by every means in his power, any matured and feasible plan which has this object in view. But in regard to the route to which you advert, commonly known as Captain Sprye's route, I would remark that as the line passes through an insignificant portion of the King of Burma's territory, the responsibility of opening it out cannot fairly be laid upon His Majesty."* Although the proverbial golden silence is here observed regarding the route from Mandalay to Momien, *viâ* Bhamo, it is not difficult to see that the Envoy thought that the only feasible route, which it most probably is. Certainly, judging from the past, and the troubles we have experienced in our various missions of exploration, the route from Assam to Sze-Chuen—strongly advocated by

* *Eleventh Annual Report of the Chamber of Commerce for Halifax and District*, 1872, p. 12.—See also *Our Burmese Wars, &c.*, p. 364, where there is also a note on the deputation from the Associated Chambers of Commerce, February 28th, 1873, to the Secretary of State for India.

Sir George Balfour—also deserves serious attention from the Imperial Government and the merchants of England. Of the route from Assam (Sudiya) to Sze-Chuen, he writes: "We then join a part of China singularly free from troubles. A dense population and great resources in minerals, and very much in want of the tea which Assam can supply." And again: "I admit that in minerals Yunnan is rich, but in population very scanty, say from sixty to 100 per square mile, whereas Sze-Chuen has from 200 to 250, and is close to Sudiya,* in Assam." The population of Yunnan, therefore, would appear to come nearer to that of Chin-India generally, where, in a surface of 700,000 square miles, there are only about thirty-six persons to every square mile; while Sze-Chuen—taking Sir George's figures—approximates to Great Britain with, say, 240. British and Upper Burma both sadly require population. In the event of our one day being compelled to possess the country to the northward of Pegu, what a boon it would be to our Eastern Empire if there was a steady emigration into our new conquest from Sze-Chuen of some 2,000,000 people! What an impetus it would give to trade and mining operations in Upper Burma; while if Pegu only had another two millions of peaceful inhabitants, from the well-disposed trading Shans, and other useful tribes, as remarked in my former work,† Southern Burma alone would have nearly as large a commerce as a fourth of that of the whole of India!

* Sudiya lies towards the extreme north-east of Upper Assam, or say, direct north-east from Rungpore, while Sze-Chuen lies north and north-east of Yunnan, and east of Sudiya.

† *Our Burmese Wars, &c.*, p. 352. For the value of Upper Burma, see page 369.

Really, the commerce of this portion of our Eastern Empire deserves the most serious attention of Englishmen, who have always prided themselves on being the leading merchants of the world. In commercial importance, in my humble opinion, there is no other Eastern question can approach it.

It is now upwards of eight years since the question of trade with south-western China was prominently brought before the British public. The local advantages of a route through Upper Burma, *viâ* Bhamo, were then strongly insisted on; and, in addition to other signs of a growing interest in the project, a valuable paper was read before the Society of Arts on the subject. It was then considered that the means of turning "the stream of life and commerce away from the old route by the Straits of Malacca and the Chinese Sea, in a new direction, as well as a better and more secure one," must first be found in easy steam communication; and then, with Burma as the highway, Great Britain and India would have no difficulty in tapping the resources of south-western China, and also other adjacent States. Canals and roads would come after, and so would railways; but, somehow or other, the subject for a time lost its interest. Now it should be revived ten-fold, not only on account of the continued prosperity of Pegu, or British Burma, but from its becoming tolerably apparent, by the state of the political barometer in the East, that the days of Golden-Foot rule at Mandalay are numbered. At the time above-mentioned, our Government had only contemplated making a railway from Rangoon to Prome. Now, that is finished, and the snort of the iron horse should go bravely on to the northward! *

With reference to the Burmese Embassy to England, some eight years ago, I have already referred to Captain Sprye's route to south-western China. An *Edinburgh Reviewer*, in a most interesting article on the "Trade Routes to Western China,"† writes: "His project aimed at connecting the port of Rangoon on the Irawadi with Esmok, a Chinese town in the extreme south of Yunnan, by means of a tramway which should be carried diagonally across Pegu and Burma, passing by the town of Shwégyeen, on the river Salwen [The reviewer here is in error; it should be the Sittang], and thence proceeding to its terminus, at what the projector believed to be an important *entrepôt* of Chinese trade." But, as it turned out, this Esmok was in reality no centre of commerce—except for some good tea—but a mere frontier post on the verge of the Chinese dominions; "and that the route by which it was proposed to reach this point abounded in well-nigh insuperable obstacles." It is about twenty years since the Chambers of Commerce first took up the idea of this route, which, though far from comparable with that *viâ* Bhamo (the emporium of commerce between Burma and Yunnan), to which attention was first called by Dr. Williams, is, nevertheless, honourably associated with the name of Captain Sprye, who did his utmost to advocate the opening

* The railway, connecting Rangoon and Prome—163 miles—was opened for traffic May 1st, 1877. See *Our Burmese Wars, &c.*, p. 388 (*note*).

† *Edinburgh Review*, No. 280, 1873, p. 300.

of trade with Western China. In time to come, probably both routes, and others that at present we know not of, will be available for capitalists from England and India. Trading centres will multiply in Burma and south-western China; and France, in Cochin-China and Tonquin (*See* Note II.), jealous of our vast power and resources from the possession of Burma, will, sphynx-like, with earnest eyes be looking on at China's old exclusive propensities giving way, till at length, through the force of our transcendent commercial power, in a future century all European nations will turn their eyes to Chin-India, where took place the first step towards bringing 400,000,000 of the Celestial Empire, at John Chinaman's own request, under the grand Imperial sway of England. Four hundred millions—an additional third of the human race—thrôwn on our hands! What shall we do with them? Could there possibly be a more interesting question? Home Rule will then have died a natural death. And the Englishman, too, will wonder how, towards the end of the nineteenth century, western and central Asia occupied so much, and eastern Asia so little, of our attention. The keen Chinaman, and especially the ever-busy Shan, as far as we are concerned, are at present far too little known among us. Tasteful Shan ladies, with their love of jewellery and elegance of design, may yet give a fashion to Belgravia; and the Shans being famous workers in straw, may yet produce hats for the Park rivalling the Tuscan in quality, and in shape that of England's far-famed beautiful Duchess. Our blacksmiths may yet take a lesson from the Shans in the forging of a sword "from iron brought from Yunnan," and British merchants will be delighted to observe that "among the arts in which this self-sufficing people are proficient is that of manufacturing cotton cloths." *

Of course the concurrent commercial interests of British and Upper Burma and China are also those of India and England; and when western China is really opened up to British enterprise, it will probably be one of the greatest boons which commerce ever received. The force of civilisation, if not war, must eventually knock the Golden Foot entirely out of the way. Our present relations with Upper Burma are in a very unsatisfactory condition; and "the events of the last few years have produced coolness and distrust between the British and Burmese Governments. The violence," continues an admirable critic on the situation, "offered to the exploring-party to Yunnán, under Colonel Sladen, the determined attack led on that by Colonel Browne, the murder of Mr. Margary in Chinese territory, &c., have all contributed to widen the breach, which has ended in the withdrawal of the British Resident." But, on the whole, he thinks that the occupation of Upper Burma—with an area of not less than 130,000 square miles, including the tributary Shan states, and numerous wild and troublesome tribes—"would involve difficulties which it is not desirable, except from dire necessity, to encounter. If we can have a free right of way through for trade with China, with the good-will both of Burma and China, that will be far better for British material interests and British honour than the violent act of annexation."†

* *Edinburgh Review*, No. 280, p. 313.—"Trade Routes to Western China."

† *The Athenæum*, No. 2729, February 14th, 1880, p. 212.

It is clear that something decided must soon be done; for Commerce is a fearful sufferer by the present state of Burmese affairs. Even the few manufacturers of Mandalay have fled. The silk clothes and silver-work are no more. Lead recently circulated for copper; and the State lotteries have added to the ruin of the country.

The concurrent commercial advantages of India and Burma become more and more fixed on the mind when we compare the two countries. In a Review of the Trade of British India with other countries, for 1878-79,* we find it stated that "although India possesses a long coast-line of over 9,000 miles, and about 300 harbours, the foreign trade of the empire is practically confined to the five ports, which are the capitals of the five great littoral provinces, viz. Calcutta, Bombay, Madras, Rangoon, and Kurrachee, all of which, excepting Madras, are excellently situated as central marts for the distribution of articles of commerce. To Rangoon naturally flow by the Irawadi, all the products of Upper Burma and of Pegu, the most valuable of our possessions in the Burmese peninsula; while the railway already open (for 163 miles) between Rangoon and Prome, offers further facilities for the conveyance of merchandise." And it is still more interesting to find that intelligent Englishmen are gradually becoming alive to the fact that the most thriving place, commercially, in the Indian (or Eastern) Empire, considered relatively to its size, is Rangoon. And there can be no doubt that British

* By J. E. O'Connor, Calcutta, 1879. A most interesting paper for mercantile men to read, and which is quoted at considerable length in *The British Mail*, March 1st, 1880.

Burma, even at present, is the most prosperous province in the Empire, with a people free from religious and caste prejudices, more fond of "personal comfort and adornment" than either Hindus or Mahomedans, and consequently more ready and eager in the pursuit of civilised commerce than their more apathetic neighbours.

It is fairly well known that much of the foreign trade of India is shared between England and China. Still the proportion of the trade carried on directly with England is not increasing, but slowly the reverse. At present, Indian trade with China is practically confined to the opium trade. What a much more noble trade would that be coming from the profitable manufacture of cotton in western China, and its dispatch, *viâ* Rangoon, to India! With the expert Chinese, such manufacture, aided by the other valuable mercantile productions of Yunnan and Sze-Chuen, would probably pay well in the end; and it has been truly said that the Chinese are better adapted for profitable cotton manufacture than the people of India. China is at present compelled to import cotton, in which India has the advantage of the flowery land. In the omnipotent article of cotton, then, until China be compelled to grow more, there is ample room for the spinnings of India, Burma, and Manchester; and no greater impetus could be given to this most useful trade (or branch of industry), and the furthering of general acute and bold commercial speculation in other commodities throughout eastern Asia, than would be derived from opening up, through northern Burma, the long neglected provinces of south-western China. Such a consummation would be the first grand wedge driven into the mighty mass of Chinese or Mongolian seclusion, making a rent which, commencing with our humble conquests of Arakan, Tenasserim, and Pegu, might eventually bring 400,000,000 of the human family under the direct civilising influence and control of Great Britain.

CHAPTER V.

DU HALDE ON TRADE WITH CHINA: AND HOW RUSSIA GOT IN THE WEDGE.*

> "What implement lacks he for war's career,
> That grows on earth, or in its floods and mines,
> Eighth sharer of the inhabitable sphere)
> Whom Persia bows to, China ill confines,
> And India's homage waits, when Albion's star declines!"
>
> CAMPBELL.—*The Power of Russia.*

WRITING on the subject of the Chinese trade, Du Halde forcibly asserts that the riches peculiar to each province, and the facility of conveying merchandise by means of the rivers and canals, "have rendered the domestic trade of

* Written in 1873–74. Regarding the famous Du Halde, it may be stated that this eminent Jesuit missionary and traveller flourished early in the eighteenth century. The pages of Du Halde, in his great work—full of important information concerning the south-western and other provinces of China—are never tedious, and always instructive. It is entitled *A Description of the Empire of China and Chinese Tartary, together with the Kingdoms of Korea and Tibet. Containing the Geography and History (Natural as well as Civil) of those Countries. From the French of P. J. B. Du Halde, Jesuit.* The work is dedicated to His Royal Highness Frederick Prince of Wales, and consists of two enormous tomes, folios printed in London in 1738 and

the Empire always very flourishing." He thinks the foreign trade scarcely worth mentioning, for the excellent reason that the Chinese, having all things necessary for the support and pleasures of life among themselves, need not seek them in the land of the stranger. When China was governed by its own emperors, the ports were shut to foreigners. The Tartars, when they became masters, opened them up to all nations. To give a full account of the Chinese trade, he speaks of the traffic carried on among themselves and their neighbours, also of European commerce with China, which, early in the last century, was in a very confined state, forming a remarkable contrast with that of later years. Truly, in the old days of our acquaintance with the East, Civilisation was making a desperate struggle to be born; for there can be no genuine civilisation where exclusiveness is paramount. The prospect of affairs is brighter at the present time, and if commercial men only assist the Government in the endeavour to better trade and promote social intercourse in comparatively unknown regions, we may, even in the nineteenth century, hear of a British-Chinese Chamber of Commerce in Yunnan

1741; printed for Edward Cave at St. John's Gate—a portal leading us to think of the early days of Dr. Johnson. Du Halde notices particularly the matter of the commercial importance of Yunnan and Sze-Chuen. After looking at these valuable provinces, the present writer thought it interesting to give some remarks on the clever manner long ago adopted by Russia in introducing the *political commercial* wedge into China, founded on the pages of the ubiquitous and learned Jesuit. At the present time (1880–81) the relations between Russia and China are of great importance to Englishmen—more important even than a war being the Chinese concession of opening the whole of their western frontier to Russian trade!

or Sze-Chuen. China, Japan, Burma,—what an interesting study it will be for us, or for our children, to watch in such remarkable countries the grand development of Free Trade, brought about by the steady law of progress. But, above all, as Pegu, or Lower Burma, is ours, and well sustaining her rank among British provinces in the East, let us consider that we are not utilising our valuable and hard-won possession in Chin-India, while we leave a stone unturned in the matter of furthering British and Indian trade with Upper Burma and the south-western provinces of China. While the Brahmapootra of Assam, and any canals that may be cut, or lines of railway that may yet run through that fertile province to near the Chinese frontier, would greatly assist Indian trade, the Chinese rivers, and the noble Irawadi (Burmese), with convenient lines of railway as proposed, would soon, as we have already hinted, make Rangoon the Liverpool of the East. But we must utilise the possessions we have, more than we do, if we would keep pace with the times and increase our commerce abroad!

In Du Halde's time the inland trade of China was so great, that the commerce of all Europe was not to be compared with it; the provinces were like so many kingdoms, communicating to each other their wealth and produce.

Thus the several inhabitants became united among themselves, and plenty reigned in all the cities. Whatever commodity one province lacked was readily supplied by the other; and all these riches, readily conveyed from place to place along the rivers, were sold in a very short time. For instance, we read of a dealer arriving in a city, and in three or four days selling six thousand caps "proper for the season."

The Mandarins themselves had their share in business, and some of them put their money into the hands of trustworthy merchants to improve it by means of trade.

There was not any family, even the poorest, that could not, with a little good management, find means to subsist very easily by traffic. As a matter of course, like the old pedlars of Europe, and the hawkers of Anglo-India, the Chinese have long been known to be addicted to over-reaching; but when the incredible crowds of people to be seen in the generality of their cities, and at their fairs, are considered, and all busy in buying or selling commodities, dishonesty is not to be wondered at. It has for ages been no worse among a certain class in the East than in the West. The fact of trade flourishing in nearly all the provinces of China makes the people negligent of foreign trade. Such is the opinion of Du Halde. But it is not so now. There is a growing liking for the trade of the foreigner. Japan used to be the grandest centre of Chinese trade; and it is likely to become so more than ever if we do not do more to encourage the Chinese. When merchants went directly to Japan from the ports of China—Canton, Amwi, or Ning-po—then they imported drugs, bark, white sugar, buffalo, and cow-hides. They used to gain a thousand per cent by their sugar. Then there were also numerous sorts of silks—satins, taffeties, and damasks, of different colours, especially black; some of those pieces which cost much in China, fell considerably in Japan.

Silken strings for instruments, sandal-wood (much prized by the Japanese for its perfume), European cloth and camlets were in great demand, and had a quick sale. By this traffic the Chinese used to gain fifty per cont., while the enterprising Dutch gained more.

The commodities, which the Chinese traders loaded their vessels with in return, consisted of fine pearls—precious according to beauty and size—by which they sometimes gained a thousand per cent.; red copper in bars and wrought copper, of which there is a great sale in China; sabre-blades, much esteemed; flowered paper for fans; porcelain and japanned goods not equalled in any other part of the world. The Chinese merchants also brought very fine gold from Japan, and a metal called *tombak*, by which they gained fifty or sixty per cent. from the Dutch at Batavia.

As it is now highly probable in these days of the triumphs of Western civilisation in the East—of which Japan is so wonderful an example – that British trade will flourish wherever properly opened and secured, the following remark by Du Halde is significant:—"Could the Europeans depend upon the honesty of the Chinese, they might easily carry on a trade with Japan by their means; but they could not possibly do any good that way, unless they bore them company, were masters of the cargo, and had a sufficient force to prevent their insults."

The merchants of Amwi used to carry on a fair traffic with Manilla, which if it could only now be diverted into Indian, Burmese, or English channels, would be of great benefit to us all. We read of the Chinese taking to that island a great deal of silk, striped and flowered satin of different colours, embroidery, carpets, cushions, night-gowns, silk-stockings, tea, china-ware, japanned works, drugs, &c, by which the regular fifty per cent. was sure to be made.

But the trade which the Chinese, in Du Halde's time, carried on most regularly was that to Batavia, as they found it "most easy and gainful". They put to sea from Canton, Amwi, and Ning-po, towards the eleventh moon (in December), with such merchandise as green tea, china-ware, leaf gold, and gold thread, drugs, copper, and *tûtenak* (or *tuttenague*), a metal partaking of the nature of tin and iron, and now well known among us in India and in England.

The Chinese imported many luxuries and necessities from Batavia. When we hear at the present time (1873–74) of English hats, postage stamps, and compulsory education being adopted in the rising island of Japan, we must not forget that things European have long been in favour there as in the Celestial Empire; and that long before Du Halde wrote, John Chinaman could be seen with his bale of European cloth from Batavia, dwelling on its merits, and selling it at a good price to the merchant of Japan.

It is strange to think that about 140 years ago, the greatest trade the Chinese drove abroad was that with Batavia They likewise went, but very seldom, to Achen, Malacca, Ihor, Patana, Lijor (belonging to the kingdom of Siam), to Cochin-China, &c. The trade carried on at Ihor was the most easy and profitable.

The trade carried on in China by the Europeans is

particularly remarked on by Du Halde. They had the liberty of scarce any port except that of Canton, which was open to them at certain times of the year. Not that they went up as far as the city itself, but cast anchor at Whang-pû, a place about four leagues short of it, in the river, which there was so crowded with a multitude of vessels that it looked "like a large wood." "Formerly," writes Du Halde, "cloths, chrystals, swords, clocks, striking-watches, repeating-clocks, telescopes, looking-glasses, drinking-glasses, &c. were carried thither. But since the *English* come regularly every year, all these are as cheap as in Europe; and coral itself can hardly be sold there any longer without loss: so that at present there is no trading to advantage with anything but silver, in China, where considerable profit may be made by purchasing gold, which is a commodity there." Du Halde considers the gold of China profitable. That to be met with at Canton comes partly out of the provinces of China, and partly from foreign countries, such as Cochin-China and Japan, and was nearly all melted over again in that city. The gold of Cochin-China (which we have allowed the French to get hold of) is described as "the most fine and pure that can be." The Chinese divided their gold by alloys, according to the custom of Europe. The other commodities imported by Europeans were excellent drugs, several sorts of tea, gold-thread, musk, precious stones, pearls, quicksilver, &c.; but the trade carried on in China by the Europeans consisted chiefly in japanned-works, china-ware, and silks, with regard to which the indefatigable Jesuit deals at considerable length.

But enough has now been said to show what the Chinese trade was in Du Halde's time. Its vast increase with India and England during the most palmy days of the glorious old East India Company (in spite of unsuccessful embassies), is a matter of history. Within the last half-century we have had Chinese wars, and numerous fortunes made by opium, silk, and tea; but now, through Assam and Burma, we can bring the Chinese provinces nearer to us than ever. Let us, then, be wise in time, and do our utmost to make use of them. Let England, in every conceivable way, boldly carry her civilisation and commerce into Western China, and she will be sure to succeed; and, succeeding, there will be no grander check on the wily schemes of Russia in Eastern or even Central Asia!

It is interesting at the present time, while the Mahomedans are receiving such severe checks* in the Celestial Empire, to note the treatment suffered by the sons of Islam, in the Chinese provinces 140 years ago. In a description of the province of Kyang-Nan (in which is Nankin), we come to a city called Whay-ngan-fu, not very populous, "in danger of being drowned" by the extraordinary increase of water, the ground it stands on being

* Official news from China, received in India about the middle of 1873, confirmed the intelligence that Talifoo had fallen, and that the Imperial Government had re-asserted its authority in the province of Yunnan. The restoration of the whole province was shortly expected. The disorders in the adjoining province of "Kneichow," (Quey-chew?) with Yunnan forming one "government-general," were also coming to an end. A telegram also announced that Momein had fallen, and that the Panthays had been completely defeated. A Chinese General had reported to the King of Burma that the capital of the Panthay (Mahomedan) country had fallen.

lower than the canal; and two miles from it there is a populous borough, the port of the river Whang-ho, where the people are very busy. Here one of the great Mandarins used to reside, named Tsong-ho, or *Surveyor-General of the Rivers*, or *Grand Master of the Waters*. "Beyond the Whang-ho there are certain towns along the canal, where the Mahomedans have unsuccessfully endeavoured to draw a trade; their mosques are very high, and not built in the Chinese taste. Notwithstanding they have been settled there for so many generations, they are still considered as of foreign origin, and from time to time meet with insults. A few years ago, at Hang-Kow, in the province of Hu-quang, the people, provoked by the indiscreet behaviour of some of them, destroyed the mosques which they had built there, in spite of all the magistrates could do."

The Christians, at and before this period, were very differently treated, and French Jesuits, as well as Russian politicals, met with occasional high marks of favour and attention. Russia did not receive Christianity till the tenth century; and in the middle of the fifteenth that Empire was redeemed from its subjection to the Tartars.

With reference to China and Russia, two remarkable events happened during the sixteenth century. In 1552, St. Francis Xavier, the Apostle of the Indies, left Goa for the purpose of converting the Chinese.* The country was then very hostile to strangers; but he persevered, and

* Jesuit missionaries first entered China about the middle of the fifteenth century.

died before he could reach the gates of Canton. It was not till the end of the sixteenth century that Siberia was added to the Russian Empire, which, till then, was bounded by the limits of Europe. In 1671, Christianity got a firm footing in China; and the zeal of Louis Quatorze, some years later, fanned the flame for a time; at which period, also (1683), P. Verbiest was travelling in western Tartary, and eventually (1688) another famous Jesuit, P. Gerbillon, who gives us some information about the Russians.

The wedge is now about to be introduced. A clever French Jesuit missionary and a Russian envoy are shortly to appear on the stage. It came about in this way: The Russians having by degrees advanced to the very frontiers of China, built a fort at the confluence of a rivulet with the great river styled by the Tartars *Saghalian úla*, and by the Chinese *Ya long Kyang*. The Chinese Emperor's troops took and razed the fort; but the Russians rebuilt it in the following year. They were again besieged, and being apprehensive of the consequences, "desired the Emperor to end the war amicably, and to appoint a place for holding a treaty." Their offer was kindly accepted; and in the beginning of 1688, the negotiation was entrusted to two grandees of the Chinese Court, one a captain of the Life Guard and a Minister of State, and the other a Commander of an Imperial Standard, and uncle to the Emperor. In addition to several Mandarins of different orders, they were to be accompanied by Pére Thomas Pereyra (a *Portuguese* Jesuit), and Gerbillon, who wrote a most admirable account of the strange journey. We question if there is a more curious chapter in literature than this account of Gerbillon's travels in Western Tartary.

The Lamas met the Ambassadors. Among the former was observed a young Lama, "pretty handsome," writes Gerbillon, "very full-faced, and of so white and delicate a complexion that I suspected it was a woman. He was at the head of the troops, and distinguished by a hat with a very large brim, made of I know not what materials, all gilt, and running up to a point; another of these Lamas had likewise a gilt hat, but smaller, and quite flat at the top." From such description we get an idea of the origin of the gilt hats worn by the chosen troops from Ava, who encountered us at Rangoon in the Second Burmese War.

But we must not lose sight of the Chinese Ambassadors about to meet the Russian. After beholding a "counterfeit immortal," who drank Tartarian tea from a silver pot carried by a Lama, meeting wild mules, observing the Tartar way of hunting, and finding plenty of game coming across wolves, yellow goats, and salt-mines, also noble "forest-trees," and eventually arriving at the Great Wall, which Gerbillon describes, the Emperor is met on his travels; and His Majesty (travelling to and from Pekin), is most attentive to the Jesuits.

On the 23rd of May (1688), an Envoy arrived at Court from the Russian Plenipotentiaries, to name a place of treaty upon the frontiers. This Russian Envoy behaved with civility, and the French and Chinese Ambassadors speak of his wit and judgment. He assured them "that the Emperor had retaken all Hungary from the Turks,' and gave other exploits by the King of Poland and the Czars of Russia. He acted his part so admirably that the Jesuits judged this Envoy to be either an Englishman or a Dutchman, "for he had nothing of the Russian pronunciation." The Chinese Emperor, too, was pleased with the conduct of the Russian Envoy, whose diplomacy, even then, was becoming celebrated in Asia. The important affair on hand was now in a fair way of progress. But we have only space for a few notes on the limits of empire proposed by the Russians while getting in the wedge. The Russian Plenipotentiary proposed the *Saghalian Ula*, or Black River (as it is called by the Tartars, and *Onon Amur* by the Russians), for the boundary between the two Empires, so that what lay to the north of it should belong to Russia, and what lay south of it to the Empire of China. The Chinese Ambassadors would not consent to this proposal, because several populous cities and countries with valuable mountains were on the north side of the river. They assigned other limits, and only demanded that the Russians should not pass beyond Nipcha, which they would leave them "*for the conveniency of their trade to China.*"

The Russians answered this proposal with a laugh, that they were very much obliged to China for leaving them "a place which could not be disputed." The conferences at length were broken off, the missionaries were allowed to interfere, new limits were again assigned, and the Russians again receded from their agreement, till eventually we find both parties agreeing about the limits, but which, up to the present day, appear never to have been definitely settled.

In the treaty of peace at this time, admirably drawn up by the Chinese Ambassadors and the missionaries, it was thought that nothing could influence the Russians more to an inviolable observance of peace than their knowing that the Chinese swore it in the name of the TRUE God, which, by command of the Emperor, was done, and the oath is given by Gerbillon, "the better to show their genius." This remarkable document commences: "The war which has been carried on by the inhabitants of the frontiers of the two empires of China and Russia, and the battles fought between them with great effusion of blood, disturbing the peace and quiet of the people, being entirely contrary to the Divine Will of Heaven, which is a friend to the public tranquillity; We, Ambassadors Extraordinary of the two Empires," &c.

After such a treaty as that drawn up in 1689, we are forced to go back to a question put by a Chinese noble to the Jesuits, when discussing European affairs, regarding what faults the Europeans could find in the Chinese. The reply was ready, and is pretty much the general idea at the present time: They passed in Europe for an ingenious people, but very effeminate, and given to over-reaching in trade. To the "very effeminate" we decidedly object; and if they were so then, they are, as a nation, not so now. And it is clear that, at present, the Chinese would much like to see the Russians entirely clear of China, as they were even in Du Halde's time anxious to get them out of Mongolia.

China and Burma are the countries we should now look to with an especial interest, at a time when we think over the present Russian doings in, and the future of, Central Asia. In St. Petersburg, very naturally, the conquest of Khiva and the other khanates is only considered "the beginning of the end." The occupation of many other places than Bokhara will become "a necessity" to the "eighth sharer of the inhabitable sphere." But, confining ourselves on the present occasion to the eastward, we believe that the Russians are now aware of the rapidity with which the Chinese are organising their army and navy after the European fashion. "It is supposed," writes a shrewd 'political' from Berlin, that with the troops and vessels even now at the disposal of the Pekin Government, it would be practicable for them to re-occupy the Amûr country!" The wedge, therefore, would seem to be loosening; and, through the lever of a well-organised system of trade, we may soon see it rooted out altogether.

Burma and Yunnan, and Assam and Sze-chuen, must now become known to the wealthy British merchants. Everything would seem to be in their favour. The deputation, a few months back,* to the Duke of Argyll, from no less than fifty Chambers of Commerce—in which the wise and liberal advice of paying for a railway survey out of the Imperial Treasury, or by a combination of the merchants and manufacturers of this country, was given—met with great encouragement; then came another deputation † to His Grace, regarding trade with Central Asia, headed by General Eardley Wilmot, chairman of the Council of the Society of Arts. And now (in the month

* February 28th, 1873. † April 25th

of July), while we are writing these notes, railways for China are announced. It is said to be in contemplation to present the Emperor of China with locomotives, carriages, &c., so as to induce His Majesty to encourage a proposed short line at Pekin, which will, of course, gradually be extended to or near Nankin, Canton, Yunnan (to one of the most convenient towns in the province) and Ava, when the noble Irawadi could do the rest by light steamers to Rangoon. We had better take care for fear that extensive railway operations, once begun in the Celestial Empire—as if in imitation of the Shah of Persia—may be a reproach to us for our delay. With all the appliances of science at our command, what an infinitely better position we now hold for trading with and civilising comparatively unknown countries than in the days of the East India Company! And yet it is no exaggeration for anyone who reads the history of British commerce to say, that while other nations were expending their men and treasure to aid conquest, a single "Company of merchants trading to the East Indies" effected very much of what was necessary to make the East and West known to each other. But for that glorious old Company—deserving a monument if ever Company deserved one—with its munificent spirit and fearless and able servants, how slight our knowledge might now have been of Persia, India, China, Burma, and Japan! To Peter the Great belongs the credit of having put in the most lasting wedge, or of having created the power of Russia. To the East India Company we must give the honour of having secured for us the government of more than a sixth of the millions of the globe.

Commerce promises soon to become a mightier herald of peace than of war: but in neither commerce nor war, in Central Asia, China, or Chin-India (Burma), must too great dependence be had on treaties; and the fewer we make, or allow others to make, the better.* An able Indian statesman recently remarked to us that, had we made no treaties, we would ere now have turned the Russians out of central Asia. He continued: "The worst thing for us has been it being proclaimed in the East that we are at peace with Russia. At peace with a progressive power? Impossible!"

We must progress also, with the light steamer and the canal boat, and railway carriage, if not with the sword and the gun. Commerce, with its battles of competition, is one of the mightiest engines of the day "for all men's good"

In conclusion; by our speedily assisting the introduction of works of utility, such as canals and railways, into China, we shall have a mightier and sharper wedge than Russia has yet been able to insert; and when it is considered, as has been affirmed, that, with so many other advantages already noted, the Chinese coal-fields extend over 400,000 square miles (while the English cover only 12,000), what a splendid field is open to the tact and enterprise of the conciliating British statesman and the generous British merchant!

* It was rumoured that the French Government had entered into a treaty (very advantageous) with Burma.

CHAPTER VI.

THE FORESTS OF BURMA.

MANY years ago a writer on Burma remarked that it was impossible to enumerate the various kinds of trees which in Ashé Pyee rear their heads in proud magnificence. Of course, the chief noticed was the teak, which, although rare in Hindustan, and hardly mentioned in any of our accounts of Siam, "constitutes the principal glory of the Burman forests." It was not without considerable interest that the present writer found, in the Proceedings of the Supreme Council in Calcutta (23rd December 1880), leave asked to introduce a Bill "to amend the law relating to forests, forest-produce, and the duty leviable on timber in British Burma." Mr. Aitchison, the Mover (late Chief Commissioner of the Province), drew the attention of the Council to the importance to the Government of forest conservation in Burma, for the purpose of securing a permanent supply of teak for the requirements of India, and for export to Europe and elsewhere. "Notwithstanding the enormous increase in the use of iron, and the high price of teak timber, the consumption of the latter had steadily increased, and Rangoon and Maulmain were the two principal ports of supply for India and the world." A large quantity of teak was imported annually into India from Burma. "In Java and the neighbouring islands there were also teak forests, but the supply from them was insignificant. The chief sources of supply were Upper Burma, Siam, the Karen-nee country, and British Burma." And the far larger portion of timber from these forests "found its way to Rangoon and Maulmain, by the Salween, Sittang, and Irawadi rivers." To give an idea of the present increased supply, Mr. Aitchison compared the statistics of the first eight years after the annexation of Pegu, with the figures for the five years ending 1878-79. "The imports into Rangoon and Maulmain for the first period were 85,056 tons of fifty cubic feet; for the last period, 276,749 tons. The exports for the same periods were 76,763 tons, as compared with 134,563 tons. During the last-mentioned period, about two-thirds of the teak exported from Rangoon and Maulmain were to Indian ports, and of the imports, about four-fifths came from forests beyond the British frontier."* One of the most important of forest products was kutch. From reckless felling the tree was scarce in British Burma. After, in a most interesting manner, explaining the necessity for

* See also Sir Arthur Phayre on Teak Timber in the Supplementary Chapter. It was originally intended that Chapter VI. should be on the manufacture of paper from the bamboo. It was afterwards thought better to incorporate the subject with remarks on Sir Arthur's paper on British Burma.

legislation, Mr. Aitchison concluded with the remark that the Bill (which had been under consideration for five years) "might appropriately be described as the Indian Forest Act of 1878, with such changes as were necessary to adapt it to the special circumstances of British Burma."

On the meeting of Council, 6th January 1881, it was moved, and agreed to, that this Bill be referred to a Select Committee.

From various notes compiled at the outbreak of the Second Burmese War (1852), the following may be selected as giving some idea of the importance attached, for a long period, to the growth of teak in Burma:—

Its wood is at least equal, if not superior, to the British oak, as a material for ship-building; for besides being as easy to work, it is said to be more durable. This valuable timber abounds in most of the forests of the Burman Empire, both to the north of Ummerapoora (or Amarapúra, "City of the Immortals"), and in the southern provinces. Colonel Symes* observes, that without the timber trade to Pegu, the British marine in India could exist only on a contracted scale. He estimates the shipping at Calcutta at 40,000 tons; and observes, as a proof of its importance, that during the scarcity of the

* Colonel Symes was sent as Ambassador to Burma in 1795, by Sir John Shore, Governor-General of India (Lord Teignmouth), with the view of re-establishing diplomatic intercourse with the Burmese Empire. The mission, however, was a decided failure. The Colonel published an interesting narrative, and in 1822 was despatched on a second mission to Ava, "which," writes General Albert Fytche, "proved even a greater failure than the first." It is said that he "failed to estimate the real character of the Burmese people, whilst he over-rated the government and resources of the country."

year 1795, when Great Britain was menaced with the horrors of famine, 14,000 tons of shipping, mostly India-built, freighted with rice, brought a seasonable supply to the City of London, and greatly reduced the price of that article. The indigenous timber of Bengal is found to be unserviceable; but some of the finest merchant ships ever seen in the Thames have been built at Calcutta, of teak wood from the forests of Pegu.

Forest conservancy, then, as well as prudent irrigation and extensive railway communication, must ever occupy a conspicuous place in the world's agents for the prevention of famine; and, considering the relative positions of India and Burma (the dry and the moist countries), how, at any time, as in the recent distressing Indian famines, want may be sorely felt in the land of the Veda and the Koran, every cry for assistance will surely be met, as heretofore, from the fertile region of Gautama. In such a case, one might fancy the waving of the trees signifying their acquiescence in the good work—waving "in sign of worship" (as sung by Milton)—at being the means of a Power ever ready and willing to save. Burma can not only furnish you with timber to build your ship, but also with an endless supply of food to freight it with. It may be observed, in a general way, that the trees of this country are superb; and so are the flowers, ever blooming, and flourishing, and beautiful. The English traveller in Burma may become sated with hills and dales, and trees and flowers; and the ubiquitous American here sometimes discovers scenery reminding him of his own sublime and ever-matchless prairie lands. Doubtless, he is rarely sated with the "sylvan scenery" of various parts of Burma, which, according to the romantic and contemplative Earl of Beaconsfield, "never palls." The great statesman, with his fondness for trees (in this respect like Burke and other famous men), would certainly have admired those of Burma, from the noble teak down to the wayward bamboo, with its dense columns, in the jungle or forest, arranged like the aisles of a cathedral. The forests of Burma are, of course, filled with nats, or spirits, like the forests of Scandinavia and India, or all over the world. Such arboreous sprites were probably at first inclined, in Pegu and Tenasserim, from the prospect of not being disturbed, to view the British Conservators with favour; but they must now take a different view of the subject.

Not long ago, when the present writer was in Burma for the second time—1863–64—forest work in a great measure consisted in clearing away jungle from around young plants to protect them from fire, cutting away creepers and parasitical plants, and removing obstructions to the due development of teak. During the above year, this work was carried on with extreme diligence in the Prome, Tharawadi, and Sittang sections:—15,286 teak, and 56,333 other kinds of trees were girdled; 304,756 young teak-trees were cleared; and 72,841 trees of other kinds were cut down; 108,689 creepers were cut. And here it may be interesting to state that as the botanical productions of Ashé Pyee are unrivalled, it is almost worth a visit to Burma to see the "great variety of creepers and wonderful luxuriance of the undergrowth in the forests." Ferns and orchids, the rapid-growing bamboo, with its fantastic forms;

and Flora's own gem, the finest indigenous tree in Chin-India, *Amherstia Nobilis**—all will give the diligent and inquiring traveller food for meditation and delight.

* See *Our Burmese Wars, &c.*, for a description of this beautiful tree, p. 309.

CHAPTER VII.

NATIONAL CHARACTER.

THAT the national character is very closely associated with the condition and welfare of a people is a fact which few men in their senses will attempt to disprove; and it is, perhaps, to be observed even more in the East than in the West. The "bold peasantry, their country's pride," as the poet styles them, must be looked on, wherever we go, as the grand motive power of those forces which must ever move onward, whether the country of their action be Ireland or British Burma; and then security to industry is necessary to all countries alike. A shrewd educationist, some fifteen years ago, thus described the condition of the people of British Burma: "Their social condition is generally similar throughout the three divisions. Everywhere in the plains the land is held independent of any superior, and the estates average from eight to ten acres in extent."* With

* General Albert Fytche corroborates this statement in his interesting work, *Burma Past and Present* (1878).—"Occupied land in the plains is an allodial possession held by small peasant proprietors, whose holdings, on the average, do not exceed ten acres." —Vol. i. p. 309.

reference to the climate, the people have plenty of food and clothing. The houses of the peasantry, whether on the hills or on the plains, are built of bamboo, and have the floors raised on platforms, so as to be above the reach of the annual flood. They are never built on the ground. The remote hill tribes are still in a savage state of isolation and independence, but even the wildest grow cotton, and weave cloth of strong texture and of various colours. All the tribes, as a general characteristic, are frank and truthful in the ordinary affairs of life; they are also very hospitable. Since the British conquest, the people generally have acquired a considerable amount of personal property. The small landed proprietors are independent and prosperous, and the condition of the labouring classes is comfortable; still, among the Burmese and other indigenous people, there is no class that can properly be called wealthy. This is a pleasing picture of a people whose national character is described at some length by a writer, before 1852, whose sketches are compiled from the best authorities*: "The general disposition of the inhabitants is strikingly contrasted with that of the natives of Bengal, from which they are only separated by a narrow range of mountains. The Burmans are a lively, inquisitive race, active, irascible, and impatient. All the children of Europeans born in the country are considered as the King's subjects, and prohibited from ever leaving it; consequently, are doomed to a life of immorality and degradation. The females of Ava are not concealed from the sight of men;

* Colonel Symes, Major Canning, Captain Cox, Dr. Leyden, Dr. Buchanan, &c. &c.

but, on the contrary, are suffered to have free intercourse as in Europe; in other respects, however, there are many degrading distinctions, and the Burman treatment of females generally is destitute both of delicacy and humanity. The practice of selling their women to the stranger is not considered as shameful, nor is the female dishonoured. They are seldom unfaithful, and often essentially useful to their foreign masters, who are not allowed to carry their temporary wives along with them. Infidelity is not a characteristic of Burman wives, who in general have too much employment to find leisure for corruption."

This old opinion rather chimes in with General Fytche's high commendation of woman amongst the Burmese, whose position is a much higher and independent one than amongst Mahomedans and Hindus. "She is with them not the mere slave of passion, but has equal rights, and is the recognised and duly honoured helpmate of man, and, in fact, bears a more prominent share in the transaction of the more ordinary affairs of life than is the case, perhaps, with any other people, either Eastern or Western."

Recent writers have also discoursed on the preliminaries of that serious thing in Burma, as elsewhere, called marriage; but which, in the land of the Golden-Foot, a French philosopher (Balzac) would never have styled, as in his own country, "a science." As in most Oriental climes, and occasionally in Europe, the demonstrative precepts are of too simple, natural, and affecting a character to admit the use of such a mighty word. And as to love in the question, the libel of Moore, so sweetly sung, on the French woman whose heart "sets sail on the ocean of wedlock, her fortune to try," is certainly not more applicable to the Burmese dark-haired bride of Ashé Pyee :—

> " Love seldom goes far in a vessel so frail,
> But just pilots her off, and then bids her good-bye ! "

Future historians of our Burmese conquests may possibly enlarge on that woudrous and, to many sober judges, unaccountable power of fascination—for beauty here is rare, and certainly never could be " matchless deemed "—exercised by the Burmese women, after the First and Second Burmese Wars, over susceptible Europeans, as if they had been spared by the jinjals of the enemy only to be the victims of a " basilisk " even more " sure to kill." Among the Burmese, marriage is purely " a simple civil rite." According to one of the best and most recent authorities, the author of *Burma Past and Present*, women are generally married " about seventeen or nineteen years of age, to the man of their choice of about the same age or older, the parents very seldom interfering more than to advise." The practical caution displayed in the following process would reflect credit on the cleverest manœuvring mother of Belgravia during the height of the London season :—" When a couple have agreed between themselves to marry, the mother of the man, or his nearest female relative, is generally first sent to sound the mother of the girl privately, and if she appears to approve of the match, some of the suitor's elderly friends are sent to propose the marriage formally to the girl's parents, and adjust the settlement. On the parents giving their consent to the marriage, the *corbeille de noce* is furnished by the bridegroom according to his means, and the marriage takes place almost immediately." Then there is a grand feast, with a *pooay* or play. "The happy couple eat out of the same dish before the assembled guests; after which the bridegroom presents the bride with *hla-pet* (pickled tea, from Thein-nee), the compliment is returned, and the ceremony is practically brought to a close."* It may now be well to resume the study of national character in the older writers:—In their features the Burmans bear a nearer resemblance to the Chinese than to the natives of Hindustan. The women, especially in the northern parts of the empire, are fairer than the Hindu females, but are not so delicately formed. The men are not tall in stature, but they are active and athletic, and have a very youthful appearance, from the custom of plucking the beard instead of using the razor. Both men and women colour their teeth, their eye-lashes, and the edges of their eye-lids with black. With further reference to marriage, the law prohibits polygamy, and recognizes only one wife, but concubinage is admitted to an unlimited extent. When a man dies intestate, three-fourths of his property go to his children born in wedlock, and one-fourth to his widow. The Burmans burn their dead. In their food, compared with the Hindustanis, the Burmans are gross and uncleanly. Although their religion forbids the slaughter of animals in general, yet they apply the interdiction only to those that are domesticated. All game is eagerly sought after, and in many places publicly sold. Reptiles, such as lizards, guanos, and snakes, constitute a part of the subsistence of the lower classes. To

* *Burma Past and Present*, vo ii. pp. 69–70.

strangers they grant the most liberal indulgence, and if they chance to shoot at and kill a fat bullock, it is ascribed to accident. Among the Burmans the sitting posture is the most respectful, but strangers are apt to attribute to insolence what, in their view, is a mark of deference. Gilding is forbidden to all Burmans, liberty even to lacquer and paint the pillars of their houses is granted to few. In this empire everything belonging to the King has the word *shoé*, or "gold," prefixed to it; even his Majesty's person is never mentioned but in conjunction with that precious metal. When a subject means to affirm that the King has heard anything, he says, "it has reached the golden ears"; he who has obtained admittance to the royal presence has been at the "golden feet." The perfume of *utr* of roses is described as being grateful to the "golden nose."* Gold among the Burmans is the type of excellence; yet, although highly valued, it is not used for coin in the country. It is employed sometimes in ornaments for the women, and in utensils and ear-rings for the men; but much the greatest quantity, is employed in gilding their temples, in which decoration vast sums are continually lavished. The Burman Sovereign is sole proprietor of all the elephants in his dominions, and the privilege to ride on, or keep, one of these animals is an honour only granted to men of the first rank. In Hindustan, female elephants are prized beyond males, on account of their being more tractable; but in Ava it is the reverse, females being never used on State occasions, and seldom for ordinary riding. The henza, the symbol of

* See *Our Burmese Wars and Relations with Burma*, p. 45 (*note*).

the Burman nation, as the eagle was of the Roman Empire, is a species of wild fowl, called in India the Brahminy goose. It is a remarkable circumstance that there should not be such an animal as a jackal in the Ava (Burmese) dominions. The Burmans of high rank have their barges drawn by war-boats, it being thought inconsistent with their dignity for great men to be in the same boat with common watermen. It is customary, also, for a person of distinction journeying on the water, to have houses built for his accommodation at the places where he means to stop. The materials of these houses are easily procured, and the structure is so simple, that a spacious and commodious dwelling, suitable to the climate, may be erected in little more than four hours. Bamboos, grass for thatching, and the ground rattan, are all the materials requisite; not a nail is used in the edifice, and "if the whole were to fall, it would scarcely crush a lap-dog."

Notwithstanding the well-formed arches of brick that are still to be seen in many of the ancient temples, yet Burman workmen can no longer turn them; which shows how easily an art once well known may be lost. Masonry, in the latter ages, has not been much attended to; wooden buildings have superseded the more solid structures of bricks and mortar.*

Of course, bricks and mortar, under our rule, are now commonly used in many of the public and other works in British Burma. But the days of the grand old brick pile

* See *An Account of the Burman Empire*, Calcutta, 1852. For more relating to Burmese national character, &c., see *Our Burmese Wars, &c.*, pp. 154, 156, 189, 191, 328.

—like the temple of the Golden Supreme at Pegu, and the Shwé Dagon Pagoda at Rangoon—are gone for ever.

At the close of this chapter, it was interesting to read as bearing on a general view of the Burmese national character—of "Festivities in Burma" in October 1880, when there were grand doings in Mandalay. At the full-moon of Thadingyoot, the end of the Buddhist Lent, there was a "Kodau," or "Beg-pardon day." On this eventful day, all the officials have to come to the palace and "do homage and worship at the Golden Feet;" as in England, during Lent, everyone is supposed to fast, be pious, and "improve his mind generally." It was presumed that the October "Beg-pardon day" at Mandalay augured well for the future of King Theebau and his people.

CHAPTER VIII.

THE SHOE QUESTION.—COURT ETIQUETTE IN BURMA.

AT the Court of Ava compliance with the oriental custom of removing the shoes has always been required from persons admitted to the presence of the King. It is not surprising that the representative of the Chief Commissioner who, like others, had to conform to the etiquette of the Court, should have desired exemption from a practice so distasteful. But the question was never considered of sufficient importance to be made the subject of special discussion with the King. When, however, the Burmese Ambassadors visited Calcutta in 1874, in connection with the question of Karennee, on which the two countries had very nearly gone to war, Lord Northbrook,* who received them with suitable formalities, expressed his hope that in the reception of the British officer at Mandalay an etiquette would not in future be required, which was unsuited to English habits and scarcely in keeping with the position of the British representative.

* Then Viceroy of India; now the Right Hon. the Earl of Northbrook, First Lord of the Admiralty.

Shortly afterwards the status of the British Agency at Mandalay was raised, an officer of high rank, with the powers of a first-class Resident or Ambassador, being appointed to represent, not, as heretofore, the Chief Commissioner, but the Viceroy of India. He was instructed by Lord Northbrook's Government to discontinue the practice of removing the shoes. The King, however, evaded the difficulty by transacting business with the Resident mainly through his ministers, instead of by personal interviews. When Mr. Shaw attended the funeral of Mengdon Meng, the local Rangoon press shouted joyfully that the Shoe question was at last finally and for ever settled. "Whether," says the author of the *Notes* before quoted, "they ever acknowledged that they had halloed before they were out of the wood, I know not, but it is a fact that no 'Kulla,' or other person, can go into the presence of the 'Golden-Foot' without removing his shoes, and endeavouring painfully to perform the umbilical trick of prostration."* The Burmese official custom of etiquette, then, still holds good. "I believe," remarks the same writer, who has a quiet touch of humour about him, "that so long as there is a King and a palace, this etiquette, that everyone entering the palace and the audience hall will have to remove his shoes, endeavour to recline gracefully on his umbilicus, and be as ''umble' as Uriah Heep, will prevail, even unto the end."

In a capital little essay on "Oriental Etiquette,"† it is observed that the custom of removing boots in Burma is

* *Upper and Lower Burma*, pp. 18–19

† See *Globe*, July 31st, 1880.

"an ingenious device to exalt the monarch of the Golden-Foot, and degrade his subjects, and strangers, too, before him. It is carried further at Mandalay than at any other Asiatic Court." Again: "Our diplomatic difficulties with the Burmese Court have been considerably intensified, at different times, owing to the insistance of the Lord Chamberlain at Ava or Mandalay that our envoy should take his boots off, and the reluctance of our proud and diffident representatives to appear in public in their stockings. The British, however, are not by any means the only people whose feelings have been hurt by this unpleasant discourtesy; and Asiatic, as well as European, ambassadors have been in the most ancient times subjected to the inconvenience. The first Chinese invasion of Burma (1284 A.D.), was brought about entirely by the 'shoe difficulty.' The Chinese envoys to the monarch Nara-thee-ha-hadé had insisted, in spite of remonstrances, on appearing in the royal presence with their boots on. They ought to have known better, for at Pekin such conduct would have been considered the height of bad manners; and, as far as they were concerned, their infraction of Burmese etiquette had a very unpleasant ending. They were not allowed twice to insult the 'Lord of all the White Elephants,' but were waylaid in a quiet part of Amarapúra, and had their throats cut; a summary mode of proceeding which brought an army upon Burma from the Flowery Land."*

It was recently announced that King Theebau and his Council had settled the shoe difficulty in "an amusing way." By means of long ranges of planking, like boxes, the

* See also *Our Burmese Wars, &c.*, pp. 395, 406.

King will not see anybody's feet. The Golden Foot himself will appear on a grand dais. Ambassadors or foreigners will be seated on chairs; but they must not stir till His Majesty is gone. Whether true or not, the idea is certainly no very bad one.

As to shikhoing, it is also written: "The Burmese officials all 'shikhoe' to Royalty, that is, make an obeisance by raising the two hands to the forehead and bowing the head to the ground On Colonel Phayre, our envoy to Mandalay, objecting to do this, the Woondouk said: 'When at Calcutta at the Government House you told me to bow to the Governor-General, which you said was *your* custom. I am only telling you what *ours* is.' Formerly, our envoys to Burma were obliged to double their legs behind them, it being contrary to the existing etiquette to turn the foot, covered or uncovered, towards the King."

Thus is the world, notably East and West, in some measure subjected to the tyranny of Etiquette. Of course the science is necessary to keep good society together; but excess therein is simply making fools of ourselves by rule. Perhaps Shakespeare had some such view in his mind when he wrote of "new customs," which may also be applied to old—

> "Though they be never so ridiculous,
> Nay, let them be unmanly
> Still are followed."

CHAPTER IX.

GAUTAMA.*

HAVING attempted, while in England, to give the British public some idea of the worship of Jagannáth and his celebrated shrine, it was strange enough to find oneself, so soon after, far away from Europe, far away even from wild, romantic Orissa, in a land of war, endeavouring to make something of another of those "*stratas* of pseudo-religious fiction in which are preserved the *débris* and the fossilized skeletons of the faith."†

The origin of Gautama is a moot point among the Burmese. One of their theories or traditions runs thus:—At the creation of the world by the Supreme Being, some angels, or inhabitants of the other world, came down below and tasted of the earth. One of them found the new material so excellent that he ate so much, he could not

* Revised from *Rangoon: A Narrative of the Second Burmese War.* London, 1852.

† *Orissa, and British Connexion with the Temple of Jagannáth.* London, 1851.

again ascend. He therefore remained on earth as Gautama, watching over mankind, to the present day, through all their innumerable vicissitudes.

Jagannáth and Gautama, both are believed to be incarnations; the former, one of the popular incarnations of Vishnu, the latter of Buddha. But Buddha, that quiet, sleepless philosopher, who has given so much trouble to men of science, is supposed by many of the Hindus to be the ninth incarnation of Vishnu. Jagannáth and Gautama, then, one would suppose, are not so very distinct. But they *are* very distinct in practice; and this is an "Asian mystery." Even the far-famed temple of Jagannáth is situated, as remarked by Colonel Sykes, "on or near the site of a celebrated relic temple of the Buddhists;" there is every reason, therefore, to believe that the modern worship of Jagannáth has a Buddhist origin. As the priority of Buddhism, the original patriarchal system, is now pretty generally admitted, it is well to see what those Brahmans, who consider Buddha an *avatar* of Vishnu, think of that extraordinary sage. He seems to us the Luther of Antiquity in the East. He exerted himself, according to the Indian history, in restoring the religion of his country—India—to its original purity.

This was not tolerated, as it tended to destroy Brahmanical influence; sin, in consequence, abounded more and more; the righteous were detested, persecuted; and in the fourth, fifth, and sixth centuries of the Christian era, the followers of the religion of Buddha were expelled from Hindustan. This religious and contemplative creed, in its present form, probably originated in Central India; but every date and computation regarding the era of Buddha differs. It is placed as far back as 1330 B.C He may have been some great and wise king, eventually deified by his subjects and meeting with extraordinary veneration, amounting to superstition, such as is practised throughout Thibet, Siam, Cochin China, Burma, Tartary, Japan, even to the present day. To reconcile dates,* say that two Buddhas, or rather, Gautamas, are believed to have dwelt on earth.

Many Buddhists think that the present universe has been ruled successively by four Buddhas, of whom Gautama (or Gaudama), whose doctrines now prevail in Ceylon, Ava, and some other places where the religion of Buddha is acknowledged, is the fourth. A fifth *Maistree* Buddha is yet to come; he, a greater than any hitherto, is yet to come. And in India, there is "Kalki," the tenth incarnation of Vishnu, yet to take place. The "Preserver," mounted on a white horse, with a scimitar in his hand, is to renovate creation with an era of purity. If it be not too presumptuous to advance such a supposition, these strange incarnations are likely to be realized in British power, British civilisation, and British enterprise in the East. [Strange! While revising this chapter, we read of that able and energetic general, Skobeleff, in a recent engagement with the Turkomans, having a famous *white horse* shot under him, to the dismay of the superstitious soldiers. Question

* The dates of the Siamese, Japanese, and Ceylonese (Singhalese), are 544 and 542—the first two agreeing in date; and Monsieur Bailly and Sir W. Jones nearly agree with the Chinese, in assigning to the era of Buddha the dates of 1031, and about 1000 B.C. There must, it has been supposed, have been two Buddhas—one, perhaps, the incarnation of Vishnu, the other the original Buddha (or Bûdha), probably a king of India.—*Orissa*, p. 13.

for Russo-phobists: Is *Kalki* to be realised in British or Russian power in the East?]

Gautama is supposed by many to have established the sect of Buddhists. He was greatly offended with the conduct of the Brahmans on a particular occasion, which was the cause of his separating from their communion, and establishing a new religion. So says tradition. "This Gautama," writes Colonel Vans Kennedy, in his erudite *Researches*, "may have been merely a learned Brahman; for it certainly seems much more probable that in India a Brahman should be the founder of a new sect, than that it should owe its origin to the son of a king."

But the Buddhists *wholly* disavow the ninth incarnation of Vishnu. They insist that the worship of Buddha possesses a far higher claim to antiquity than that of the deities of the Brahmans, who, they maintain, came from other countries, and established their own religion, mainly by the power of the sword, on the ruins of the more ancient one of Buddha, which had for ages before prevailed.* In a former work † we stated that, with all its errors, a seeming purity, an honesty, a sincerity of purpose, belong to Buddhism, which we search for in vain in Brahmanism. The Brahmans appear before us in dark colours as a set of despots, shorn of all their scientific glory, whose chief delight is to fetter the human intellect by domineering over the inferior masses of mankind. Among the Buddhists of later centuries, including those of the present time, the adoration of a *Great Supreme*, unseen, is more apparent than among the Brahmans. The present Brahmanical

* Coleman. † *Orissa.*

system, which has so long existed, is founded on outward display, licentiousness, and mammon. Yet this neglect of the spirit pervading all things is forbidden in the principal *shastras*, and by various Brahmanical authors, where it is stated that "it is for the ignorant to view God in wood and stone; the wise behold him in spirit alone." Buddhism is supposed to have been introduced into the kingdoms of Ava and Pegu by emissaries from Ceylon.

According to the Chinese it came into their Empire about sixty-five years after the commencement of the Christian era, during the reign of Ming-ty, of the Hân dynasty. "That monarch, considering a certain saying of Confucius to be prophetic of some saint to be discovered in the west, sent emissaries to seek him out." On reaching India they discovered the sect of Buddhists, and brought back some of them with their idols and books to China. The tradition is, that Buddha was both king and priest in a country of the west, with a queen whom he made a divinity.*

And now Buddha awakes from a state of felicitous nonentity, † and assumes his operative and creative qualities; so let us at Rangoon behold him incarnate as Gautama. The most common image, from the colossal down to the diminutive, is that which sits with crossed legs,

* *The Chinese*, by Davis. See also *Our Burmese Wars, &c.*, p. 2.

† *Niebban*, in Burmese, is annihilation. Alluding to Bandoola, in the First Burmese War, having a superstitious fear, the writer remarked that such was "inseparable from a Burman and a believer in *Gautama*, in which religion, spirits, charms, transmigrations. *Niebban*, or Nervâna—annihilation, and yet, as Gautama mentions, an 'eternal city,' hardly perfect annihilation—form the leading features."—*Our Burmese Wars, &c.*, p. 45.

the right arm easily depending, or on the knee ; the left arm is laid across the body The ears have elongated lobes reaching to the shoulders; and the hair is twisted into a fantastic knot on the top of the head. There sits the creature, clad in an effeminate robe, gazing tranquilly. It is often mistaken for a female. To get a good view of other specimens, let us survey the large, upright images.* Many of them stand twelve feet in height, and have the right hand over the breast, while the left holds up a graceful flow of drapery. The head is encircled with ornaments. There is a touch of female beauty about the faces of some of them. These figures, perhaps, were designed to represent the past, the queens of successive Gautamas throughout many generations. The gilding appears to be of a superior quality. Strange enough it is that the Burmese excel alike in forming a beautiful image, and in fabricating from stone or wood some winged monsters which are absolutely terrible to look upon. Such are some of those which stand out around the great pagoda.

In the creed of Gautama, there is nothing like the Brahmanical caste. This is a very important point. Comparing Brahmanism with Buddhism, a writer remarks:—"Imperfect as Gautama's moral system undoubtedly is, it must be acknowledged free from numerous gross Brahmanical sources of error. *Unshackled by caste,* and resting their hopes on individual merit, his followers are characterised by greater independence of conduct, and a somewhat higher, less clouded ethical knowledge." And

* Soon after the capture of the Great Pagoda, nearly all those "comely" creatures were removed.

again: "It may strike the heart of a Christian heavily, to see prayers offered up before the uncouth idols of Gautama; yet, after having witnessed Hindu rites and festivals, there may be some consolation in the far more amiable features which the service of Gautama assumes, and in the freedom of his followers from the debasing effects of impure rites, and scenes of barbarous and revolting cruelties."* There can be no doubt of the truth of these remarks, and they augur well for the future enlightenment and consequent civilisation of Burma.

The changes that the various religions of the earth have undergone, must always form matter of interest to the student of history. But all arrive at the same Omega—there is but one God, Jehovah, the Lord of all. With regard to the caste, excluded from the creed of Gautama, but the effect of which on our own Anglo-Indian empire is a matter of serious importance, Colonel Sykes gives some interesting information in his *Notes on Ancient India*. It is supposed that the divisions of caste were anciently "secular and not religious, as the four castes, as they were called, existed equally amongst the Buddhists, as amongst the Hindus." Brahmanical caste, however, is considered to be *a divine ordinance*, whilst the Buddhist is regarded *simply as a civil institution*. Strictly speaking, there is no Buddhistical caste. Consequently, we are warranted in stating, that the religion of Gautama is unshackled by caste.

By the simple introduction of one letter to the present name, it will be observed that the mystic syllable AUM

* *Calcutta Review.*

appears in the word Gautama. It literally signifies three in one. The Brahmans apply it to their triad of *Brahma, Vishnu*, and *Siva*. The Buddhists apply it to *Buddha, Dharma*, and *Sanga*. According to the interior doctrine, *Buddha*, or the Intelligence, produced *Dharma*, the Law, and the two united constituted *Sanga*, the Union, or combination of several. Such is the Buddhist Supreme Head, or God, the Law, and the Church. These three are supposed by M. Remusat to have been represented by images in China, during the grand processions many centuries ago. Then "all the images were of gold or silver, ornamented with precious stones. When the images had arrived within 100 paces of the gate (in this instance, of the city of Khotan), the King took off his crown, *changed his garments*, and advanced barefoot towards it (*i.e.* the supreme image of Buddha), accompanied by his suite; falling at its feet, he adored it ('a gross corruption of the principles of Buddhism, which taught the worship of the Supreme Intelligence only'), burning at the same time perfumes, and scattering flowers." *

There is little or no difference in the manner in which these processions are ordered in many parts of China, even at the present day. The priesthood assembled, worshipping, chanting, striking gongs; the priests with shaven crowns, and arrayed in the yellow robes of their religion,

* Quoted in the author's *Idol-shrine*, from *Notes on Ancient India*, By Colonel Sykes, F.R.S. With reference to the above, Orientalists have remarked as singular facts the carrying supposed Brahmanical gods in procession in a subordinate capacity to Buddha; also that the chief gods of modern Hindu worship, Vishnu and Siva, are not mentioned; while Indra and Brahma, who then figured, are now in the background.

their "lowering look of bigotry," incense burning in the temple, counting of beads and tinkling of bells—what a glimpse have we of the importance attached to outward worship in all this display!

The worship of Gautama in the Tenasserim Provinces, and other portions of the old Burmese Empire, is at the present time celebrated in a similar way. In the religious procession there may be cars, dressed out with rude grandeur, as at Jagannáth; but without the noise and the indecencies and the fanatic madness of Indian worship; or it may be simply a foot procession, when well-dressed Talaings (Peguese) and Burmese proceed on particular occasions to their numerous pagodas, "bearing offerings of flowers, of fruits, of flags, of glittering umbrellas," and present their offerings at the altars, or place them around and against the pagodas and image-houses.

The books of the Buddhist priests, we are informed, mentioned a country called Sylân (Ceylon) in which, near the sea, there is on a certain mountain (Adam's Peak) the print of a foot three cubits in length. At Rangoon, we found a colossal foot of Gautama; it was discovered at the base of one of the large images, and it certainly is a great curiosity. It is of solid white marble, about five feet in length, and ten or twelve inches deep. Several strong European soldiers could scarcely move the huge foot. It was hoped that the British Museum might be yet enriched by the presence of this colossal symbol. The handsome *saumies,* as the Hindus style them, brought in for sale, we did not find of much value; but they are curious. The coating of silver was generally very thin.

The figures are represented sometimes holding a small pot, or a basket of eggs. Perhaps they are intended to illustrate how the disciples of the Phongyees are employed out of school-hours. The inhabitants of villages most willingly present these pupils, out of respect for their teachers, with rice, fruit, and other eatables. A *Kioung*, or monastery, is a suitable residence for one or more Phongyees. These are built at the expense of the town or village. Round the *Kioung*, the *Dzayat* is built for the use of travellers.

The dependence of the priesthood of Gautama on charity reminds one of the usages of the primitive Christian professors—" Go your ways: behold I send you forth as lambs among wolves. Carry neither purse, nor scrip, nor shoes: and salute no man by the way. And into whatsoever house ye enter first say, Peace *be* to this house." * Such were the words of the Divine Teacher of mankind.† Mercy and charity are two remarkable features in Buddhism. The Phongyees are the national instructors. " Any layman may turn Phongyee, and *vice versa*, a Phongyee may lay aside his yellow cloth and re-enter upon a secular life." In China there are numerous monasteries attached to the temples of Fo, or Buddha. The mendicant priests therein resemble the monks of the Roman Church. Celibacy is a principal vow on entering the priesthood. It is of course the same with the Phongyee. The Phongyees of Burma are a remarkable class of men; but yet for all their wisdom,

* St. Luke, x. 3, 4, 5.

† For some remarkable Burmese General Orders, during the First War, in which there is wording similar to that in the Old and New Testaments, see *Our Burmese Wars and Relations with Burma*, pp. 437–438.

they do not hesitate to believe that the mother of Buddha or Gautama swallowed an elephant in a dream, whence one reason of the veneration for elephants in this golden land.*

Buddha's birthplace and residence is supposed to have been Gya, in Behar. Gautama—styled also Gautom, or Gaudma—the saint or philosopher, is said by the Burmans to have flourished 2,300 years ago, and taught in the Indian schools the heterodox religion and philosophy of Buddha. His image, we read, is called Gautama, "a commonly-received appellation for Buddha himself." The Burmese, then, are followers of "Boodh," whose image is worshipped throughout the country under the name of Gautama. It is also written that Gautama was born about B.C. 626, having previously lived in millions of worlds, and passed through millions of conditions in each; that he became a "Bûdh" in the thirty-fifth year of his age, and remained so forty-five years. "There is no evidence," writes Mrs. Mason, "to show that Buddhism, as it now is, had any existence in the days of Gautama. On the contrary, the ancient Pali inscriptions, made two or three centuries after Gautama's death, prove that it had not then; for they show that certain birds and beasts were allowed to be killed for food."—

In fact, the study of Gautama is inexhaustible; and it may be strongly recommended to those perverse disturbers of the Established Church of England—the Ritualists—at the present time (1880). It might even be advisable to recommend that young would-be priests about to take Holy Orders should first pass an examination in Buddhism—the original patriarchal system—in order that, by treading

* End of chapter in *Narrative*.

the long extent of backward time in its history, they might have the chance of wondering how, towards the end of the enlightened nineteenth century, able and clever men can be guilty of such tremendous clerical follies, follies unworthy even of the dark ages. But, putting these aside, there is much that is wonderful in the study of Buddha or Gautama. According to M. Manupied, he is almost foretold in the prophecies of Isaiah, or rather, it is asserted that the prediction concerning the birth of Buddha, as discovered by a Chinese traveller (Fa-hian), is only an enlarged edition of Isaiah's prophecy on the coming of the Saviour:—" 'A sa naissance les dieux firent paraitre trente-deux signes ou présages relatifs á cet événement' . . . voici les plus remarquables. 'Les monticules et les collines s'applanirent . . . les arbres secs se couvrirent de fleurs et de feuilles . . . les terrains sans eaux produisirent des lotus grands comme les roues d'un char . . . cinq cent *eléphants blancs* (regardés comme des animaux dangereux) qui s'étaient pris d'eux mêmes dans les filets se trouvèrent devant le palais. . . Cinq cent lions blancs, sortirent des montagnes de neige, et se trouvèrent liés à la porte de la ville . . . . les tourments des enfers furent interompus,'" &c. &c. It would be difficult to find a more striking resemblance than that offered by these two prophecies, on which the writer has before dwelt at length (See *The Idol Shrine*, p. 48); and here it may be remarked, while writing on Burma, the above-mentioned "White Elephants" have, of course, something to do with the veneration paid by the Golden Foot and his subjects to the White Elephant at the present day.

Here it may be of interest to remark that, notwithstanding the Burmans are members of the sect of Buddha, and not disciples of Brahma, "they nevertheless reverence the Brahmans, and acknowledge their superiority in science over their own priests." The King and all his chief officers have always in their houses some of these "domestic sages," who supply them, with the skill of political Guy Mannerings, with astrological advice. Perhaps these scientific gentry have done more harm to King Theebau than is supposed; above all, that of teaching him to undervalue British power and influence, on which depends the regeneration of Upper Burma.—But a word or two more on Gautama. As will have been seen, it is a remarkable and interesting study; especially as, in the words of General Fytche, "the singular analogies that exist between the rituals, institutions, and outward observances of Romish Christianity and Buddhism is very startling." Buddhism tinged with Romanism, then, or *vice versâ*, is a curious fact; Gautama identified with the Saviour of Mankind; Maha Maria—"the great Mary"—the supposed mother of the great Eastern teacher; the curious circumstance (also mentioned by General Fytche) connected with the legend of Gautama, "that of being entered as a saint in the Roman Calendar, and ordered to be worshipped as a saint on every 27th November, under the title of St. Josaphat;*—all these things, and many more, regarding Buddha and Gautama, are well worthy of the study of every Christian or searcher after knowledge.

* See *Burma Past and Present*, vol. ii. chap. iv. One of the most interesting chapters on Buddhism ever written.

SUPPLEMENTARY CHAPTER.

SIR ARTHUR PHAYRE ON BRITISH BURMA.

It was not without great pleasure that Anglo-Burmans in this country received the announcement that Sir Arthur Phayre would read a paper on British Burma before the Society of Arts (Indian Section), May 13th, 1881. If local knowledge were ever to unroll the ample page on such a subject—knowledge of yesterday and to-day adorned by the rich "spoils of time"—there surely could be no better expositor than this experienced and distinguished administrator of Chin-India. As, doubtless, the paper read by Sir Arthur Phayre has drawn the attention of many to Burma, who before regarded the country without much hope or favour, it may please the readers of this little work if we commence a supplementary chapter with a brief sketch of his career. It is the career of one of "a class of public servants which has never been equalled upon earth." Such was the eulogy bestowed by a high authority on the many illustrious men produced under the system of the old East India Company; and certainly, when we look at their actions, the difficulties they had to encounter, and the vastness of the splendid dominion in which they laboured, the praise seems not undeserved.*

Sir Arthur became an ensign in the Bengal Army on the 13th August 1828, a lieutenant in 1835, a captain in 1843, major in 1854, and lieutenant-colonel in 1859. He was appointed to the Bengal Staff Corps in 1861, and five years later held the rank of colonel. In 1870, he was a major-general, which rank he held with the honourable adjuncts of K.C.S.I. and C.B. In 1877, he became a lieutenant-general, which rank, with the additional distinction of G.C.M.G., he now holds.

From the first he was essentially a political officer, for, as in the cases of Malcolm and Munro—Sir John and Sir Thomas the Great—the duties of drill and discipline were second in his mind to the more noble work of settling the affairs of kingdoms.

It was during the Second Burmese War, 1852–53, not long after that "brilliant feat of arms," the capture of Rangoon, and when the important towns of Bassein, Prome, and Pegu had fallen into our hands, while the energy of the great pro-consul, Lord Dalhousie, was in the ascendant, that Captain Phayre was looked upon as the only man fitted to be the future administrator of the conquered kingdom. Released from the tyranny of the Golden Foot, it was thought that the administrative talents of the Bengal captain—who had turned the swamps of Arakan into the granary of the bay, and whose *forte* lay in

* See the author's *Sketches of Some Distinguished Anglo-Indians*, p. 135.

making a little kingdom a great one—would soon render Pegu a most important and valuable British possession. The reading by the new Commissioner (middle of January 1853) of the Governor-General's proclamation, annexing Pegu to the British territories in the East, no doubt, Sir Arthur considers not the least important action in his busy life; while hardly less remarkable was another, when, a year or two afterwards, in the marble hall of Government House, Calcutta, Major Phayre, as interpreter, by desire, and in the presence of the Governor-General, announced to the Burmese Envoy—who had come by command of the King of Ava to seek restitution of the whole of the captured provinces—that "AS LONG AS THE SUN SHINES IN THE HEAVENS, THE BRITISH FLAG SHALL WAVE OVER THOSE POSSESSIONS."*—A capital lesson for those short-sighted political sentimentalists who would talk of giving up any of the really useful and profitable, and, it may be said, humane conquests of Great Britain.

When Sir Arthur Phayre had finished his work in Pegu, he was (1860) appointed the first Chief Commissioner of British Burma—or Pegu, Arakan, and Tenasserim. No better representative of His Excellency the Viceroy could have been appointed; and in March 1867, when he gave up his high post to General Albert Fytche, Pegu might have been looked upon as possessing a model administrator. Within a period of fifteen years (from 1853), British Burma had attained a prosperity which rivalled that of any province in India; and in the ten years, from

* See *Our Burmese Wars, &c.*, p. 322.

1855–56 to 1864–65, the revenue was doubled. At the same time the population—which had been essentially reduced through the devastating wars which for centuries had desolated the entire region from Chittagong to Siam—increased from 1,252,555 to 2,196,180. Where, in the history of national statistics, have we more splendid results than these? The official report on the administration for 1866–67 does Sir Arthur Phayre full justice. The details of his labours are most carefully noticed; and this was only fair to a master of detail in administration. His intimate knowledge of the Burmese language, and scholarly acquaintance with the dialects of the races in, and contiguous to, British Burma, and his close study of their history and characteristics "rendered him an authority on the philology and ethnology of the Indo-Chinese nations"—perhaps, we venture to add, the soundest that England can boast. Mr. Coryton, in a letter to the Liverpool Chamber of Commerce, after Sir Arthur Phayre's retirement from British Burma, quoted a fine passage from the report abovementioned, which must not be omitted from this brief sketch:—"His constant accessibility and courteousness to the people of the country, whatever their position, gained for him their confidence and respect to an unusual extent. He was careful of the rights of Government, but zealous and watchful over the interests of the native population." To this we may add, that in the all-important matter of education there could not be a more zealous advocate for the diffusion of its blessings. For this alone he will ever be remembered by the people of Pegu, to whom he strove to give a national system of education, founded on the best principles; while for his works among them in general, Peguese, Burmese, and Karens (Deists chiefly inhabiting the hills), for many generations to come, will, as in the case of the "Munro Sahib" in southern, and in that of "Jan-Malcolm Sahib" in Central India, make it apparent to the inquisitive traveller in their region, that whoever mentioned the great Chief Commissioner—as Dr. Johnson said when extolling a celebrated poet—mentioned him with honour.

In 1874, Sir Arthur Phayre was appointed by Lord Carnarvon to the Governorship of the Mauritius. The appointment was considered an honour to the Indian army; and many of us saw in the laudable action of the Colonial Secretary that the clever and experienced Anglo-Indian was "no longer to be left out in the cold." After visiting the Cape, where, at the time, trouble was paramount, and confusion facing misfortune everywhere, he returned to England about the middle of 1879, leading a comparatively retired life, till he appeared before the famous Society of Arts, where we are now to welcome him.

A better selected chairman could not have been found for the occasion than Sir Rutherford Alcock, K.C.B., Vice-President of the Royal Geographical Society; while the able and ever-zealous Mr. Trelawney Saunders, Geographer to the India Office, was ready to point out the various places alluded to by the distinguished lecturer on the map.

Sir Arthur Phayre commenced by an allusion to the rapid progress made in material prosperity by British Burma during the last twenty years.

Statistics of trade and revenue were not available for a

later period than 1879–80. The population by the census of the present year had just been received, but he did not propose to do more than briefly refer to some of the statistics "for a few years preceding that above mentioned." We were reminded that Burma is inhabited "mainly by people of the Burmese race, and which is as distinctly the country of the Irawadi and its tributaries as Egypt is the gift of the Nile." Politically, it is divided into two parts: British Burma and Independent Burma. Sir Arthur proposed, on the present occasion, to refer only incidentally to the latter. The following passage, and other passages to be cited hereafter, will supplement any deficiencies of information made by the present writer while treating the same subjects in this little work, and elsewhere: "British Burma was formed, to speak generally, from the union of three maritime provinces, two of which, Arakan and Tenasserim, were annexed to the British Indian Empire in 1826, and one, Pegu, which became British territory in 1852. The province has a direct sea-coast line, extending about 900 miles along the eastern shore of the Bay of Bengal. Though for such an extent the number of ports is limited, yet the outlets of the great rivers give at Akyab, Bassein, Rangoon, and Maulmain, admirable positions for trade with other countries. The province has an area of about 94,000 square miles, being a little larger than Great Britain." The reader will already have seen it mentioned (in the Third Chapter) that British Burma is about half the size of Spain. This was stated on the assumption that the former had an area of only 90,000 square miles. The concise nature of the following information, coming from such a learned authority, adds much to its interest at the present time, when China and the Indo-Chinese races would seem to be, as it were, emerging from darkness into a marvellous, and, it is to be hoped, lasting light: "The Burmese people, who, including the Talaings, or Peguans, form about five-sixths of the population of British Burma, are classed by ethnologists as Mongoloids. The numerous hill-tribes, Karens, Khyengs, Kamis, and others, belong to the same family. The Burmese, by their physiognomy as well as by their language, show that they belong to the same family as the Bhote, or people of Tibet The connection from the one to the other, though their countries are so far apart, may be traced by similarity in the physical form and speech of tribes dwelling on the south-eastern border of the great plateau of Tibet, and bordering the way along the courses of rivers to the country of the middle Irawadi. The Burmese language may be roughly described as monosyllabic, though this classification can only be applied to it with considerable modification. The Talaing people, who chiefly inhabit the delta of the Irawadi, may no doubt be traced to the same original seat as the Burmese; but their ancestors appear to have left it at a much earlier period than the forefathers of the latter. Their language, which now differs materially from that of the Burmese, has become nearly extinct, and there is, perhaps, a larger Talaing-speaking people in Siam than in Pegu." Leaving such matters for the euridite Max Müller and his students to solve, we now come to the population of British Burma. Elsewhere allusion has been made to the sparseness of population * in

* See *Our Burmese Wars and Relations with Burma*, p. 328.

the country when it fell into our possession, as well as to the causes of such a scarcity of life-blood in Ashé Pyee, —life-blood so necessary to develope the resources of a land teeming with all the accessories of wealth and prosperity. "The total population of British Burma, by the census of this year, amounts to 3,704,253 souls.* In order to show the great increase in population which has taken place, it may now be stated that in 1855–56, the population amounted to 1,252,555 souls. Probably the number may then have been understated from defective returns; but, even supposing that the deficiency reached to so much as a quarter of a million, about one-fourth of the whole, the fact will remain that, in a quarter of a century, the population has nearly trebled. This, no doubt, has resulted largely from immigration from Upper Burma; but the people are also increasing from natural causes, consequent on freedom for their industry, the absence of war, and, it is believed, generally improved sanitary condition from better food and clothing." These authoritative remarks, coupled with what the present writer has already said on population in this little work, as well as in his larger one, it is to be hoped will go some way towards exhausting the interesting subject.

We now turn to the latest information regarding the revenue of British Burma, the increase in which is even more remarkable than that of the population. "The amount of imperial revenue—that is not including what is collected

* This is an increase of thirty-four per cent. since 1872. Rangoon contains 132,004, and Maulmain 46,472, an increase in the former of thirty-six per cent., and in the latter of fourteen per cent.

by municipal rates—raised from this population amounted, in 1879–80, in round numbers, to £2,100,000. That is a far greater proportional amount than is paid by any other province under the Government of India. It may, at the same time, be noted that the amount collected in 1855–56 was, in round numbers, £531,792. While, therefore, in twenty-five years, the population has nearly trebled, the revenue has nearly quadrupled." This extraordinary increase, Sir Arthur Phayre felt assured, "has resulted from general increase of prosperity, and not from excessive taxation." The only item on which the first Chief Commissioner would wish to see a reduction in the annual revenue is "on that arising from the consumption of opium. The quantity consumed might be very much reduced by Governmental action, with great advantage to the community,"—and, he adds: "I learn, within the last few days, that measures have been adopted for that purpose." Thus, we have the first dawn of local option, but of a different kind to that already alluded to,* in British Burma. Opium-eating and smoking will yet become a great Eastern question; and, doubtless, the same wise people at home who style alcohol "the devil in solution," will name the former drug "the devil in pieces!"

The next important subject for consideration, while handling the question of progress in the prosperity of British Burma, was "the continued regular advance in the area of cultivated land." To this reference has already been made in a previous chapter; but, bringing down the

* See introductory remarks to Chapter III. See also Note IV., on "Opium in Burma."

statistics a year or so later, the result seen in the following figures becomes of remarkable interest. In 1855–56 the total area of cultivated land paying revenue to Government was 1,075,374 acres. In 1879–80 the area was 3,364,726 acres. The value of rice exported by sea was, in 1855–56, £1,482,475; and in 1879–80, £5,274,311.' It must have been highly gratifying to Sir Arthur to record such progress—a progress, it may be safely said, unexampled in the colonial history of the British Empire. Let us suppose, for a moment, that a similar degree of progress in the area of cultivated land had taken place in Upper Burma and the adjacent countries—to say nothing of their valuable mineral and other resources—in 1881, would not the whole of Burma really be deserving of the appellation of Ashé Pyee, the superior country? Statistics, like facts, are "stubborn things," and cannot be got over by futile sophistry, or lamentable indifference. Every Englishman should say of British Burma, looking to the future, Sooner or later, next to India, it must become "the brightest jewel in the British crown."

At a time when a Land Bill was demanding all the intellect and energy of great statesmen to make it palatable at home, it was pleasant to hear a word or two from Sir Arthur Phayre about land in Burma, which remarks will render the brief information already given on the subject by the present writer more complete.*

The very beginning is worthy of notice; but as the great Irish Land Bill will surely be passed, or become law

* See beginning of Chapter VII.

before this little work is published, whatever useful matter is contained in the following extract will be too late to give a hint or add to the already overwhelming number of amendments:—"The right of property in the soil is independent to the governing power, and is so laid down in Buddhist Scriptures. The average area of each estate on which rice is raised is not more than seven or eight acres. That is the area available for cultivation. Grazing-land is that which is left wild round each village, and is common to the landowners thereof. All owners exercise the right of sale, lease, gift, and mortgage, though sale outright is very seldom made. There appears to be an objection to it, which may almost be called religious, irrespective of the rights of heirs, which cannot be alienated; and when land is sold by deed, it is generally expressed that the object of the purchaser is to build a pagoda or other religious edifice thereon. This is supposed to justify the sale. Rice land is occasionally let from year to year, on verbal agreement, the tenant agreeing to pay ten per cent. of the produce."

It is pleasing to think that there never has been, nor ever will be, a Land League in Burma! In respect of such "a rapid fire,"* at least fair parts of the East are superior to bright portions of the more civilised West. Some Liberals of the present day, and, doubtless, many Conservatives, will be of opinion that a few cautious statesmen like Sir Thomas Munro of yesterday, and Sir Arthur Phayre of to-day, with vast Eastern experience, could have framed a good Land

* "A solid league—a rapid fire."—*Grattan.*

Bill at home, though wanting the finish of the master-piece yet to come.

It was pleasing to hear it asserted by Sir Arthur Phayre, that the development of commerce in British Burma "has kept pace with the increase of population and cultivation." The trade of the province "may be classed as (1) that carried on by sea with foreign countries, and with British India; and (2) that carried on by river navigation, or by inland caravan traffic with independent Burma, China and Siam." He compared the sea-borne trade of 1879-80 with that of 1871-72; for both years all imports and exports of goods on account of the Government being excluded. The imports and exports for 1871-72 amounted to £8,249,558. In 1879-80 they reached the large sum of £15,555,312. (*See also* Chapter IV., on "Concurrent Commercial Interests"; likewise *Our Burmese Wars*, &c., pages 314, 350,* 472.)

It was not considered necessary to do more than mention the principal articles:—"The two of most importance to the United Kingdom are the cotton and silk piece-goods, the cotton twist and yarn of British manufacture. The value of those goods imported in the year 1871-72 amounted to £1,385,011, and woollen goods to £88,372. In 1879-80, the value of the former amounted to £2,006,453; and woollen manufactures to £225,915. When I say these were of British manufacture, it should be noted that, strictly speaking, 97 per cent. of the goods were shipped from the United Kingdom. Considering the population of British Burma small in comparison with

* Note on Revenue and Commerce, written in October 1879.

that of most provinces in British India, this is a very large proportional amount of annual consumption."

After the rice exports from British Burma, the value of which has already been given, "the next article of importance is teak timber, which is probably the most valuable wood known for ship-building and industrial purposes. There has been a considerable falling off in the export of teak timber within the last five years. In 1875-76, the value exported amounted to £432,389 ; and in 1879-80, to only £273,967."

Sir Arthur Phayre's remarks on teak timber are very valuable; and they must commend themselves to all intelligent readers. It is always pleasing to gain information of such a useful and practical character :—

"Teak timber exported is grown both in British territory and beyond it. The teak forests in British Burma are the property of Government, and are carefully conserved. No care appears to be taken of those in Independent Burma, or in Siam, and it is to be feared that the destruction now going on must in a few years render it impossible to find large-sized timber in those countries, in such positions as to be available for the market. In the districts of British Burma, which were annexed in 1826, similar waste was allowed. It was only in 1852, when experience had shown the absolute necessity of guarding against indiscriminate felling of trees, that the Marquis of Dalhousie issued orders for the formation of a forest department in the province. First under Dr. McClelland, and afterwards under the present Inspector-General of Forests in India, Dr. Brandis, successful measures were adopted for the conservancy of forests. This it was which led to the formation of a Forest Department for all India, which it is now acknowledged has been of vast benefit to the empire.

"The growth of teak trees in British Burma is secured partly by planting in suitable localities, and by guarding against destructive agencies all young trees whether planted or of natural growth. The principal destructive agencies are:—Fire, which, in the dry season, unless prevented, frequently spreads over hundreds of square miles, and kills young trees; parasitical plants; and the method of clearing ground for cultivation on mountain slopes carried on by the hill tribes, who indiscriminately fell trees and burn them in one mass. The latter enemy to forest conservancy is, perhaps, the most difficult to deal with, as there is great danger of exciting the ill-will of the hill tribes by interference with what they have from time immemorial considered their right. Great caution, therefore, is necessary, and has been observed in carrying out measures necessary to check the destruction of trees by that means. Teak trees which have arrived at maturity, that is at the age of eighty to ninety years, are girdled two or three years before they are intended to be felled. The rise of the sap being thus intercepted, the trees die, and they become thoroughly seasoned while still standing. They are then capable of being floated down the streams and rivers without delay after having been felled. During the last five years there has been a material decrease in the yield of *teak* timber in the forests of British Burma. This will be seen from the following table of the actual quantity brought down during each year:—

	Tons.
1875–76	46,597
1876–77	46,431
1877–78	39,081
1878–79	22,763
1879–80	17,585

"It must not be supposed that the diminution in the annual supply brought to market indicates a diminution in the actual number of mature, or full-sized teak trees existing in the forests. The reduction proceeds from various causes, and it may be confidently pronounced that the effect of the forest conservancy in British Burma has been to render available for public use a valuable natural product, while guarding against wasteful felling, which would, in a course of years, extinguish the supply for future generations. Various other timber trees are cared for in the forests of Burma, which it is not necessary to enumerate. Cinchona trees have been planted, but the result, as yet, has not been favourable."

Before proceeding with Sir Arthur Phayre's paper, it may prove interesting to well-wishers of British Burma to learn that, in a report* on forest conservancy in that country,

* Drawn up by H. Leeds, Esq., Officiating Conservator of Forests, British Burma.

for 1863–64, there are some useful hints regarding forest administration; and in an order by the Government of India thereon, it is said:—"The report exhibits the state of forest administration in British Burma in a very satisfactory light. The result of the eight years' working of a strict system of conservancy is a surplus of 6¾ lakhs of rupees (nearly £70,000), and the steady growth of the net revenue gives promise of a continuation of this prosperous state of affairs." Thus has prosperity in many phases crowned British efforts in Burma—a strong argument in favour of our giving every attention to that country.

As regards teak timber floated down the rivers into British Burma from the neighbouring countries, the first Chief Commissioner observed "that the quantity is about four times that derived from forests in British territory. But, as already stated, as no conservancy is exercised in those countries, the supply, before many years, will probably be much reduced." To this it may be added that, both in Upper or Independent Burma, and in Siam, King Theebau and the young king of many names, would find it greatly to their advantage to possess a well-organized forest conservancy, for it would doubtless prove a strong symptom of real progress in Chin-India; while proud and selfish monopoly's head would soon disappear if the two mighty sovereigns of "earth and air" were to invite over a band of scientific European miners to develop the resources of their superior countries, when the concurrent commercial interests of Great Britain and Burma, and even Siam and China, would probably be established for ever! The gold mania at present raging in southern India may, ere long, be succeeded by a more powerful one in India beyond the Ganges.

"Other articles exported from Burma are cutch, cotton, and petroleum."

Sir Arthur Phayre now alluded to one abundant natural vegetable substance, which "promises to become utilized, and to add to the products exported to other countries. I allude," said he, "to the manufacture of paper from bamboo fibre, which has been undertaken by Mr. Thomas Routledge. This enterprise will turn to good account a plant which grows rapidly in every part of British Burma; and there are many tracts where plantations of it may be farmed for the object in view. The material would be exported in the shape of fibrous paper stock."—"*All honour to the man,*" says shrewd, philosophic old Carlyle, while descanting upon Goethe, "*who first through the impassable paves a road!*" There will be more to say about the manufacture of paper from the bamboo, and Mr. Thomas Routledge, by-and-bye.

It must be of great interest to British merchants to learn that "the inland trade of British Burma with Independent Burma and the Shan States is only yet in its infancy; but it has made great strides within the last few years. The progress during eleven years has been gradual, and is shown by the following figures":—

1869–70.

Value of exports	£1,283,588
Value of imports	905,308
Total	2,188,896

1879–80.		
Value of exports	... ...	£1,880,052
Value of imports	... ...	1,983,354
Total	... ...	3,863,406

In order to show the value of the inland trade of British Burma in articles of British manufacture, and its progressive increase in eleven years, the following statement of the value of exports of textile and fibrous fabrics is given:—

	1869–70.		1879–80.
Cotton piece-goods ...	£44,549	...	£191,821
Silk piece-goods ...	9,025	...	168,936
Woollen piece-goods...	7,941	..	43,524
Cotton twist and yarn	49,281	...	157,924
Total ...	110,796	...	562,205

After remarking that the great bulk of the trade with Independent Burma is carried on by the river Irawadi, Sir Arthur Phayre considered the statement worthy of notice, that, "notwithstanding the unsatisfactory state of the relations of the British Government with the Court of Mandalay, trade between the two countries has not materially suffered." This may be very true, comparatively speaking, but it is hardly so in a progressive point of view. Supposing our relations with Burma had been of the best, and King Theebau, since ascending the throne, had adopted the principles of Free Trade, and even carried out the views of a shrewd M.P. of the present day, "that treaties of commerce, instead of advancing Free Trade, tend to retard its progress,"* would not the results of the trade between British and Upper Burma have been far greater? "The great object," Sir Arthur continued, "of establishing and maintaining a direct trade with Yunnan has not been accomplished. The main obstacle to success may be attributed to the Chinese merchants settled in Burma, and to the Chinese local authorities on the border. The opposition of the former arises from jealousy of foreigners, and what every other people similarly circumstanced shows, dread of losing a profitable trade."

A noble kindness towards the Burmese Government comes forth in the succeeding remarks, which many will admire, though others may be somewhat sceptical as to what is said about Theebau's "engagements":—"On the whole the Burmese Government has been faithful to its treaty engagements with the Governor-General of India, and with prudence and avoidance of aggressive conduct, which is certainly not likely to arise from the Burmese Government, there is no reason for doubting that the interests of both countries, as regards friendship and commerce, will be maintained." There is also, it may be added, no chance of aggression on the part of our present Liberal Government. The writer's opinion of King Theebau has not, however, materially changed.

Turning now to the "Statement"† so ably compiled in the India Office, it is there written in singular opposi-

* Mr. Agnew. M.P., writing on the subject of the French tariff, June 1881.

† Exhibiting the moral and material progress of India during the year 1878–79; ordered by the House of Commons to be printed, 13th September 1880.

tion to Sir Arthur Phayre's remarks above quoted:—"During the greater part of 1878–79, our relations with Upper Burma were much strained, and trade was injuriously affected" (page 113). Under any circumstances, there can be no doubt as to "the necessity of placing our relations with the Court of Mandalay on a proper footing."* The re-appointment of a Resident at Mandalay has probably long been under the serious consideration of Government; and when the time comes, it is to be hoped that King Theebau will have undergone a complete moral revolution. Without this, the renewed presence of patient diplomatists at the capital will be utterly useless. The Golden Foot is young; there are still hopes of him; and when such an authority as the ever-zealous and successful first administrator of British Burma is of such an opinion, it is hardly wise not to augur, even for King Theebau, something of a bright future.

Sir Arthur Phayre next gave a sketch of the "means for ready locomotion and conveyance of produce," as, of course, "directly connected with trade and all material progress." When we first occupied the province, the rivers alone afforded internal communication.

In Arakan and Tenasserim, rain was the Siva (destroyer) of the roads. The "great annual rainfall constituted a serious obstacle" to their construction and maintenance. The prospect of return or benefit in a thinly-populated country was remote.

Nothing was lasting, save that mighty highway of Pegu,

* See article on "British Burma," in *Allen's Indian Mail*, May 16th, 1881.

the Irawadi, ever flowing on in silent majesty, heedless of any progress but its own. "Made roads for wheeled vehicles were unknown. Made lines of metalled road," modestly remarked Sir Arthur, "have, under the British Government, been constructed, but only to a small extent. The total length of these does not exceed five hundred miles. The building of village and district roads to connect with main lines will yet occupy many years. A railway has been built from Rangoon to Prome, a distance of 163 miles. The success of the line after four years has been greater than could have been anticipated, considering the bulky nature of the products to be carried, and the nearness of the river to the line. The net earnings, by the last account, were four per cent. on the outlay. The chief source of profit appears to be by passenger traffic." Again, as regards the navigation of the Irawadi by the steamers of the Flotilla Company, it was satisfactory to hear that "it continues uninterrupted, notwithstanding occasional reports of unfriendly relations with Independent Burma. In 1879–80, there were made 129 trips up, and 121 down, between Rangoon and Mandalay." He was not aware of any trips having been made to Bhamo—the famous mart already mentioned (Chapter IV.), where Burmese and Chinese influences commingle. A canal, to connect the Pegu river with the Sittang, "completes the water highway between Rangoon and Toungoo, and is a great advantage to trade." At this point of Sir Arthur Phayre's paper, it may be observed that, at the end of last year a Report was presented to the Supreme Council, Calcutta, on the Bill "to regulate the navigation of the Pegu and Sittang canal, and to provide for the execution of works necessary for its maintenance. With increased navigation of the above canal, and that afforded by the Pegu and Sittang rivers, and the completion of a railway (alluded to by Sir Arthur), from Rangoon to Toungoo (now, it is said, fairly taken in hand), communication in British Burma will be vastly augmented, not only in the interests of commerce, but also in those of the security of the province. With a railway from Rangoon to Prome on one side, and the newly-projected line on the other, with the noble Irawadi, the smaller rivers, and the numerous creeks, with which the country abounds, at our disposal, Upper Burma, south-western China, and even distant, but ever-approaching, Russia—perhaps with a chosen legion of Tekke Turkomans, under some future Skobeleff—would be fairly shut out from successfully attempting a descent on Rangoon. "The coast of British Burma, and the several ports, are well provided with lighthouses. There are seven, and one light-vessel." Not the least remarkable information in this most important paper, is that regarding the Irawadi embankment, which may be here given entire :—

"Among remunerative public works, the embankment of the Irawadi takes a prominent place. An exhaustive report thereon has been made by Mr. Robert Gordon, C.E., under whose direction the works now are. The object of the embankment was to protect cultivated and cultivable land from inundation. This has, to a considerable extent, been effected. But as is to be expected in dealing with a great river, having a rise of about forty feet when in flood, and an extreme discharge in the rainy season, thirty miles above the head of the delta, of two millions of cubic feet per second, many complications have arisen, and the question of further embankment is still under consideration. In the lower part of the delta there are some thousands of square miles which can be made culturable by an embankment, and where the difficulty from the destructive force of current is much reduced. Mr. Gordon has, with reference to the periodical rise of the Irawadi, the rainfall in the eastern Himalaya, and the discharge of water by the rivers entering the Brahmapootra from the north, in Assam below Sadiza, concluded that the Irawadi is the continuation of the Sanpo of Thibet. This is one of the few great questions in the geography of Asia which has still to be solved, and which has been a subject of controversy since the time of d'Anville."

The next subject, especially to one who had held an educational post in the country,* was of intense interest.

In the annals of Indian administration there is hardly any subject so remarkable as Education in British Burma. Take a report for any year, and there is always something wonderful to tell—astonishing progress made by both sexes of a most interesting class of the Mongolian race, caused by a rare desire and aptitude for learning; and all this is carried on in Ashé Pyee with so little expense, and without half the fuss or noise of more civilised countries, that in a few years it is quite possible that not many of the population will be perishing for lack of knowledge. What the Board Schools have done for education at home, the Monastic system—with the improvements grafted upon it by Sir Arthur Phayre—has done for British Burma. A mighty triumph over ignorance has certainly been accomplished. True enough, before the British advent zealous American and other missionaries had done their teaching work "excellent well;" but the master-hand was wanting which was to put the numerous odd pieces of the cabinet together, to

* Inspector of Government and Aided Schools in the three seaport towns—Rangoon, Maulmain, and Akyab. The Inspector commenced his duties on the 1st May, 1865, and submitted various reports.

delight and surprise the friends of universal progress. A remarkable year for education in British Burma was 1865; and, to say nothing of what the writer witnessed at the seaport towns, among other wonders, through our occupation of the country, Dr. and Mrs. Mason—of whom America may well be proud—had opened in that year a Karen Young Men's Normal Institution, to train teachers for the mountains of Toungoo, and a Karen Female Institute, at the same place, for the instruction of the daughters of Karen mountaineers. In the former institution the subjects taught were the English and Burmese languages, arithmetic, geography, drawing, land surveying, and the study of the Holy Scriptures. Many of the boys could survey well with the chain and cross-staff, while five of them could use the prismatic compass, and the study of plane trigonometry and the use of the sextant received every attention. In Mrs. Mason's institute there were sixty-six pupils at the examination of January 1866. On this auspicious occasion, "Karen mountain chieftains sat for the first time as judges, and awarded prizes to Karen young women for attainments in scholarship. There were present also, strange new visitors in nine Manu Manau chieftains from beyond the eastern water-shed, and two Gaiko chiefs from near the northern boundary. In all, there were forty-one chiefs and elders present from the mountains, with fifty students and jungle teachers." Here was at least one grand educational result in Burma, achieved, nearly sixteen years ago, by zealous workers, of a class too often labouring on in distant lands "in the front of severest obloquy."

Sir Arthur Phayre, then, leaving the Irawadi, next

directed the attention of his hearers to a notice of the present state of education in British Burma, the very commencement of which is full of information, and well deserving of attention by all Englishmen :—

"Elementary knowledge of reading and writing is more generally diffused among the people of Burma than is the case in India, and even in some countries of Europe. This has resulted from the fundamental principles of Buddhism. For the Buddhists, having originally protested against Brahman exclusiveness in matters of religion, and as regards the acquisition of knowledge by those outside their own body; and having contended for the right of all to rise by personal merit to ecclesiastical and secular eminence, and to inherit a higher reward by transmigration, the doctrine led to a general diffusion of instruction among the masses of the people. Hence in Burma all the male children are taught letters; the national schools are the Buddhist monasteries, and the schoolmasters or the directors of the studies are the rahâns or monks. There are also in some towns lay schools, in which both boys and girls are taught. The rules of Buddhist monks prevent their teaching girls; but female education is, among the higher classes, carried on in families, as well as in lay schools. The great importance of attention being directed to the indigenous schools of British Burma will be seen from the number of scholars in the monasteries and lay schools, the heads of which have agreed to Government inspection. The number is 70,858 boys, and 3,330 girls."

The medium of instruction in these indigenous schools is the vernacular language of the country. In the majority of instances the instruction does not go beyond the now famous "three R's"; but a knowledge of arithmetic, so dearly prized in England, is not considered of much importance in the Burmese monasteries, as forming no part of religious knowledge, from which the gifted Bishop of Natal might take a salutary hint. "The object of the Government in connection with the monastic schools has been to avoid all interference with the religious teaching, and to induce the head monk of each monastery to admit inspectors, in order that the secular studies shall be more systematically pursued, and the course be more advanced than hitherto. For this purpose, elementary books on arithmetic, geography, and other subjects, have been supplied, and are used. The monastic schools are far more numerous than the lay, there being in 1879-80, 2,693 of the former, to 355 of the latter." Of course, the chief difficulty lay with the monastic schools; but it appeared to have been admirably overcome. In these, prizes were awarded; while the girls in the lay schools were "distinguished for their zeal and aptitude."

The Chief Commissioner (Mr. Aitchison) in his resolution on the educational results of the year (1879-80) had observed:—"After some years of only partial success, the Education Department has, mainly through the instrumentality of Burmese inspectors, got the teachers of monastic schools to accept with gladness, which now seems to be heartfelt, the visits, the inspection, and the guidance of our educational officers." Success could only have been attained, from first to last, in the opinion of Sir Arthur Phayre, "by a rare union of tact, discretion, and earnest perseverance on the part of those to whom the work was entrusted. For the result, the Education Department of British Burma, under the direction of Mr. Hordern, may well be proud."

In addition to the primary vernacular schools, and secondary schools,* of the Missionary Societies, which receive aid from Government, "the Government have also second-

* In which the English language is taught.

class schools in each district, while in Rangoon there is a High School, which has lately been affiliated to the Calcutta University." Some of the pupils, we were informed—doubtless with a feeling of pride on the part of him who had fanned the flame while in its infancy — "are now reading for the First Arts examination."

The conclusion of the paper was in every way worthy of the writer:—"Considering that the most populous part of Burma, which furnishes the great majority of students, has been a British possession for less than thirty years, it may be pronounced that the advance made in sound education has been satisfactory, and is evidence of the capacity of the people, and their desire for improvement." Sir Arthur Phayre had now placed before the Society of Arts and an attentive audience, in which were men—a few of them highly distinguished—of various callings, and of many shades of opinion, "the several points in the present condition of a people differing in race, in language, and in religion, from the people of India"; and he trusted that the result would appear favourable to their moral and material progress. "IT IS EVIDENT THAT THE COUNTRY AND THE PEOPLE HAVE BEFORE THEM A GREAT FUTURE." Let Great Britain look to this fact, enunciated by so high an authority, and do all she can to benefit herself, India, and Ashé Pyee, ere it be too late!

Of course the usual "discussion" followed the reading of Sir Arthur Phayre's paper. To not a few present, who were met to join in it, a grand feature appeared to be the utter abnegation of self displayed throughout the eventful narrative. The everlasting I (so pleasant to minds of small calibre), or the "Alone I did it!" was quite out of the question. It was enough for others to know who had done it nearly all. Like chivalrous Outram, he had shown, in the various incidents of a stirring yet studious life, this abnegation of self "with an uncompromising resolve to do his duty"; and the people of British—perhaps also aided by those of Upper—Burma, in a few years, may think of erecting a statue to the great Administrator, bearing on the pedestal what has been said of Alexander Farnese, Prince of Parma: "'Untiring, uncomplaining, thoughtful of others, prodigal of self, generous, modest, brave.'" *

If we did not know that reticence was a valuable ingredient in modern statesmanship, some present might have been inclined to find fault with Sir Arthur for saying so little regarding our relations with Independent Burma; but more would probably have been out of place in the Society of Arts. As in all such cases, it was the authority which made the paper chiefly valuable. And like a true soldier, both as to time and materials, he stuck to his marching-orders.

Sir Henry Norman, K.C.B., commenced the discussion by happily remarking:—"To speak of Burma was to speak of Sir Arthur Phayre; for the two seemed to be inseparably connected." Again: "He hoped the railway systems now projected in British Burma would be carried out; and he was quite sure they would be not only profitable to the State, but would conduce to the prosperity and progress of the country."

* Quoted by Dr. James Burnes (brother of Sir Alexander) in March 1861, regarding Sir James Outram.

Mr. E. G. Man, in his eulogistic remarks, said, with regard to the statement in the paper, "that there was no communication at present, and none last year, between Mandalay and Bhamo, he believed steamers had been running between these places up to the present time." He could endorse every statement made with regard to the destruction which had taken place amongst the teak forests. He also alluded to education, and had not the slightest doubt that there was a great future before British Burma.

Mr. William Botly made a few interesting remarks "on the influence of forestry on the climate and agricultural interests of the country."

Mr. Pfoundes wished to know from Sir Arthur Phayre more about the old literature of Burma, and "whether it was much affected by the ancient Chinese, or by the more modern Chinese under the Buddhist; or if there were any traces of old Arabic literature. He believed, also, there was a wide field in Burma for anthropological investigation."

Mr. Thomas Routledge was very glad "to have an opportunity of adding a few remarks to the very interesting and instructive paper" just read. As these remarks are of a highly novel and useful character—in an age of paper as well as questions—they are given *verbatim*, from the Society's Journal, in the Notes (No. VI.). We should all take an interest in the manufacture of paper from the bamboo.

Mr. F. Barlow had just returned from a three months' tour in Burma. He had evidently made the most of his time. "The Burmese were the most charming and interesting people he ever saw, except the Japanese, whom, in some respects, they much resembled." This versatile and pleasant traveller seemed to have some tinge of the old "age of chivalry" about him when he remarked, "the women were exceedingly pretty, and dressed in the most graceful and becoming way." As to the men, they were "always cheery and nice, and you became friendly with them at once; very different from the natives of India." The following remark must have somewhat alarmed the able and energetic paper manufacturer above mentioned:—"Whether Mr. Routledge would get over the labour difficulty he did not know, but he never saw a Burmese man work at all." The women did everything.

Mr. Barlow also said a word or two on the subject of opium. He had seen its bad effects; but it was a question, he thought, "whether a total prohibition of opium in a malarious country would be wise. It was probably a useful drug in its way, and with it, as with most other things, moderation would do no harm; it was the excess which did the mischief." Shortly before citing this remark, a notice appeared in the papers that a lady in Lancashire had indulged in laudanum to the extent of six ounces a day!—leading us to think that anti-opium legislation was even more required in England than in China or Burma. This amusing traveller would hardly have found the men "cheery and nice" had they indulged in too much opium.

Mr. Christian Mast had felt great pleasure in hearing about a foreign country like Burma. To night they had heard "that the real means of civilisation, namely education, commerce, and trade, seemed to be employed in Burma, and the rulers seemed also to enter into the spirit of the people, and not to run counter to their inclinations." He was much struck with the skill displayed by the "Governor" in these respects. This intelligent native of a foreign country—an Englishman by naturalisation—considered "the Buddhists were highly civilised, and their civilisation was older than the English." In a few words he brought forth the grand secrets of all our Colonial and much of our Imperial greatness—knowledge of the people, and conciliation.

Sir Arthur Phayre, in reply, said "he was glad to hear it stated that steamers had gone up from Mandalay to Bhamo last year as usual, as it showed the trade with the frontier of China was likely still to go on, without any further interruption. The time he alluded to was 1879–80, when, according to his information, there had been no steamers." With regard to the literature of the Burmese, so far as he knew, "the ancient Burman literature had not been influenced by China; but he spoke with great diffidence. He believed the Burmese were taught letters by Buddhist missionaries from India—probably from Gangetic India—but the present literature of the country might be said to be derived almost entirely from the Pali literature of Ceylon. From that, a vernacular literature had arisen; much as, they might suppose, the literature of England arose or had followed from the Latin used in the Middle Ages. He had lately heard that remarkable discoveries had been made as to the extent of the Pali literature. While he was in the country no researches were made on the subject; but within the last two years, a German gentleman had been appointed Professor of Pali in the High School of Rangoon, and he had made some very remarkable discoveries as to Pali works existing in the country, and also as to translations into Pali from the Sanskrit, and again from that into the vernacular."

To these valuable remarks the writer would venture to add, for general information, that the common language of Ashé Pyee is called the Burman, and is written from left to right in circular characters. The language in which all the religious works of the Burmese are composed is called the Pali, and is written in the Sanskrit character. The Burmese use the palmira leaf, and for common purposes the iron style. "Their religious and other books of value are written with lacquer, or sometimes with gold and silver, and the leaves are splendidly gilt and ornamented."*

Perhaps the most important part in the discussion was taken by Sir Rutherford Alcock himself, when he brought the experiences of a long and useful career spent in Eastern lands to bear on the various subjects.

The Chairman said that, "so far as his information extended, and certainly what Sir Arthur Phayre had adduced confirmed the impression, whatever discussions there might have been at the time, or difference of opinion as to Lord Dalhousie's proceeding in annexing the territory of Burma, the inhabitants had been only gainers by the process. Not only had their numbers more than doubled, but the commerce had quadrupled; in fact, there appeared to be all the evidence of improved government, and of the perfect freedom of development necessary to the welfare of the people. Certainly, if they had any doubts as to the mode of proceeding in different regions, it was a

* The Rev. A. R. Symonds.

great satisfaction at least to know that there could be no question as to the results on the welfare and happiness of the people that came under our rule. Mr. Routledge had given some very interesting facts with reference to paper-making which had especially interested him, the 'bamboo' being a very old friend of his. He had spent a great many years in two countries where there was this singular state of things. In China, where rags abounded, they never used a bit of rag in paper, but it was entirely made of bamboo. In Japan, where also they had abundance of rags—in fact, they were a perfect drug in the market—they neither used them nor bamboo, of which they had plenty also, but the bark of the mulberry-tree, with some twigs of other shrubs. The bamboo paper, which was well-known to artists many years ago, being specially favourable to fine proof impressions from copper-plate, was called India paper, because it was brought home in India ships; but it was really China paper, and there it existed to this day. That colossal empire, like other methageria, moved very slowly, and had not shown the slightest disposition to use either rags or mulberry bark. The bamboo paper had one objection, that it was exceedingly perishable and brittle; it tore with the slightest effort, whereas that shown by Mr. Routledge was cured of this defect. Japanese paper also, though often as fine as cambric, was almost as difficult to tear. Of course, both in China and Japan, the paper was made for Indian ink, which, again, was really Chinese ink. The Japanese, with their marvellous development of industry in the last ten or twelve years, had now got various paper-mills on the European pattern, and made a good deal of paper entirely of rags or rag mixed with other ingredients. The Chinese, on the other hand, went on making their bamboo paper as they did 3,000 years ago, and for aught he could see, would go on doing so for another thousand years. Mr. Routledge's bamboo paper was much superior in many respects to that of the Chinese, though they had been using it so long. He supposed it would be necessary to have crushing machinery wherever the chief supplies might be drawn from, in order to reduce the bamboo to some manageable condition for freight."

The following concluding remarks by Sir Rutherford on the subject of bamboo are very graphic and forcible:—

"The Chinese were rocked in bamboo cradles when they were young, fed with bamboo, and beaten with it when they were growing up; they lived under it in their houses, and, in fact, without bamboo one could scarcely understand how a Chinese population could exist."

It is so, but in a lesser degree, with the Burmese. The learned Chairman continued:—

"There did not appear to be any trace of race hatred or religious fanaticism in Burma, to prevent harmony between subjects and governors, as there were in China, where missionaries were continually being massacred, and their houses burnt over their heads. He had not heard of anything of that kind in Burma, and he presumed the Burmese were a more easily governed race, or had less race prejudices. They must all rejoice at the great progress which Burma had made under the auspices of Sir Arthur Phayre; and, in conclusion, he would propose a cordial vote of thanks to him for the very excellent and interesting paper which he had given them."

More appropriate remarks than these could not have been uttered by any other public man; and the hearers of the distinguished Chairman were quite alive to their truth and merit.

Sir Joseph Fayrer, F.R.S.—who was serving at Rangoon in 1853, from which capital the present writer had marched northward not long before young Ensign Wolseley (Sir Garnet) first distinguished himself by leading the storming party at Donnabew*—said "he was aware it was not usual to second the vote of thanks on these occasions. . . . ." He could "hardly express the great pleasure it gave him to be present that evening, when he thought of twenty-eight years ago, at which period he had the honour of serving in Rangoon with Sir Arthur Phayre, the latter being the first Commissioner and he the first Medical Officer. At that time he could hardly have anticipated that at so distant a period he should have had the great

* March 19th, 1853. See *Our Burmese Wars, &c.*, p. 276.

gratification of seeing Sir Arthur looking in such excellent health, and of hearing from him so gratifying an account of the country he had so admirably governed. The population had been doubled, probably more than doubled; the revenue had been quadrupled; everything had prospered. The nation was happy and contented, and had preserved its individuality. Its religion was undisturbed; the people had been peaceful and contented throughout the whole of that part of Burma which had had the good fortune to be under British rule. They might, indeed, congratulate Sir Arthur Phayre upon this state of things, as no one could doubt that it was mainly due to his administration."

The vote of thanks passed unanimously, and the proceedings terminated.

Long will this eventful meeting of the Society of Arts be remembered, as it may be termed the first really great public effort to draw attention to Burma—*Ashé Pyee*, the superior country—the future seat of British enterprise in the East.

MISCELLANEOUS RECORD.

(*From February to October* 1881.)

HAVING led the knowledge-seeking English reader thus far in Ashé Pyee, the author believes that now, in spite of what has been styled "a various and abundant crop of anxiety,"—Ireland, the Transvaal, and Central Asia—he will be interested in some occasional notes, chiefly on Burmese affairs; while, should he be that "man so various," an English politician, he may be able to pick up something worth making a note of, which he may produce before or on the realisation of a bright future in store for Burma.

KING THEEBAU AND THE ENGLISH NURSE.—King James I. had a very kindly feeling towards his old nurse. Sir John Malcolm, also, never forgot the services of that truly domestic functionary, who had actually brushed him up for appearance before the mighty Court of Directors. An English nurse in King Theebau's family must have had a rare opportunity of acting the part of a female Theophrastus with reference to the Golden Foot, that generally wayward child of a larger growth. Although not his "old nurse," the King must have had some regard for her.

Early in February it was announced that this fearless nurse in the Royal Family of Burma took a more favourable view of King Theebau than previous visitors to Mandalay had brought back. She owned he drank to excess, but he never seemed much the worse, and he was always kind, except when he got angry. On this it was shrewdly, but severely, remarked:—"Unfortunately, his fits of anger are very frequent, while his conduct is so bad, at the best of times, that it could scarcely be worse under any circumstances." It is to be hoped that the young King will have become "slow to anger," as well as a Free Trader, before the re-establishment of a British Resident at Mandalay. Probably, during the English nurse's residence, the loss of Pegu, and all his fine ports, preyed on the Golden Foot's mind with greater force than they would do now, and hence one chief and constant source of irritation; but, as Lord Dalhousie said, Pegu is irrevocably ours, the domestic record above given may lead some able judges to think that the wisest step which could be taken by King Theebau, when His Majesty might have an opportunity of mastering the intricacies of Free Trade, Fair Trade, Protection, or Reciprocity—all *versus* Monopoly*—would be to throw himself and his kingdom into the arms of the great and wise, and humane and liberal nurse, BRITANNIA.

GOSSIP FROM RANGOON.—Gossip, when not too idle or ill-natured, is a pleasant thing, and has frequently presented

* That is, in the Burmese, or Golden Foot, sense of the word; although, according to Sir W. Lawson, England was only saved from revolution by sweeping away the system of "Protection, Monopoly, and Cruelty."—Sept. 1881.

valuable materials to the historian and the essayist. Shortly after we became settled in Rangoon, or following its capture (April 1852), the gossip of the camp formed an abundant source of amusement and information. Without it there could have been neither book nor newspaper. Nearly thirty years have, perhaps, made little difference in the gossiping propensities of Rangoon, much to the satisfaction of able newspaper correspondents and others, who now retail the favourite article, from the Liverpool of Chin-India, with unceasing vigilance, for the benefit of mankind. The "very age and body of the time" cannot be given without a certain share of gossip. At the beginning of February it was reported in London that H M.'s 77th Regiment had arrived in Burma from Madras, to relieve the 89th, which had been about two years at the frontier and three in Rangoon. A popular journalist, evidently not averse to gossip, follows up this announcement by an amusing illustration of what he considers "the curious kind of convenience and economy aimed at and secured in the management of things military, as mentioned by the Rangoon correspondent of the Lahore paper, in connection with the arrangements for conveying the 77th Regiment to, and the 89th Regiment from, Burma" According to the worthy Rangoon purveyor of news for the Punjab, the 89th, about to embark for Vingorla, had a detachment at Port Blair (Andaman Islands). "For some sapient reason the *Tenasserim* steamer, which was to have called at Port Blair and dropped a detachment of the 77th and picked up the 89th men, was ordered to come on straight to Rangoon. It might save trouble if she took a detachment of the 77th, called at Port Blair on her way to Vingorla, and took on the 89th men with their regiment, but that would give too little trouble, so she is to go straight to Vingorla, the 77th detachment is to be sent out from Rangoon by a small steamer, and the 89th brought back to find their comrades gone." And then, according to this gossiping yet severe critic, the 89th men were to be forwarded on to Belgaum, "by the longest route that could be found for them." Doubtless, many officers of long service, in India and elsewhere, have experienced trials of temper from mistakes similar to the above, which—be the case in point wholly true or not—like an ill-judged time for marching, or an inefficient manner of moving troops, must sometimes occur, especially in working the complex machinery of our vast Eastern empire. Again, about the same time, "The famous Yandoon order, or proclamation, stopping the sale of glutinous rice, vermicelli, pickled fish, &c., on account of there having been some cases of cholera, has been rescinded by the Chief Commissioner of Burma, and the author of it told to confine himself to his legitimate duties, of which interference with the food of a whole people is certainly not one." Still, the origin of the order has its humane point of view, as it is well known, when cholera is about, the consumption of suspicious rice, pickled fish, or fish paste (*ngapee*), tends to invite destruction by the pitiless and ubiquitous "angel of death" in the East.

Valuable exploring information now breaks forth through the aid of gossip. EDUCATE! was Lord William Bentinck's grand panacea for the ills of India and the Hindus. If he were among us at the present time it is difficult to say how far he would be satisfied with the result. EXPLORE! should certainly be the cry in Chin-India; for without fearless exploration we shall never be able to give fair-play or fair trade to commerce in the East. The *Pioneer's* Rangoon correspondent writes:—

"I am glad to hear that one of the results of the protracted stay of a gentleman connected with the Bombay-Burma Trading Corporation in Mandalay is likely to be the exploration of the Chindwin river in a steam-launch. The Burmese Government have given their sanction to the trip, but as it is said their authority does not extend very far inland from the course of the river, it will not be altogether a trip without danger. The Chindwin river flows into the Irawadi near Myinjan, and from the large body of water discharged it is thought it must be navigable for a long distance from its mouth. Unfortunately, the wild Kachins who live about these parts have a bad name for cunning and cruelty. Revenue is collected from them by the Burmese with great difficulty, and reprisals are not unknown. If they take it into their head to annex the exploring launch when she anchors, as she must do to get fuel, it will not be easy to get out of the difficulty. But with the danger and difficulty attending the exploration, there will of course be the honour and glory of being successful pioneers of trade and civilisation; and with the example of Stanley in Africa, the first navigator of the Chindwin will doubtless be able, by a happy combination of the *suaviter in modo* with the *fortiter in re*, to set at rest for ever the question of the navigability or otherwise of this important river. It is to be hoped a surveyor will accompany the launch, so as to be able to map the route of the steamer."

Nothing important came of all the foregoing hopes and aspirations, however; so we must just have patience. In Sir Arthur Phayre's opinion, the chief essential for extending the commerce of Chin-India is exploration; and the British Chambers of Commerce must, therefore, throw themselves more heartily into the subject. We have not only got Russia to contend against, but, in her dreams of colonial power, Germany as well. Great nations are only now beginning to find out the value of colonial power.

THE FORCE IN BRITISH BURMA.—A high authority in military matters wrote about the middle of February :—

"As the British Resident has been withdrawn from the capital of the King of Burma, and as the Chief Commissioner of British Burma is of opinion that Theebau's troops need inspire no dread, the garrison there is to be reduced. The *Madras Times* learns that a force of 2,000 British infantry and 3,500 Native infantry, besides artillery and sappers, is considered sufficient for keeping the peace of the country, and for repelling possible attacks. This garrison of 5,500 infantry will not answer in case it should ever become necessary to move a hostile force upon Mandalay. In this case the Commissioner is of opinion that additional Native battalions will have to be sent from India. The re-distribution of the Madras Native regiments in British Burma will, in future, stand thus :—One regiment in Rangoon, one regiment in Moulmein with two companies at Port Blair, two regiments at Thayetmyo and Allanmyo, and one regiment at Toungoo. The removal of the 44th Foot to Madras has been deferred for the present, and when it is withdrawn, there will be left in Burma the 77th and 43rd Foot, together with four batteries of artillery."

Even more important than the necessary force for British Burma are the military qualifications of the officer commanding it. He must not be an old man, nor even one well on in years, to stand the climate. He must not be a very young and venturesome general, or his longings after Mandalay, and even Pekin, may be, in these days of peace and non-annexation, of an unpleasant character. But he must be a middle-aged, practical warrior—if possible, one who has seen something of Burmese warfare—a near duplicate of the Cabul and Candahar hero, Sir Frederick Roberts, to serve in a far more interesting country than Afghanistan, with a visage on which we can read at least something of the famous inscription under Warren Hastings' picture in Calcutta—even more required in a great general than in a great civilian—*mens æqua in arduis*. There is every probability, before very long, of some most important movements taking place in Eastern Asia, which will throw action everywhere else in our Eastern empire completely into the shade; so let us always be prepared for an emergency in which a mere revolution in Mandalay may only play a small part. It has been well said that it is dangerous to argue probabilities; but there can be no harm in arguing in favour of constant preparation and circumspection in "India beyond the Ganges."

Our Political Resident in Mandalay.—On the 25th February, in the House of Commons, Lord Hartington stated, in reply to Mr. R. Fowler, that there was no immediate prospect of our Political Resident being reinstated in Mandalay. [The withdrawal of the British Resident from Mandalay—for some time an expected event—took place on the 6th of October 1879, under instructions from the Indian Government. See *Our Burmese Wars, &c.*, pages 426, 466].

Cotton Duties.—The Governor-General of India extended the exemption from all Custom's duties notified on March 13, 1879, to the class of grey cotton piece-goods containing no yarn of higher number than thirties, except in the border. This notification, published in London at the end of February, took effect on February 10th. Probably, King Theebau, when reading such an announcement, said to himself: "What a strange Government to take off any possible duties, instead of laying them on as I do!" But John Bull has not yet taught the Golden Foot the grand lesson of the universal producing and satisfying power of Free Trade. Should he eventually master the "burning question," and assist us in exploration and commerce, surely all his past sins will be forgiven. But to teach King Theebau such a lesson will be difficult, as the Golden Foot, "true to his cloth, would not reduce his frontier duties, nor forego any one of his monopolies." —*Our Burmese Wars, &c.*, page 381.

MUNNIPOOR.—GARROW HILLS.—Towards the end of March, it was published that the Indian Government might be called upon to assist the Raja of Munnipoor (Munipur) in repelling an invasion threatened by the Burmese. In anticipation of such service, a wing of the 10th Native Infantry, then at Shilong (the sanitarium of Assam, in the centre of the Jynteah hills), which was under orders to proceed to Benares, had been directed to stand fast, so as to set free the 44th Native Infantry, to advance into Munnipoor. The 34th Native Infantry in Cachar had been ordered to hold 300 men ready to move. As a reward for good service rendered by the above Raja during the late Nága campaign, and on previous occasions, we could never render too much assistance to the chief of this plucky little independent* kingdom, lying between Burma and Assam. The Munnipooreans, or people of Cassay, are much prized as clever workmen; and owing to their superior skill in the management of the horse,† the Burmese cavalry in the first war was almost exclusively composed of them. Away, in a north-westerly direction, we come to the Nága, the Cossyah and Jynteah, and the

* Munnipoor was constituted an independent country by the British, in order to form a neutral territory between our frontier and that of Burma.

† Munnipoor is the original home of the game of Polo.—See *Imperial Gazetteer of India*, vol. iv. p. 516.

Garrow hills. At the same time that Munnipoor was threatened, disturbances broke out among the Garrows (or *Garos*), who were reported to be in open rebellion; and a strong body of police was ordered to the hills in consequence. So far back as 1835, this remarkable tribe* was described by Howard Malcolm. Formerly numerous, they became reduced by their warlike habits. Their territory was then about 130 miles long, by thirty or forty broad, and they raised large quantities of cotton, and carried on a considerable trade with the English. Their houses are built on piles, like the Burman; and although the women do much servile work, they have a voice in all public business, and, according to the above missionary, "possess their full share of influence." It is not improbable that some female agitator among them, as if taking an example from the West, was at the bottom of the rising in the Garrow hills. Having thus touched on a part of our eastern frontier, it may also be recorded that, at this time, the Government of India "decided on the retention of the Angami Nága country, lately annexed." It may here be remarked that, some eight or nine years ago, during the Looshai expedition, the present writer was bold enough to advocate that, in order to keep watch on Upper Burma, we should possess all the country bordering thereon towards India, which it was thought would be the best means of preventing any restlessness or intrigue among the frontier tribes being caused by the Burmese. Even the Looshais, it is said, are now being "pressed up" into Cachar by

* Some most excellent papers on the Hill and Frontier Tribes of Assam, have been recently published in the *Homeward Mail*.

tribes advancing upon them from Independent Burma, which action must be a frequent cause of anxiety to the Chief Commissioner of Assam and his political officers.—(For some information regarding the Looshais and the Nágas, see *Our Burmese Wars, &c.*, page 420).

UNIFORM FOR THE BURMESE TROOPS.—Information also reached us in March that the first instalment of the European-made uniforms for King Theebau's "Invincibles" arrived at Mandalay on the 31st January. They were considered to be after the pattern of the Italian army. "Indeed," adds the *Rangoon Gazette*, "it would not be surprising if they were found to be cast-off raiments of the Italian army, cleaned up nicely, as they understand how to do in Europe. All the same, they will doubtless pass as new." The Burmese, like ourselves in a great measure, have long been strange in the matter of costume, civil and military. Let the reader turn to the first edition of Major Snodgrass' narrative of the Burmese war, published in 1827, by the famous John Murray, for whom Lord Byron clomb up Pindus, and who said that "every man had a book in him." The frontispiece represents (in a rough wood-cut) a meeting of the British Commissioners at Neoun-Ben-Zeik, the principal figure being the Kee-Wonghee, or Prime Minister. Nothing can be more absurd or fantastical than the appearance of this mighty personage. It is a gigantic specimen of humanity, his chest covered with embroidery, in his right hand a long patriarchal staff or club, his left reposing on a rich, probably gold and silk, waistband, the skirts of a rather theatrical costume, calculated to show off his height, reaching to his knees only, the head surmounted by an extraordinary helmet, somewhat after the German fashion, with a long spike at the apex, from which seems to fly something like a small flag, denoting his supremacy. This helmet is variously worked, with a scolloped rim, and has a chin-strap well down on the neck instead of on the chin. In his rear are assembled British officers and Burmese officials and soldiers, all of whom, especially the British, it is evident from the Kee-Wongyee's severe countenance, he has just been surveying with the supercilious sneer of a high Burmese scorn. The British officers of rank, wearing huge cocked hats, coatees with epaulettes, and swords, and looking uncomfortable, are ranged on the right of the temporary building of the Grand Assembly (near Prome); while on the other side are the Burmese Commissioners in dresses of somewhat the same pattern as that of the Kee-Wongyee, but more humble, and in their rear the umbrella and spear bearers, with a few military officers in grotesque costumes, as a sort of guard of honour. Such is an imperfect sketch of fifty-six years ago. Now that Italian uniforms (and, doubtless, other) have got to Mandalay, we may expect from Ashé Pyee, ere long, aided by wonderful Japan, a lesson in the art of military dress.—(For a remark or two on Burmese costume and equipment, see *Our Burmese Wars, &c.*, page 405.)

THE NÁGA TRIBES.—As a record of what actually occurred in March, lovers of such subjects may be glad to read that, on the 8th of the month, at a meeting of the Anthropological Society in London, Colonel Woodthorpe, R.E., read an interesting paper on the Nága tribes. He touched briefly on the supposed derivations of Nága, none of which he said were satisfactory or important, "as the word 'Nága' is unrecognised by any of the tribes except as a name given the tribes inhabiting the plains; and went on to state that the Nága race might be briefly divided into two great sections, the kilted, or Angamis, and the non-kilted, including all the other tribes; and that though the latter differ among themselves in many minor particulars, yet there was a general family resemblance, whereas the Angami differs from all the other tribes in every way, personal appearance, dress, customs, method of cultivating the land, and, as far as it is known, in language, which probably would be found to be the only safe guide in determining ultimately to what family of the human race these Nága tribes generally belong." In these anti-drinking, anti-opium, and anti-smoking days, the following observations are interesting:—"Very few among the Angamis smoke, but all are great drinkers of a fermented liquor which they brew from rice, no Angami being seen without a mug of this beer in one hand, from which he takes constant sips, either through a reed or with a bamboo spoon, all day long." * This may be considered as fine an example of *personal*, if not *local option*, as could well be desired. And, as to the great temperance movement in England—headed by so many distinguished philanthropists—should such an engine of reform ever want an

* This is hardly worse than, if so bad as, the state of a Highland glen, some five-and-twenty years back, when an M.P. (for Glasgow) declared, to the amusement of the House, he knew of such a glen, where "not one, or two, or three, of the glen got drunk; but the glen got drunk altogether."

illustration of EXCESS in poor humanity, the would-be orator for the million will hardly be able to find a more devoted toper than the Angami Nága.

RUSSIA AND CHINA.—There has, for a long time, been something mysterious in the relations between Russia and China. In time, the Flowery Land will gain information which will be of use to it; for so much diplomatic business with the great Northern Power must result in a practical knowledge of the Russian motto—*Znaj Rus Kago.** An acute military chronicler wrote in March of the present year, that, "notwithstanding the improved relations between Russia and China, warlike preparations are still being made by both Powers." The strange feature in such proceedings was considered to be, that the Russians should have selected Shanghai as the most suitable port for fitting out some of their war-vessels with torpedo netting beams. Again, "the Chinese, on their part, not satisfied with our naval architects, who have given them their admirable 'Alphabetical' gunboats, are employing the Germans to furnish them with another class of vessels—larger than gunboats and smaller than corvettes—built for speed and little draught of water." The latter qualifications are indispensable in all steamers built for service in the rivers of Eastern Asia. Russia and China, ere long, will be as familiar in people's mouths as Russia and Turkey and Russia and Merv are at the present time.

COREA.—About the same time, Corea began to occupy slight public attention. The extensive peninsula of Asia,

* Know the Russian.

between China and Japan, has long been unknown to our countrymen, the exclusive and suspicious character of the people rendering it difficult to get at them. Corea, however, would now seem to have a bright future before it; and it should not be neglected when we consider that here can be got wheat, rice, iron, paper made of cotton, and numerous other useful productions. As with Burma, the Prince of Corea is a vassal of China. Their customs are chiefly Chinese; but their language is different. They are infinitely more Chinese than the Burmese The rapid progress of Japan has begun to teach the Coreans that they may as well be of use to mankind while they live. Thus civilisation at the present day may be said not unfrequently to flourish by example. It was thought that the ubiquitous Russians were going to establish themselves on the coast of Corea, with the view of developing their empire in the Pacific. But England will surely look to such intentions in good time. With the French at Tonquin, the Russians in Corea, and the Germans where the great Prince may put them before he shuffles off this "mortal coil," our Eastern Empire might suffer by competition from such Powers.

Burmese Dupes.—Early in April, many English readers were entertained by a remarkable case from the land of the Golden Foot, which was said to be "probably unique in the annals of the law." There are dupes in Burma as well as in England, where, occasionally, the

"pleasure is as great
"Of being cheated, as to cheat;"

and the victims of thimble-riggers and card-sharpers find their match in Ashé Pyee. The incidents are characteristic enough, and may here be briefly stated: A tattooer, by name Sayah Oung Ban, offered to give a charmed life to three Burmans, by tattooing them with a certain device which would defy injury to their persons. Neither sticks nor stones to assail them, nor cords to bind them, would, under this device, have any effect. They paid four rupees for the gift, and furnished a suitable offering of cocoa-nuts and plantains for the Nats. They were to be tattooed on a running stream; and for this purpose the party went into a boat lying in a creek. After the operation, the dupes were told that they were now quite safe, and that even if bound with cords, and thrown into the river, nothing could befall them The cords would come adrift of themselves. Two of the Burmans were sceptical, but Oung Ban bound the third with cords—the dupe having strong faith in Sayah. Bound hand and foot, he was pushed off the prow of the boat into the creek, about ten feet deep. They watched for his re-appearance, "but were disappointed naturally," while the Sayah's accomplice made off at full speed, and had not been apprehended when the case was published.

RAILWAY AND TELEGRAPH IN CHINA.—In the first quarter of 1881, it was fully believed that the difficulties between China and Russia had been settled. The Russian squadron in Chinese waters had been ordered to disperse, and five additional vessels that had been ordered to China had received instructions to return to Russian waters. It was stated that the war scare—extended over so many months—would have one highly beneficial effect. Within the next two or three years, there was to be a railroad between

Tientsin and Pekin.* The construction of an overland telegraph line was another remarkable innovation among a people "unchangeable in the midst of change." It was sanctioned from Tientsin to Shanghai; and there was good ground for supposing that before long the railway would find its way to the capital of the Chinese Empire. When China begins to thoroughly understand the value of the rapid transit of troops in times of war and rebellion, and the vast importance of sending messages by "the wings of the wire," it will be high time to take more interest than we do in the affairs of Eastern Asia. Meanwhile, we are wisely doing our best to perfect the railway and the telegraph in British Burma.

THE OPIUM TRAFFIC.—On Friday, the 29th of April, there was a discussion in the House of Commons on the opium traffic. The argument was, of course, that England should not sell to the Chinese "a drug which, when consumed too freely, does harm to the human constitution." The tendency to exaggeration, among philanthropists, on this question is really very sad, for, as has been before remarked (Chapter III.), excess in anything is bad, particularly in tobacco, wines, and spirits. With the opinions of a writer in a popular evening journal, under the head of "The Opium Craze," it is impossible not to agree; it was pleasing to see what the present writer had previously said corroborated by so able a journalist. Because men, east or west, cannot practise self-denial, are some of the good

* After the destruction of the Woosung line, a few years ago, there seemed but little hope of hearing the snort of the iron horse in China.

things of this world, which a kind Providence has furnished, to be entirely set aside? Is it likely, if teetotalism were really a rational institution, that the mighty Founder of Christianity, and the great Apostle of the Gentiles would, respectively, have turned water into wine, and recommended its use? To be moderate and sober in what we eat and drink, and thereby crown our lives, is not less wise a maxim than "He that resisteth pleasure crowneth his life;" but such can never be interpreted to mean that an Oriental may not consume his piece of opium, or an European not enjoy his glass of ale or wine. A gentleman, who can say a really good thing, recently remarked to the writer, who, in the capacity of what Charles Lamb styles "a lean annuitant," was enjoying his lunch, consisting of bread, cheese, and ale, that such a simple repast was excellent "for brain power." If such be so, Messrs. Bass and Allsopp most assuredly deserve the thanks of the present generation for increasing the extent of such a valuable human commodity, the good effects of which will surely descend to generations yet unborn. But to return to the London journalist. With reference to India's opium trade with China, if it ceased to-morrow the "morality" of the Chinese would not be improved thereby. "Opium is now consumed largely in parts of the Celestial Empire to which no foreign imports ever penetrate; and it is also a fact, established beyond controversy, that the indigenous manufacture of the drug grows year after year. If, therefore, England were to agree to sacrifice many millions of the revenue of India by abolishing the trade, the only result would be to cause an enormous development of the local manufacture." Would it not be better, then, to "leave well alone" in this matter, at least for the present? Of course, it would be well that the Chinese should grow more cotton—especially in south-western China—and less opium, to increase a trade which it is to be hoped will be opened up to us ere long; but when the exclusive barrier is fairly broken down, that will surely come, civilisation following hard after the change, just as the tone of an Englishman's house is improved by having a fair proportion of books, pictures, newspapers, and music therein, and not an excess of meat or drink. As to the opium traffic in Burma (*See* Note IV.), even were the Indian Government less anxious than they are to prevent its abuse, there is little to be feared in the matter. The Phongyees and the spread of education are safe-guards of no ordinary importance against excess. Although, as an able reviewer well remarked, we hold Pegu by the "simple fact of being there," we certainly have not made the people either drunkards or excessive opium-eaters. Strong drinks are, perhaps, more relished in Upper than in Lower Burma, and in China they are even more in favour than in the land of the Golden Foot. A famous "political" and traveller in the Flowery Land relates an amusing instance of Chinese liking for cherry-brandy. But an example of colloquial *circumlocution* may first be given, showing what a wide circuit words had to make before reaching the proper comprehension. The Colonel (for he was of that rank) spoke in the language of Hindustan to a Mussulman who understood Burman. He delivered it to a Burman who spoke Chinese. "This Burman gave it to the first official domestic, who repeated it to his master in the Chinese tongue." The Colonel continues: "Our wines, port, claret, and madeira, all excellent of their kind, were served up; these, however, were too cold for Chinese palates. My visitants did not seem to relish them; but when cherry-brandy was introduced, their approbation was manifested by the satisfaction with which each of them swallowed a large glassful of the liquor." Even from this showing, it is plain that the Chinese are fond of spirits as well as opium. In Upper Burma, we know there is a liking for the former, or both. It is probable that if opium became difficult to procure, European wines and spirits would soon have a good sale on the river, but especially at Mandalay. From spirits to wine or ale, would be a grand step of reformation, for spirits are even more injurious to the Oriental constitution than opium. Since the departure of our Resident, King Theebau, while musing over his isolated position, and occasionally thinking what a good thing it would be to get on well with the English, has frequently relished his glass of good wine, shouting forth to his admiring and, perhaps, jovial councillors, in the language of the Persian poet, Hafiz, to the "lovely maid of Shiraz":—

"Boy, let yon liquid ruby* flow,
And bid thy pensive heart be glad,
Whate'er the frowning zealots say;
Tell them their Eden cannot show
A stream so clear as Rocnabad,
A bow'r so sweet as Mosellay."

* This beautiful simile of wine—so admirably rendered by Sir W. Jones—is especially applicable to Burma, where the ruby is the most favourite "precious jewel," and it is especially selected to place inside the images of worship.

As King Mengdon, his late father, was a great reader, it is not unlikely that Theebau has a literary turn, and, to show us that His Majesty is not so bad as he seems, or is reported to be, he may yet write his version of the entire song above quoted, of which four lines may be anticipated:—

"Whate'er the mighty English say—
Tell them their Indies cannot show
A city not ten times as bad
As Gautama's own Mandalay."*

HEAD WATERS OF THE IRAWADI.—Early in April, a record of some importance was received at the India Office, entitled "Report on the Irawadi River," by R. Gordon, Esq , M.I.C.E., M.I.M.E., Executive Engineer, Henzada Division. The Report is published in a folio volume, with upwards of thirty maps and sections, and is a lasting monument of Mr. Gordon's industry and talents in the certainly not dry subjects of Hydrography and Hydrology. The author of the present little work has already, in his third chapter drawn attention to the supposed sources of the Irawadi, and has also endeavoured to give a full account of the etymology of the name of this noble river. Mr. Gordon's thirty-third paragraph in Part I. of his work has some interesting remarks on "the determination of the Thibetan sources of the Irawadi." To give some idea of the extent of his researches on the entire subject, it may be mentioned that the book consists of four parts; the first

* So called from the hill Mandalé, below which it is built. The city is about three miles from the Irawadi, and is especially watched over by Gautama. "The city, with its walls and moat, is considered by the Burmese impregnable."—See *Our Burmese Wars, &c.*, p. 403.

containing 126 goodly paragraphs, the second 95, the third 328, and the fourth 256, with various appendices. Such a huge volume on one river is apt to remind one of Lord Macaulay's famous review of Dr. Nares' *Lord Burleigh and His Times*, which, in bulk, was considered hardly suitable to modern times, but which might have been called "light reading" when the span of human life was far more extensive than at present, or before the Deluge. Authors of books and reports should now more than ever study the allotted age of man, in case a "big book" may be thought a "big nuisance."* The thirty-third paragraph, before-mentioned, is a sort of key to the whole question; and its commencement runs thus:—"It is a more difficult matter to distinguish which portion of the area of the great Thibetan highlands to the north is drained by this particular river. One degree further north than the Irawadi has now been traced, no less than five great rivers are found running parallel to each other from north to south, the distance between the two furthest apart—the Bramapootra and the Yang-tse-Kiang—being less than 200 miles. Between these lie the Irawadi, the Salween, and the Mekong; and any adjustment of territory to one or more of these must be so arranged as to provide a suitable area for all."

The following remarks on this interesting subject have been communicated to the present writer:—

"Mr. Gordon's voluminous report on the Irawadi river

* Or "big evil." So thought the author of the *Opium-eater*, De Quincey; or, if memory serves aright, he styled BIG BOOKS the *impedimenta* of the Intellect on its endless march.

discusses vigorously the vexed question of its origin. Among his authorities he refers to the map of the mountains of India by that well-known, pains-taking geographer, Mr. Trelawney Saunders, prepared in 1870. That work treated particularly on the ranges of the Himalaya and Tibet, and it merely exhibited the views then generally accepted by geographers with regard to the Irawadi. But in a later map of the Himalaya and Tibet on a larger scale, Mr. Saunders appears to have studied expressly the connection of the great streams of south-eastern Asia with the Tibetan rivers as delineated by the Lama surveyors, and he has in that map derived both the Salween and the Cambodia rivers from Tibet. The sources of the Irawadi are still retained in that later map, among the unknown regions, reputed to be covered with perpetual snow, on the east of Assam. In cutting a passage for the Irawadi, so as to connect it with the Sanpu without intruding on the course of the Nu or Salween, Mr. Gordon does not hesitate to destroy Wilcox's delineation of the rivers which descend to the Bramakund from the east, and are said to water the Chinese and Lama stations bearing the names of Chusi and Rooema. It may be well to note that the missionary Desgodins adopts Wilcox's hydrography in the maps which he has published. But Mr. Gordon places Chusi on the Nu or Salween, and Rooema on the water-parting chain which he has imagined between the Sanpu-Irawadi and the Nu-Salween in that part. It would be interesting to know whether Mr. Gordon has any authority for thus dealing with those places, which, being the reported seats of the Lama and Chinese authorities respectively, must be regarded as of considerable importance in any attempts to penetrate this sealed territory. A native explorer, trained and despatched by Major Sandeman, of the Indian Survey Department, has recently made an instructive journey on the Irawadi, between Bamo and the route followed by Wilcox in 1825. He traced an eastern branch for some distance, and heard of another branch, also from the east, which falls into the former near 26° 30′ north latitude. It is said to rise in a large lake. Snowy mountains were also reported. There can be no doubt that whichever way opinion may incline with regard to the question of the connection of the great river Sanpu, whether with the Irawadi or with the Bramapootra, it is impossible at present to speak with much confidence on either side. It is no doubt difficult to account for the vast volume of water which finds its exit by the Irawadi, if its sources are of confined to the southward of the twenty-eighth parallel north latitude. Hence the inducement to connect the Irawadi with the Sanpu, which, even according to Mr. Gordon, is the only one of the Tibetan rivers that can be supposed to fall into it. But has it been sufficiently considered that, although the Irawadi basin—confined to the south of 28° north latitude on the north, and by the course of the Salween on the east—is extremely small for the production of such a body of water, yet that it is a region of perpetual snow, probably falling in excessive abundance, so as to supply a great stream even in the winter months, and one vastly greater, when the intense heat of a tropical sun is employed in vain to deprive all the snow of its quality of perpetuity. It is impossible to turn aside from reflection upon this hitherto inscrutable problem without expressing a hope that its solution will engage the perseverance and energies of the Indian Government, and that the cordial aid of the Government of Pekin will also be enlisted. No doubt the distinguished minister who now represents China at the Court of St. James would be willing to help towards a proper knowledge of this frontier question. It may be suspected that the Mishmees, who turned back the late T. J. Cooper, were instigated by the Lama or Chinese officials at the frontier stations of Rooema or Chusi."

EARL OF BEACONSFIELD.—Allusion has already been made to the late distinguished "author, statesman, Premier," while writing on the Burma forests; but it would not do to omit from this record that the noble Earl died in London, on Tuesday, 19th April, regretted by men of every shade of politics. During his Premiership most important events regarding the present King of Burma (Theebau) took place; and there can be no doubt that, had any "aggression" on the part of the Burmese occurred—notwithstanding time-absorbing Afghanistan—affairs in Ashé Pyee would have occupied the Premier's careful attention. His foreign policy—about which there will long be much difference of opinion—had something about it which won the hearts of the Services; and there are few intelligent men who, in some way or other, did not admire Lord Beaconsfield.

BHAMO TO ICHANG.—At the beginning of May, most welcome intelligence reached London, that at last Englishmen had succeeded in entering China, from Burma, without molestation. They had penetrated into the interior of the Empire; and the credit belonged "to two members of the enterprising body known as the China Inland Mission, Messrs. Soltan and Stevenson." They left Bhamo—eastward of Upper Burma—in November 1880, and their safe arrival at Ichang, on the Great River, was announced by telegraph from India. After alluding to the lamentable fate of the brave and energetic Augustus Margary,* and to those pioneers of commerce, Thomas Manning of seventy years ago, and the late Mr. Cooper, the chronicler of this last important event is of opinion that the two missionaries have at length succeeded in overcoming the "formidable barrier of Mandarin suspicion and dislike." This is, perhaps, rather a sanguine view of the subject, and seems to leave the possibility of Burmese obstructiveness and foul play entirely out of the question, However, it is hoping for the best, in which hope all interested in British commerce with south-west China most sincerely join. In future, no expedition to Yunnan by British officers must be undertaken, without holding the King of Burma, to the best of his power, responsible for the safety of the mission. It should leave Mandalay and Bhamo as if it belonged to the Golden Foot, and he were certain of its safe return.† With such precautions there would be no more treacherous murders, like that of

* See Chapter IV., p. 99.

† When alluding to Captain Sprye's route, it has already been said that the King of Burma declared he could not be responsible for what might occur out of his own country. But the two cases are different. The King's power and knowledge were very limited through the Captain's route; whereas nearly all facts about Yunnan, its commerce and doings, are known at Mandalay.

poor Margary, who, although killed in Chinese territory, one cannot help thinking that the deed was prompted by some one at Mandalay. But to the enterprising gentlemen above-mentioned, let us admit the fact that the honour has been reserved for them "of breaking the shell which has so long kept the frontier of Yunnan closed in our face. The hope may be indulged that, with the establishment of so satisfactory a precedent, it will now not be long before a brisk and ever-increasing trade arises between the fertile regions watered by the Irawadi and the Yang-tse-Kiang." It is now high time for the British Chambers of Commerce to work, or, if not, ere long we shall certainly have some other Power stepping in!

By the way, since writing this note, we are reminded that we must not only look to our laurels in exploration, but also to the quality of our cotton goods for sale in China. Our consuls in Chinese ports have remarked upon "the disfavour into which English cotton goods have fallen among the native population, owing entirely to the excessive sizing, which adds to their weight and detracts from their durability."

Education in India.—There can be little doubt that the educational prospects of British Burma are far brighter than those of India, and that eventually the land of Buddha and Gautama will be better educated than that of the Koran and the Veda. On the 5th of May, a meeting took place in the rooms of the East India Association, presided over by Major-General Sir William Hill, K.C.S.I., when the Rev. James Johnston, delivered an address to show that the lines laid down by Lord

Halifax, in the Education despatch of 1854, had been ignored or disregarded in the twenty-six years' operation of the Act. According to this gentleman, the elementary education of the humbler classes had been neglected, and the higher culture had obtained the lion's share of the funds set apart by the State. It was also remarked that there were 3½ millions (27 millions of the population being of school age) more uneducated children in 1880 than there were in 1854. Mr. Johnston concluded by urging that a case had been made out for an inquiry by Government into the working and results of the Education Code in India.

On April 6, a deputation from the General Council on Education in India had waited upon Lord Hartington (having been introduced by Viscount Halifax), regarding the education of the people of India. His Lordship delivered a most important address on the subject, assuring the deputation that the matter would receive the most attentive consideration of the Indian Government.

British and Upper Burma.—Before the middle of May, information arrived from Ashé Pyee and Calcutta, affording a striking contrast in its nature. Regarding British Burma, Mr. Stokes had obtained leave* to make provision for a paper currency, as with the growth of trade in that province, the want was seriously felt by the mercantile community. Mr. Stokes had also introduced a Bill to consolidate and amend the law relating to the excise revenue in British Burma. This Bill, if passed,

* To introduce a Bill to amend the Paper Currency Act of 1871.

would practically prohibit "the use of intoxicating drugs, except for medical purposes, in the province." These drugs were considered far more injurious than opium, and, originally unknown to the Burmese, were chiefly used by immigrants from India, who, in the opinion of the Chief Commissioner, Mr. Bernard, and his predecessor, Mr. Aitcheson, deserved no special consideration in the matter. It also came out that *Ganja* was smuggled into Burma by the native troops from Madras and Bengal. Thus commerce as well as health in the country were being benefited by British rule.

The picture now changes to Upper Burma, or Mandalay:—

King Theebau, the *Rangoon Times* says, "finds money growing very scarce in his capital. He was in the same predicament about *eighteen months ago,* and to replenish his failing exchequer had recourse to that refuge of all the impecunious and weak, to wit—*gambling.* Lotteries were started in the royal city, and, for a time, money flowed in very freely. Curious stories were wont to be told, however, of the fate of some of the winners. One, a Burmese lady from Rangoon, won a large sum one day, and went to the royal treasury in the palace to draw it. While waiting, a trustworthy servant of the King suddenly found out that the lady was a spy in the pay of the British. History is silent concerning her fate, but her sorrowing friends still mourn her absence. Another, a fairly-well-to-do Burman, resident in Mandalay, was sent for one evening, and left his house there and then for the last time. He has never been seen since by any of his friends, who, however, found out that he had drawn a heavy prize in one of the lotteries. The theory of the friends is that Theebau is taking care of him lest he should attempt to go into British territory to spend his money. But to leave these stories alone, the fact remains, that for a long time after the establishment of the lotteries, goodly sums, by fair or by unfair means, poured into the royal coffers, and for a time all went merry as a marriage bell. But, as everyone else but the King of Ava and his ministers knows full well, the primeval curse rests on mankind; the ground is cursed for their sakes, and wealth is only to be acquired by the sweat of their brows. Money went into the King's coffers which ought to have gone into the land, and now produce, and consequently money, is scarce. Lotteries have failed, therefore, and now *monopolies are to be tried.* Some time ago the monopoly of *jaggeri*, or *raw sugar*, was sold to an enterprising Chinaman. This product is largely used in the province in the manufacture of liquor; and by placing the monopoly of its sale into the hands of one man a fillip was given to *illicit distillation, a great deal of which goes on in the delta of the Irawadi.* The owners of *illicit stills* are mostly Chinese, and as the *jaggeri* farmer is a Chinaman, each can play into the hands of the other. The *monopoly of the sale of salt in His Majesty's dominions* has just been sold by the King to Hashin Ariff, a wealthy trader in Rangoon, for a lac of rupees a year. The absolute cruelty of this step needs no insisting on. A salt monopoly, even when worked by the Government, is not a thing deserving of special admiration; when such is farmed out to an alien it becomes an instrument of intolerable oppression and cruelty. *Of the injury done to trade by these monopolies* it is impossible to speak too strongly. And the worst of it is that neither the country, the people, nor the Government benefit in the least from these proceedings. The King gets a lac of rupees a year, certain of his ministers get presents of greater or less value, and double, if not quadruple, the entire sum is eventually extracted from the pockets of the people, ere the farmer, and his agents and assistants, consider themselves fairly paid."

After reading such a description, and making every allowance for gossip, we cannot help thinking how difficult it would be to give King Theebau clear views on Free Trade. Self-protection, as with strong Protectionists in Europe, is evidently the Burman monarch's grand theory and still grander practice; and it may be doubted if even Mr. Bright, with all his persuading logic and eloquence, could have any effect upon the Golden Foot. To English readers, it must appear that the King's doings are a few shades more unnatural than placing a duty on grain and cattle; for such as King Theebau seem to think that it is not enough to take the duty, but it may be in accordance with national custom to take the corn and the cattle also. The King is a young man, and may live to see—with his crown or without it—that no nation can prosper where the policy of Free Trade does not prevail; and, perhaps, when all Ashé Pyee is flourishing, Theebau will be found studying a translation into Burmese of the life of the great Richard Cobden, which will surely remove any remaining sympathy " with the exploded doctrine of Protection, *alias* Fair Trade, *alias* Reciprocity ! " *

CHINESE AND INDIAN OPIUM.—It was interesting to read, at a time when opium was receiving so much attention, that the native drug was rapidly superseding the Indian in many of the southern provinces of the Celestial Empire; and although an Imperial decree, issued some three years ago, absolutely prohibited the cultivation of the poppy, the local mandarins were either afraid to enforce it or " had an interest in allowing it to remain a dead letter." Missionaries from the interior reported "a large increase of the area under poppy cultivation." Of course, it is well known in some quarters, that Upper Burma receives opium from south-west China.

SAGHALIEN.—Slight allusion has been made to this remarkable island elsewhere. On the 18th of May, some interesting information regarding "the colonisation of Saghalien," appeared in a popular London journal, as a "Note of the Day," which is well worthy of notice, and shows that Great Britain must look ahead in Eastern Asia It must be kept in mind that the present writer in his occasional allusions to the progress of Russia, is very far from a Russophobist. As a retired member of one of the Services, he is not in the least afraid of Russia or any other great Power; but it must candidly be confessed that with all our inherent greatness, energy, and good intentions,

* These concluding remarks were written while this little work was going through the press, after reading Mr. Bright's birthday (70) speech, at Birmingham, of 16th November.

we are sometimes lamentably outdone in scientific and commercial enterprise :—

"The Russian authorities are going to make a strenuous effort this year to establish settlements in the islands which they annexed a few years ago from the Japanese. During the course of the ensuing summer some 4,000 convicts will be despatched thither from Odessa, and dispersed in colonies about the island. These colonies are being organised in a most careful manner, reminding one of the solicitude displayed by Robinson Crusoe in choosing proper settlers for the ever-memorable island he reigned over in solitude so long. Thus, in the steamer *Nijni Novgorod*, which is now on its way to the Pacific with 500 souls on board, there are among the prisoners forty carpenters, ten shoemakers, sixteen tailors, ten stove-setters, four smiths, two painters, and a number of other craftsmen, selected with care from the leading convict establishments in the empire. . . . . It is hoped by the Russian Government that as soon as Saghalien is dotted with settlements a large development will take place of the mineral riches of the island, and that the colony will gradually become a second Java or Ceylon. Associated as this scheme is with plans for developing Russia's political power in the Pacific, it merits the attention of the public. By the discovery of vast beds of coal in the immediate neighbourhood of Vladivostock, Saghalien has lost its orignal *raison d'être* as the coaling station of the Pacific Fleet; but the fact that, in spite of the supercession of its mines, the Russian Government persists in colonising and developing the island, is not without significance."

Mandalay and Rangoon.—Towards the end of May, some intelligence, styled "authentic," was received from Mandalay, "to the effect that the murders of the princes ceased only within the last month, or thereabouts." A well known old Mingyee and his daughter, "one of the inferior queens of the late king," were said to have been murdered. At least, after being thrown into prison, they were never more seen or heard of. There were various other arrests, with some difficulty in saving life, which still appeared rather cheap at Mandalay. The following, to English readers, must seem hardly credible; but, after what has been reported in *Our Burmese Wars, &c.*, perhaps it is correct:—"All the young princes, from nine years old and upwards, the sons, grandsons, and nephews, of the late king, who were spared in the general massacre of the princes, their wives and children, have now been put to death secretly, one by one, at various times, within the past few months; with the exception of the late War Prince's sons, who became Phongyees about two years ago, and so far saved their lives. The mother and sister of the Nyoungyan prince have lately been released from custody, but are under surveillance." But news from the Shan States now came to trouble the King's heart. The Shans were said to be gaining ground, and had inflicted various defeats on the Burmese troops. The King could spare no reinforcements; but he had sent two "Hpoongyees" to preach loyalty and submission to the Shans, who turned a deaf ear to their exhortations, and declared their determination to be independent of the King, and their resolution to form a confederacy to resist all attacks.

From Rangoon, the news was of a decidedly more civilised character—civilised, at least, as this world goes. Fortunately, as if not over-zealous in imitating the West, a "regular" murder was wanting to complete the picture. The report contained "another outbreak in the Rangoon jail"; "Homicide by soldiers"; a "Wife divorcing her husband"; and other by no means innocent amusements. In an age when, from its frequency, divorce would almost appear to have become fashionable, the divorce case according to the *Rangoon Times* may now be given. The European wife of a European preventive officer at Rangoon had written to her husband returning him her wedding ring, and stating that she had embraced the Buddhist religion, and that, availing herself of the rights of her new faith, she divorced him." This example, it was feared, would have many imitators when it became "generally known h cw easily a wife may divorce her husband."* After all, marriage, in too many cases, on either side, all over the world, is simply a repetition of Benjamin Franklin's wise story, of *paying too much for a whistle!*

Trade with Burma.—This all-important subject has already received due attention. In what old Spenser styles "Jolly June"—when none of the British possessions in the East promised a more rapid or more enormous development of trade than British Burma, "the volume of its

* Such a law would appear to be in imitation of the Burmese code of divorce, provided for ill-assorted unions, and which, according to General Fytche, "has been pronounced by Father Bigandet, the Roman Catholic Bishop of Rangoon, as a damnable laxity."—See *Burma, Past and Present*, vol. ii. p. 73.

inland traffic alone having reached about four millions"—it was announced that one important channel of trade was threatened, in consequence of an insurrection against the Chinese having broken out among the Panthays (Mahomedans of Yunnan). Seven or eight years ago, it is well known, after the latter's first great rebellion, the Chinese reconquered the province. It was thought that the rebels had at length received a decided blow. For centuries a considerable trade had been carried on between Yunnan and Burma, Bhamo, and Momien, being the trade emporiums. During the Panthay rebellion, this trade ceased altogether. "Since the Chinese have regained possession of the country, trade, particularly in cotton, was continually in progress," but seemed now to have been stopped by the new revolt. Not long ago, news reached Bombay that "all the cotton boats had returned to Bhamo in consequence of the rising." The following information may be considered supplementary to what has already been said with reference to Yunnan:—

"The resources of Yunnan are described as immense, and all who know anything of the country agree that an almost unlimited and very profitable trade might be carried on with that part of China *if only one Government, either Chinese or Panthay, could be firmly established.* The distance from Bhamo to Momien is only ninety miles, and no difficulties would be experienced in constructing a road, or even a railway between the two towns, which would bring Western China in direct steam communication with the rest of the world. Already the volume of inland trade in Burma by the Salween, or Loo Kiang river, is very considerable, and is only overshadowed by the Sittang, and, of course, that other great trade route, the Irawadi, both of which, however, are wholly river-routes, whereas the Salween, and five other routes are all partly land-routes, which is necessarily a great drawback. Last year there were imports to the amount o £29,803 received by the Salween route, and exports sent by the same route to the amount of £82,316, making the whole volume of the trade by that route of the annual value of an eighth of a million sterling."

BRITISH BURMA DINNERS.—The history of brotherhood in the army is much embellished by the grand and steady fact of the regimental dinner. To dine together, once a year, and talk over old friendships, "friends departed," or "moving accident by flood and field," is a very enjoyable recreation; and long may the rational and pleasant custom exist among us! On the 11th of June, however, it was not a regimental dinner that took place at Willis's Rooms. Although several of the company had shared in the conquest of Pegu, still the gathering was more one of the well-wishers of, and distinguished men who had served in, British Burma. General Sir A. P. Phayre, G.C.M.G., occupied the chair; and such well-known names as Major-General B. Ford, Major-General H. T. Duncan, C.S.I., Messieurs E Garnet Man and J. M. Leishman, figured as members of the committee on this august occasion. A great English wit said that if London were to be laid in ruins to-morrow, the loyal citizens would celebrate the event by a dinner. The love of dining together is so strong in the British nature, that probably nothing will ever check the honoured custom; and, while British Burma is becoming so prosperous, nothing could be more gratifying to those present at the feast than to be gathered round a chief who had done so much for the country

HUSKED RICE IN BURMA.—Towards the end of June, an interesting note was published on the Burmese and husked rice, which is worthy of insertion in this record, as showing a delicacy in the matter of their food for which we have not been accustomed to give them credit:—

"It is strange what a prejudice the Burmese inhabitants of Rangoon have to rice husked in the steam rice-mills. All they consume is husked by hand, and such rice, they say, contains more nutriment than the steam mill-husked rice. A native firm has recently imported steam machinery from Italy in the hopes of conquering these local prejudices against machine-husked paddy, but the Burmese say that they still prefer to have their paddy pounded by hand when they require rice for their own consumption. On the other hand, they are quite alive to the importance of steam machinery in the rice trade, and Burmese, both here and there in Moulmein, have of recent years gone in for steam rice-mills, though they will not consume the produce of their mills themselves. There seems to be an abundant supply of paddy and rice this year, and since Sir Richard Temple's Behar famine we have not had grain so cheap as in the present year at the commencement of the rains."*

INDIAN OPIUM TRADE.—At the end of April, it will be remembered, this important topic was discussed in the House of Commons. There can be no doubt that it is a great subject, from a moral, a financial, and a commercial point of view. It was of interest, therefore, to read the opinions of a leading Calcutta journal thereon, after the various remarks of the London press. As to the first aspect of the question, Lord Hartington showed that it was the abuse of opium which alone was mischievous. "It required a man to be moderately rich to be able to smoke immoderately"; and, "owing to its high price, Indian opium could not be used by the labouring classes." The Secretary of State for India, in the opinion of the Calcutta journalist, "made a very complete reply to Mr. Pease on the question of morality; and he expressed his

* *Homeward Mail*, 22nd June, 1881.

conviction that the use of the drug in China is, on the whole, a benefit to the people, and that evidence made it very doubtful whether the use of opium was necessarily injurious at all, or at all events more injurious than that of other stimulants." Beyond this the force of argument can no further go. The morality of the question lies in a nutshell. It is simply one of *moderation* and self-denial—which view has already been insisted on in these pages, and the present writer is firmly of opinion that "reforms of this sort must originate with the people." Now, passing on to the next phase, the journalist does not think that the substitution of "private enterprise" for a Government monopoly will necessarily tend to a decrease of revenue, "for the revenue," he says, "derived from excise and export dues, instead of, as now, from direct Government sales, will depend upon the quantity of the drug manufactured and exported; and it is reasonable to suppose that the quantity will increase." But here one point seems to have escaped the writer's mind. Until the "private enterprise" machinery got into *perfect working*, not brilliant with spasmodic operation, like the volatile electric light, there would be a great deficiency in the finances of India, at a time when money is most required in our splendid dominion, As to the commercial view of the question, he thinks that "private enterprise" will not satisfy Mr. Pease and his followers, "as the industry will still live, and probably flourish more vigorously." Again, he says, "It would be just as reasonable to prohibit or limit the manufacture of alcohol as of opium." Looking calmly at the whole subject, it is not easy to get rid of the opinion that, if not a positive eventual loss, a vast inconvenience will arise from the cessation of the Indian opium trade with China. Of course, the "private enterprise" trade could extend to China; but the Flowery Land seems more than ever bent on growing its own opium.* If they cannot get Indian opium, they may "import it from Persia, Turkey, and Africa." And all these probabilities add to the difficulty of the question.

THE KING OF SIAM.—Early in July, information was received that the King of Siam had sent an envoy to the Court of Mandalay. He was commissioned to conclude a treaty with the Burmese Government, by which Siam would retain the territory occupied by the Siamese troops, and for which she was willing to pay to Burma a compensation to the value of ten lakhs (£100,000). It was generally thought that King Theebau was so pressed for money that he would not be able to resist the chance of obtaining a good round sum. Siam is a remarkable country but little known. The monarch of many names is absolute, and considered so sacred a character, that even his name is not allowed to be uttered. It is not forty years since the Government directed its attention to the establishment of a regular army. Siam's one great river, the Meinan, or Menam, rises in the Yunnan province of China, and flows southward through Siam into the gulf of Siam, watering the whole country in its course. The capital of Siam—

* The above journalist is of opinion that, to aid the restriction on the importation of Indian opium, the Chinese Government might "revert to their old policy of prohibition or protective duties." This, even with China, in an age of Free Trade, would never do.

Bangkok—in name, at least, is pretty well known to Europeans. It is on the banks of the Menam. The population of the country used to be 3,000,000, of whom 150,000 were Chinese. After Alompra's brilliant reign at Ava, the Siamese received their independence. They succeeded in maintaining it; but were continually at war with the Burmese. Now, all feuds appeared to be forgotten. The King of Siam sending an envoy to the King of Burma, was a significant event; and, as before hinted, the two young kings may yet assist British enterprise in opening up the trade of south-west China.

THE BURMESE FRONTIER.—For upwards of two years the frontier between Munipúr and Burma had been in a disturbed condition. At the time of the restoration of the Kubo valley to Burma (1834), the frontier line was but roughly demarcated; and the uncertainty of the boundary had led of late to "constant border forays and raids." With a view to prevent these disturbances, it was generally published, at the end of July, that an expedition would be sent in the cold weather, or rather an officer to demarcate the frontier; and the Burmese Government were to be invited to send an officer to co-operate with him. The boundary line has been a chief disturber of the peace among Eastern states for centuries past; and too much attention cannot be paid to such matters. Lord Dalhousie was most particular on this point. On the present occasion, we read of a boundary made when the country was uninhabited, which does not correspond to any of its natural features. Peáce cannot possibly be expected under such circumstances.

THE RUSSO-CHINESE TREATY.—Towards the end of August, it was generally announced that an exchange of ratifications of the Russo-Chinese treaty had taken place at the Foreign Office, St. Petersburg, between the Marquis Tseng, the Chinese Envoy, and M. De Giers. Here was another clever stroke of Russian policy, of getting in the wedge, by giving back territory to China. Before the ratification, it was announced by an able St. Petersburg correspondent:—

"It may be remembered that the refusal of China to ratify the work of her Plenipotentiary was due chiefly to the fact that Chung How had been induced to give up to Russia the better part of the Kuldja territory, including the Valley of the Tekkes, and certain passes in the Tian Shan. In the new treaty the Court of Pekin has carried its point, and regained this valuable slip of land, though at what sacrifice we are yet unaware. The towns of Old and New Kuldja, or Ili, with all that lies to the east of them, come once more under the sceptre of the Boodokhan, the line being drawn, according to the above authority, from the town of Bedjin to the south and south-west to the Tian Shan, rounding off the Russian province of Semiretchinsk by the absorption of a comparative insignificant portion of Chinese territory."

FLOWERING OF THE BAMBOO.—In India it is said that the flowering of the bamboo and an abundant mango season were looked upon by the natives as signs portending great sickness and famine. It appears that the same belief holds good among the Burmese. "Both these beliefs prevail in Burma," says a Rangoon journal; and what is more to the point, Burma may be added to the list of provinces where this year (1881) the bamboo has flowered, and the mango crop has been exceptionally abundant. The belief among the Burmese at present (August) is that great famine and pestilence are threatened.

Previously, it has been considered a fact that the bamboo (each clump) flowers but once in thirty years. Few see the bamboo flower twice; and when it has flowered, it dies. How is this? Famines are not certainly confined to periods of thirty years. For information on this subject, on referring to a scientific friend, he could only remark:—"The seeding of the bamboo varies according to species—some every year—some only after from sixty to seventy years; and then death—like man, indeed, at maturity."

SILK.—Among the Government presents which, according to custom, were ordered to be sold in Calcutta in the first half of the year, were China and Burmese silks. In the month of August some most interesting information was published in London on the silk trade of China, the Chinese Government having just issued a voluminous report thereon. Silk-manufacture is of very old date in China, whence, of course, it came to Burma, or to the whole of Chin-India. It is even said to have been in a flourishing state, in the Flowery Land, four thousand years prior to the introduction of cotton from India at the beginning of the Yuan dynasty, in A.D. 1260. But at that date it began to decline. "Cotton was a cheaper material for clothing than silk, and, as a consequence, the latter, though never quite abandoned, became less and less used." But when the ships of the "outer barbarians" arrived in the Chinese ports, the demand for silk stimulated the manufacture for export, and the silk trade again rose with the prosperity of the people. It has fluctuated on several occasions, but China and silk are as inseparable as China and tea. These, in spite of rebellions, will ever flourish somewhere in China. We read that the Taepeng rebellion ruined the silk and many other industries. "In Chinkiang sericulture revived in the year 1851, the local authorities distributing, free of cost, young mulberry-shoots, and teaching the people how to grow them and breed silkworms." Chinkiang had manufactured large quantities of silk piece-goods, gauze, ribbons, and the silk damasks known as "ling pongee" and "kung pongee."* It is a sort of Coventry of the Celestial Empire. As with Burmese, elasticity is wanting in most Chinese silks, and "ignorance of how to weave a net with every thread of the same calibre." That in time they will be able to do so, and compete with the silks of India in the European markets, "need not be doubted. Already the Lyons Chamber of Commerce are getting alarmed over the prospect." It became apparent that the Chinese, as well as the nations of Chin-India, require to learn the methods of silk manufacture employed in the European factories, and obtain machinery, after which *course of silk* it has been truly remarked, "silk gowns will become common enough." (See also *Addenda* to Chapter IV.). Some years ago, the revival of a silk trade at Mandalay was attempted under French auspices. Like other commercial attempts in the same quarter, it was simply a flash in the pan, and it cannot be said that there has been any improvement in the manufacture of silk in Burma since that period. Probably Upper Burma is waiting for China to set the example, when Ashé Pyee

* See also *Standard*, August 11, 1881, on "Chinese Silk."

may yet give to the world soft and elastic silk of excellent quality.

INDIAN BUDGET.—THE COTTON DUTIES.—On Monday, August 22nd, Lord Hartington explained the Indian Budget to the House of Commons. The following is a summary, from a leading journal, of his lordship's annual statement on the finances of India:—"In 1880–81 the revenue was £2,300,000 more than in the previous year, and the expenditure £7,535,000 in excess, owing to the Afghan war. For the current year he estimated a surplus of £855,000 over expenditure. The cost of the war, including the frontier railways, up to the end of 1880–81, exceeded £20,000,000, or double the amount of Sir J. Strachey's estimate in February 1880. The total charges of the war exceeded £23,000,000. But for the war, during the last four years there would have been surpluses of revenue exceeding £9,500,000. He regretted that the condition of the revenue necessitated the continuance of duties upon the coarser kind of English goods. Though unable to make any remissions of taxations he regarded the state of Indian finance as prosperous and satisfactory." With reference to the cotton duties, the Marquis of Hartington said, after stating that he thought "it was wise to postpone any reduction, or even readjustment, of Indian taxation":—

"*As to the remnant of the cotton duties*, the total loss incurred by the reduction of those duties was, in 1879–80, seventeen lakhs of rupees, or about £170,000; in 1880–81 the total loss was twelve lakhs, or about £130,000. A heavy loss has been incurred on the class of grey goods which were dealt in a few years ago. Considerable inconvenience is caused to trade by the inspection and examination necessary under the present system, but the interference with trade is greater still; for what has happened? *While protection has been withdrawn from native industry*, a sort of protection has been directed to one class of English goods against another; and *while coarser goods are now protected or stimulated by free admission, the finer goods are still taxed.* It seems absolutely impossible to continue that condition of things, and I regret that it should have been thought necessary to continue it for another year.'

"The whole course of trade," added the Secretary of State, "has been changed by our fiscal legislation, and by the peculiarities of our tariff." Perhaps there are few problems so difficult to solve in the minds of Oriental sovereigns as our Indian budgets. Nothing would make them good financiers (particularly King Theebau) so soon, if they would only be thorough in their study.

BURMA FORESTS BILL.—To the friends of British Burma, a meeting of the Governor-General's Council at Simla, 31st August 1881, was of some importance, as the Forests Bill—already alluded to—was under consideration. Even to one who has not made the subject a study, the remarks of the Honourable Mr. Rivers Thompson, on presenting the Report of the Select Committee on the Bill to amend the law relating to forests, forest-produce, and the duty leviable on timber in British Burma, will be of interest, as tending to show with what care such matters are treated by our Indian Government. Mr. Thompson, on moving that the Bill as amended be passed, remarked that, after its introduction, the Bill had been referred to the Local Government, "the whole of the details of the Bill had been very carefully considered, and an excellent report submitted. Generally, the Bill, as stated before, proceeded on the lines of the Indian Forest Act of 1878, but there were certain particulars in which modifications were necessary to make that law applicable to the particular circumstances of British Burma."

In short, an exceptional Forests Bill was required for Burma as much as an exceptional Land Bill for Ireland. On some points the Select Committee had differed from the Local Government, as with theory *versus* practice must ever be expected. In these days of Land Bills and Land Agitation, a good remark by the Chief Commissioner of British Burma is worthy of being quoted. Referring to a particular section, he said: "On the general principles that it is a great pity ever to make a law that is not shown to be needed, and that it is inexpedient to create by legislation vague undefined rights or claims, the scope of which cannot be foreseen, the Chief Commissioner and his officers strongly advise that this section be omitted."

Mr. Rivers Thompson, in his able review, drew attention to Chapter III. of the Bill, "which was a new one, and related to the constitution of village forests. There were at present no village forests in Burma, but it was thought desirable that Government should take the power of assigning certain areas of its own in the neighbourhood of villages for the use of their inhabitants, under the condition that teak or other specially reserved trees should remain the property of Government. The establishment of such forests would be a great boon to the people; and it had been found by experience that it was quite possible in Burma to combine the protection and good management of a teak-producing forest, with a free use of bamboos or other woods required by the people for all domestic purposes." The chapter thus alluded to would give the Chief Commissioner the power of constituting such village forests, and regulating their use. Referring to Chapter IV. of the Bill, "the Chief Commissioner proposed to maintain the ancient and universally-recognised right of the State to all teak trees, wherever situate, for a period of five years; that is, for such time as would enable the Government to utilise the valuable trees, after which he considered the right might be conveniently abandoned." The Government rights in the teak tree as a royal tree are recognised in Burma, even when the tree stands on land the property of a private person.

VICEROY'S VISIT TO BURMA.—By the overland mail which arrived on the 19th September, information was received that the Marquis of Ripon, after his northern tour, was expected to visit Burma about Christmas or the New Year. Such an announcement naturally led the present writer back to two famous visits of Governors-General in days gone by. The first was by Lord Dalhousie—the great Proconsul, the ready writer, the statesman, possessing amazing decision of character. On Tuesday, the 27th of July, 1852, the noble Marquis and Staff arrived at Rangoon in the Company's steam-frigate *Feroze*. It was little more than three months since we had captured the great Pagoda; and while the illustrious party wandered round the Temple, wondering and admiring, it was pleasant to hear his lordship remark:—"I am astonished how your men got in here with such defences."* It

* See *Our Burmese Wars, &c.*, pp. 175–176.

seems strange that more should not be thought of the illustrious man who gave England so many large and important and profitable additions to our Indian Empire. About twenty years after the above visit, the popular and chivalrous Lord Mayo arrived in Rangoon. In 1870, when replying to an address from the European community in Burma, presented by the Chief Commissioner, General Albert Fytche, C.S.I., his lordship gave the first announcement of his projected visit, which circumstances eventually delayed, and it did not take place till 1872. On the 8th of February in that year, as is well known, the energetic Viceroy was murdered at the Andamans. "Not climate, not overwork this time," it was remarked. "That clear, firm intellect was never more securely seated on its lofty throne; that herculean figure never firmer in the saddle, more commanding at Durbar, more conspicuous in brilliant assemblies, more lordly and magnificent everywhere."* Should Lord Ripon, it was thought, carry out his visit to Burma, doubtless it would be of immense benefit to the "superior country."

NEW COMMISSIONER.—In September it was published in India that, owing to the creation of a new Commissionership (of the Irawadi Division), various appointments had been gazetted. Another division for British Burma will surely tend to improve our prosperous possession. Rangoon, the capital, must be proud of the addition. With its learned and highly-respected Bishops—Protestant and

* See the author's *Sketches of some distinguished Anglo-Indians, &c.*, p. 212. The allusion to Lord Mayo is in a sketch of Anglo-Indian Periodical Literature.

Roman Catholic—its Masonic lodges, its wooden residences of merchant kings, its Government buildings, its Chamber of Commerce, Rangoon has every reason to be thankful.

POPULATION OF INDIA.—Some interesting statistics on the population of India were published in London about the end of September. Already much has been said on the population of Burma. Mr. W. C. Plowden, the Census Commissioner of India, had issued a memorandum with regard to the population of that country, according to the census of the 17th of February 1881. "The only provinces or States," it is remarked, "which show a very perceptible decrease are Mysore, 17 per cent., and Madras, 2.4 per cent. These figures give mournful evidence of the check to growth in numbers which famine and consequent disease have imposed on the population of these two countries." The province which has the largest population is that of Bengal, which numbers 68,829,920. The North-Western Provinces, excluding Rampore and Native Garhwal, number 32,699,436. Madras has a population of 30,839,181. The grand total of the seventeen provinces is 218,559,918. Compared with the census taken in the several provinces between the years 1866 and 1875, this shows an increase of 12,788,565, or about 6 per cent.*

To the above may be added, from Supplement to *Gazette of India* (September 10), a few notes based on the "statement showing the population by sex," of some of the

* See *Standard*, September 28, 1881.

provinces in India, according to census of 1881. These, of course, include British Burma, with its great British Indian port, Rangoon. It is well to give the ladies the precedence. Out of twenty-three provinces, including native States, we find only four with the females exceeding the males. These are Bengal, with 34,601,015 females against 34,220,905 males (excluding population details for Sikkim and Nága Hills not censused); Madras, with 15,597,059 against 15,242,122; Mysore, with 2,100,107 against 2,086,292; and Travancore, with 1,204,024 females against 1,197,134 males. The future historian, as education progresses, will doubtless claim these as the four grand provinces — following the example of the West—for Female Suffrage! Emigration and famine, however, have been the causes of the decrease in males.

British Burma has only 1,720,220 females against 1,987,426 males in a population, as stated elsewhere, of 3,707,646. The population of British Burma, according to previous census, was only 2,747,148, or 1,311,630 females against 1,435,518 males. The population of Upper Burma—the most famous portion of Ashé Pyee in the eyes of the genuine Burmese—may be set down at 4,000,000 or 5,000,000, from which might be deducted Shan tribes, who have recently thrown off their allegiance to the Golden Foot. It has ever been extremely difficult to estimate the population of the Burman dominions. When Colonel Symes visited them in 1795, they were said to contain 17,000,000, including Arakan. Captain Cox, who succeeded him as Ambassador, does not go beyond

8,000,000 *; and Captain Canning, in 1810, considered even this last number as greatly exaggerated. (For causes of decrease in population, see *Our Burmese Wars, &c.*, p. 328.)

Tonquin.—In the *Times* of 8th October, it was announced that the Chinese Ambassador at Paris had represented to the French Government that the Chinese Government could not allow the independence of the Prince of Tonquin, as established by treaty in 1875, to be trifled with. He is a vassal of China, and pays tribute, as the King of Burma is supposed to do; so China could not allow the relations to be disturbed. There are many millions under his rule; so if France interferes, China and Tonquin may yet come down with fierce wrath on "the Eastern policy of our Gallic neighbour."—(See Note II.)

Opium Supply for Upper Burma.—About the middle of October, the following interesting note was published. Allusion has already been made in this record to the enterprising missionaries; and opium is a subject of vast interest in England at the present time:—"Two missionaries, Mr. H. Soltau and Mr. J. W. Stevenson, who have recently completed a journey of 2,900 miles in China, starting from Bhamo, in Upper Burma, and reaching Shanghai and Hankow, report that about three-fourths of the land under cultivation in some districts through which they passed was devoted to the growth of opium, and that all the fresh clearings on the hills were about to be utilised

* Of course, including Pegu, and the greater portion of British Burma.

in the same way. In Sze-chuen they were informed that the quantities exported from that province alone to other parts of the Chinese Empire exceeded the total amounts of the imports of the article from India into China. They add that Upper Burma is supplied with opium from the neighbouring Chinese province of Yunnan."

DESTRUCTION OF WILD ANIMALS AND SNAKES.—In the middle of October, some interesting reading appeared in the Supplement to the *Gazette of India* on the destruction of wild animals and venomous snakes in our great Dependency, including, of course, British Burma.

The ingenious author of a book of travels in Iceland, it is fairly well known, commenced and finished his chapter, headed "Snakes in Iceland," by declaring "There are no snakes in Iceland." Such cannot be said of Ashé Pyee. There are both wild animals and venomous snakes in Burma; and, as regards the latter, although the snake is a comfortable reptile, and, so long as he keeps out of your boot or your bath-room, the European does not see much of him unless he looks for him, still his effectual destruction is, hardly less than that of wild animals, of great importance. It is pleasing to observe that the British press is beginning to take up this subject; while the Government of India is doing its utmost to extirpate such fatal nuisances. One can hardly believe that, in Bengal, during 1880, nearly 12,000 persons—the population of a good-sized town—were killed by wild animals and snakes; and over 15,000 cattle by the same terrible agents of the Destroying Angel. The other Presidencies and Governments have also a large array of death. In British Burma, during the same year, the number of persons killed amounted to 181, and the number of cattle to 1,172. In Bombay (1880), the total number of wild animals destroyed amounted to 1,717; and snakes to the enormous number of 177,000. The total amount of rewards given for this destruction reached to nearly £1,200. In British Burma, the wild animals (in the same year) amounted to nearly 700 destroyed; while the destruction of snakes gave a return of 1,000, the total amount of rewards being under £400. The entire figures show that the total number of persons killed in the several provinces has gradually increased from 19,273 in 1876 to 21,990 in 1880. The study of snake-poison evidently requires another Sir Joseph Fayrer in India at present; while some engine of wholesale destruction, for wild animals in our Eastern dominions, remains to be invented. To think that, in Bengal alone, during last year, there were 10,000 deaths from snake-bite, and 360 by tigers, and a total in eleven provinces of nearly 3,000 from wild beasts, and 19,150 from venomous snakes, is enough to make humanity shudder, showing that, with regard to populations in the East still—

"The trail of the serpent is over them all!"

No wonder the writer of an interesting note, entitled "'Tis the land of the sun," concludes in this fashion:—"Surely something must be done in our Eastern Empire to circumvent the wisdom of the serpent and take him in his own craftiness; and love of good sport and arms of precision ought by degrees to thin down the man-stealers." To men of only moderate courage, or even invalids, a day or two of such sport might do more good to the nerves than weeks on the moors in Great Britain.

MERV AND AFGHANISTAN.—It was also published in October, that an agreement existed, in which England bound herself not to send agents to Merv, and Russia not to send any into Afghanistan. If this be the case, we shall hear of no more Missions to Cabul, like those reported in or before May last, under the auspices of the indomitable Skobeleff, who, it was said, took the opportunity of conducting the Ameer's family, and a Mission at the same time, to the then less unruly Afghan capital. In the matter of a Resident, not knowing the Ameer's real views on the subject, an analogy seems to exist between the Merv Turkomans and the Government of Upper Burma. The former were, at St. Petersburg, anxious to cement good relations with Russia. The Russians were to have free access and egress, all requisites for security of trade, person and exploration; but the Turkomans would not have a Resident. If King Theebau would act likewise, we might do without a Resident at Mandalay if a peaceful reign continued.

UNITED BURMA.—And now, in conclusion, it is pleasant to record the welcome intelligence, which became rife at the very end of October, of the triumph of the Liberal policy in Afghanistan. The Ameer has secured Herat, and the prospect of a united Afghanistan seems not far distant. Of course some of the unruly tribes will still give trouble; but a turbulent and stormy sea does not settle down all at once. "Give him time," every well-wisher of the country must say of Abdul Rahman. Any way, there is a comparative calm for the present; and our late brave and energetic enemy, Ayub Khan, is a fugitive. The Transvaal shows brighter prospects; and if the thirteen kinglets of Zululand would only agree with each other, that country also might settle down with a "message of peace" as effectual as that which has been given to Ireland. But it is to the hope of a united Afghanistan that the master Pilot who has "weathered the storm" doubtless looks with the greatest pleasure, while rejoicing at his success in navigation through a sea of troubles.* And if the triumph could only be followed by a UNITED BURMA, so much the better for humanity, commerce, and civilisation in Eastern Asia.

MAPS.—Should the readers of this little work seek for good maps of reference, they cannot do better than, for an admirable general map of Burma and the surrounding countries, refer to the Map of Bengal, Burma, and parts of China and Siam, published by the Surveyor-General of India, and to be had of Messrs. W. H. Allen & Co.; also to Colonel H. Yule's original map in his account of Sir Arthur Phayre's first mission to Ava; also to that in General Albert Fytche's work, *Burma, Past and Present*; for sketch maps of the trade routes to south-west China, those in Dr. Anderson's volume, *From Man-*

* "And O! if again the rude whirlwind should rise,
The dawning of peace should fresh darkness deform,
The regrets of the good, and the fears of the wise,
Shall turn to the pilot that weather'd the storm!"
From a Song written by Mr. Canning on Mr. Pitt in 1802.

dalay to Momien, will answer every purpose; while a good and clear map of British Burma, by Mr. Trelawney Saunders, will be found in *Our Burmese Wars and Relations with Burma*. There are also other maps of older and later date. Among the former is one by Mr. John Arrowsmith, compiled in 1858, with additions to 1875, entitled "Map of Burma and the Adjacent Countries," from which a very good idea of Ashé Pyee may be obtained.

MEANING OF ASHÉ PYEE.—No sooner had the foregoing Record gone to press, than the following concise information, by a distinguished Burmese scholar, was gladly received by the present writer; and as there have been inquiries about the title of his little work—already slightly touched on—he now gives all that can be desired on the subject:—

The literal meaning of Ashé Pyee is "the Eastern country." It has, however, a more extensive signification with the Burmese, and means the first, or superior country. The heir-apparent to the throne is called Ieng-Shé-Meng, literally, Lord of the Eastern House, meaning the first noble of the kingdom. The Burmese believe that they belong to the Suryavansa or Solar race; and the Sun rising in the East, and shining from the first on their country, that it is the first country in the world!

ADDENDA TO CHAPTER IV.

TWO PROVINCES OF SOUTH-WEST CHINA COMMERCIALLY CONSIDERED.*

I.

THE British Chambers of Commerce have for some years been interested in the prospects of trade in western China. Having recently written and circulated some "Notes" † on our opening trade with south-west China, which, we trusted, contained matter of commercial and, perhaps, also of political importance, it was satisfactory to find them appreciated by a high and influential authority, who also thought that it would be a good service to look after the route from Assam into China. Some years spent in Burma, and having devoted a good deal of time and attention to the affairs of that rising country, it was presumed might

* The MSS. of this paper (written in 1873-74) has been lying by for some eventful years; but the writer now considers it of sufficient importance for publication, in connection with what has already been said on the two provinces.

† *General Albert Fytche's Administration of British Burma: with Notes on opening Trade with South-West China.* London, 1873.

facilitate judgment in the matter of how far the new route from Assam (Sudiya) into Sze-Chuen (or Sechwen) is preferable to that through northern Burma, *viâ* Bhamo, or through Lao, on the south-east, into Yun-nan. It was likewise suggested that we should look up the famous old work of Du Halde, alluded to in Chapter V.

From an eminent living authority we learn that the before-mentioned province of Sze-Chuen is connected with the province of Kansuh, which was partly under the Governor of "Ki," or Kuldja, now occupied by the Russians, and which was the capital of Chinese Turkestan when Yarkand and Kashgar were ruled by China. From Kansuh runs the way to Chinese Turkestan. It is believed that it would pay Russia to advance into China, especially as the river Amoor and the territory in Manchooria would facilitate the advance on Pekin. Some readers may require to be reminded that Manchooria lies on the Pacific coast, opposite Japan, and that a large tract of this region, south of the Amoor river, has recently been ceded by China to Rûssia. The Japanese island of Saghalien—opposite Corea, a mass of coal—is about to share the same fate.* Russia's advance to the border of China would completely give the command of a vast commerce. Now, here is where Russia rules. Everything is sacrificed to her commercial monopoly in favour of her own traders, and it is thought, by advocates of Protection, that Free Trade would be a great disadvantage to the commercial progress of Russia. During the China War of 1841, blue cloth was

* It has since been annexed by the Russians (1880).

16

found at Ningpo, and jackets were actually made from it for our two companies of Artillery. The cloth was marked with Russian marks, but it was suspected to be English cloth!

Let us now proceed with Du Halde, particularly in the matter of the commercial importance of Yun-nan and Sze-Chuen. In the general view of the Empire of China, we learn that the kingdom is called by the western Mongols, *Katay*; by the Man-chew Tartars, *Nikan Kuran*; and by the Chinese, *Chong-qua.* The name in use with Europeans (China) is perhaps derived from that of the first Royal Family, which, carrying their victorious arms westward, "occasioned the country to be called *Tsin* or *Tay-tsin.*" On this point, Du Halde informed us that the Emperor *Tsin Shi-whang's* fleet, which, according to Chinese history, sailed to Bengal, must needs have made known to the *Indians* the name of the *Tsin*, whose power was felt at such a distance; "and that name passing from the *Indies* into *Persia* and *Egypt*, it is highly probable came thence to us about the year 230 before Christ."

The learned Jesuits pay every attention to the geography of the country; and what they consider, "beyond all dispute," the largest and finest "kingdom known to us," receives from them the following distribution of the fifteen provinces into which it is divided:—Those of *Shen-si, Shan-si, Pe-che-li* (in which is Pekin), stretch themselves along the famous wall which on the north divides it from Tartary; *Shan-tong, Kyan-nan, Che-kyang*, and *Fo-kyen*, lie along the *Eastern* Ocean; those of *Quang-tong* (Canton), *Quang-si*, YUN-NAN, and SZE-CHUEN, lie to the south and west; lastly, the provinces *Ho-nan*, *Hu-quang*, *Quey-chew* and *Kiang-si*, take up the middle part. Later geographers give three more provinces, the most important of which to us is Kansuh.

Du Halde, in his preface, alludes to the "curious travels of certain missionaries in China," whose relations prepare us for the description that follows of the fifteen provinces, presenting to our view a great number of splendid cities, celebrated on account of their situation and extent, the multitude of their inhabitants, the extraordinary concourse of the Chinese drawn thither for the sake of trade. There, also, one beholds the produce of fertile lands (which often yield two crops in one year), in corn, trees, and remarkable fruits; metals of all sorts, minerals, and precious marble, dug from the bowels of the mountains; extraordinary plants, whose roots are so wholesome, and thrive in no other climate; numerous lakes and canals, as well as large and deep rivers, which abound with all kinds of fish; stupendous bridges; in a word, "all the advantages which Art and Nature can contribute for the necessaries and pleasures of Life." *

This is really no exaggeration, as has been proved by subsequent travellers and writers. At a time when the scarcity or expense of coal is beginning to create some anxiety in England, it is almost tantalising to read, in the description of Pe-Che-Li, Che-Li, or Li-Pa-Fu, the first and chief province of the whole Empire, that its mountains afford a great deal of pit-coal; this the Chinese burn

* Preface, p. iii.

instead of wood, which is very scarce; and considering how long these mines have supplied the province, one would think them inexhaustible. And, as if to rival the old ladies of Great Britain in their ideas of domestic felicity, these remarks on coal are immediately followed up by the assertion that, " there is a particular sort of cats, with long hair and hanging ears, which the Chinese ladies are very fond of, and rear with a great deal of tenderness."

As there is something about this province which directly affects the others, it may be stated that it is rendered much more considerable by being, as it were, the rendezvous of all the riches of the Empire; and because all the northern and southern provinces strive to outvie each other in furnishing it " with the most rare and delicious things they produce." And, again: The inhabitants are neither so polite nor so much addicted to the sciences as those of the southern parts; but they are much more robust, warlike, and able to undergo the fatigues and hardships of war. The same may be said of all the Chinese inhabiting the northern provinces.

The province of Yun-nan is considered one of the richest of the Empire, and is bounded on one side by the provinces of *Se-chwen* * (or Sze-Chuen), *Quey-chew*, and *Quang-si*; and on the other by *Tibet*, some savage nations little known (then as now), and the kingdoms of *Ava, Pegu*, *Laos*, and *Tong-King*—which kingdoms, the former two especially, have undergone wonderful changes since Du Halde wrote.

* Du Halde also spells the word "Se-chuen"; "Chuen," in Chinese, a smaller river.

The conquest of Pegu by the Burmans, under Alompra (founder of the present dynasty), had not taken place; the mighty "hunter" had not invaded Siam, which his son Shembuan (in 1766), found himself unable permanently to retain; and the Chinese had not yet sent an army of 50,000 men from the western frontier of Yun-nan, which advanced far into the country, where they were hemmed in by the Burmans, the Tartar cavalry no longer venturing out either to procure provisions or to protect convoys, when the Chinese forces were attacked and almost destroyed (A.D. 1767, or 1131 of the Burman era).

Both the kingdoms of Laos (or Lao), and Tong-king (or Tonquin), might with advantage be opened out for the purposes of European and Indian commerce—the former containing excellent timber and valuable mines, and the latter has been reported on as one of the finest countries in the East for population and trade; the inhabitants, in the manufacture of silks and cottons, displaying pre-eminent skill. Du Halde makes no particular allusion to those kingdoms.

The province of Yun-nan contains twenty-one cities of the first rank, and fifty-five towns, and is watered throughout by rivers, whereof several take their rise from considerable lakes in the province, and render it very fruitful The necessaries of life are cheap. The gold that is gathered out of the sand of the rivers and torrents, which descend from the mountains in the western part of the province, amounts to a considerable sum; whence it may be judged that those mountains contain gold-mines, which would produce "immense riches" were they properly opened.

Besides the mines of common copper, found also in other provinces, there are some of a singular kind, named *Pe-tong*, which is white, both within and without. There is also red amber, but no yellow; and Yun-nan contains rubies, sapphires, agates, pearls, and other precious stones; also musk, silk, frankincense, *Lapis Armenus*, and very beautiful marble. "Some of this marble," we are informed, "which is of divers colours, naturally represents mountains, flowers, trees, and rivers, whereof they make tables and other ornaments; some think that the rubies" (and the thought is a very natural one, as Burma is famous for them) "and other precious stones, are brought hither from the kingdom of Ava."

II.

It is considered that the provinces of Yun-nan, Quey-chew, Sze-chuen, and Fo-kyen, are too mountainous to be cultivated sufficiently; but such expressions as "hideous mountains," "almost uninhabitable mountains," in these days of the triumphs of engineering, should not deter those British sons of enterprise who are anxious to open the riches and commerce of the Chinese provinces to the world. It is an undeniable fact that the mountains of China are most valuable, on account of the mines of different metals. Du Halde leads us into the secret of their being so long shut out to the Chinese, and, of course, to the European merchants: "The Chinese say they are full of gold and silver, but that the working of them hitherto has been hindered from some political views—perhaps, that the public tranquillity might not be disturbed by the too great abundance of these metals, which would make the people haughty, and negligent of agriculture."

Such ideas would have done no discredit to Adam Smith, Mr. Mill, or the most philosophical Chancellor of the Exchequer! They are just what might have been expected from a people boasting such a celebrated philosopher as Confucius (Kong-Fû-Tsë). Who can say that if we keep well with and conciliate the Chinese, and sufficiently check Russian progress and influence in parts of the Celestial Empire, that, in another fifty years, the National Debt of our glorious island-home will not fall from us like the burden from the back of Christian?

In Yun-nan, among the animals, one meets with excellent horses, most of them of low stature, but strong and vigorous. There are also curious stags, and golden hens. The people "are very strong and courageous; besides, they are of a mild, affable temper, and fit for the study of the sciences." What a splendid field for the host of public lecturers and would-be instructors of human kind now in England will be afforded if, after we have opened a steady trade with south-west China, they can only be induced to pay a visit to Yun-nan!

The commercial importance of this province, it will now be seen, is very great; and, from Upper Burma, is of course, the best route into south-west China. The three difficulties to be overcome are—first, to get the King of Burma to aid us in every possible way for his own and our benefit; second, to overcome by judicious management and conciliatory behaviour the local prejudices of the people of Yun-nan and the adjacent provinces; and third, to provide sufficient capital for surveys, railways, and light steamers. At present, the probable draw-back to Yun-nan as a trading centre is its sparseness of population. In his description of the province, Du Halde is not very full on the number of inhabitants. In another part of his great work,* however, he gives some valuable general information—as valuable at the present time as it was 140 years ago: The fifteen provinces, into which China is divided, are not equally peopled; for from Pekin to Nan-chang, which is the capital of Kyang-si, the people are not so numerous as in the provinces of Che-kyang, Kyang-nan, Quang-tong, Fo-kyen, and some others, where the great roads as well as cities are so crowded, that it is troublesome to travel; whence the missionaries, who have seen only those fine and populous provinces, have exaggerated the number of inhabitants, which, however, far exceeds that of all Europe put together. Although Pekin stands on more ground than Paris, Du Halde does not believe it contains above three millions of souls; which computation is the more certain, as every head of a family is obliged to give the magistrates an account of the number of persons that compose it, with the age and sex of each.

In short, what was done in Pekin in Du Halde's time, and had been done for many centuries before, is now effected in London by our census-paper for 3½ millions of the modern Babylon! The far-famed Smith and his Mormons should have settled in or near China; for, says

* *Of the Antiquity and Extent of the Chinese Monarchy*, vol. i. p. 240.

the learned Jesuit, several things contribute to make the country so prodigiously populous: as the Chinese being *allowed many wives*; their sobriety and strong constitutions; their contempt for other nations, which prevents their settling, or even travelling abroad (in this respect we all know that a considerable change has taken place); the goodness of the climate, which has been hitherto free from the plague; "and especially the almost perpetual peace which they enjoy" (which they have not enjoyed, however, during portions of the last century, and the present).

In describing the first city of Yun-nan, the capital of the province,* or Yun-nan-su (which has no navigable river), it is stated that the trade for metals is greater here than in any other province. The Chinese, Du Halde quaintly says, make in this city a particular sort of silk named *Tong-hay-twan-tse*, "that is, the *Satin of the Eastern Sea*, without knowing the occasion of this name.' It is made of twisted silk, is not flowered, and without any gloss. They dye it with all sorts of colours, as they do the *Twan-tse*, or common satin; but it appears "neither bright nor lively." We were going to have recommended a ribbon of the above very long name to the attention of the silk-mercers of London, who are often in a difficulty as to the best material and colour for a new ribbon; but this silk being "neither bright nor lively" would hardly suit; still, there is no doubt that the most fastidious young lady or fashionable matron in London or Paris could be suited in Yun-nan.

* A Chinese prince formerly kept his court here; but taking up arms against the Tartars in 1679, his family was ruined.

They also make good carpets in Yun-nan-su. In Du Halde's time, the province had more reputation than wealth; and, what agrees with Sir George Balfour's estimate, the shops were found to be indifferently furnished, the dealers poor, the buildings mean, and the concourse of people not very great, if compared with what is seen in most of the other capitals of provinces. But the whole country (Yun-nan) is agreeable and fertile, consisting partly in little hills, and partly in large plains. The waters are very good, the climate temperate, and the canals give an easy admittance to vessels. Commercially considered, therefore, we should certainly like to see Yun-nan opened to British enterprise; and, whatever the difficulties may be (which would with our customary perseverance be overcome), our possession of Pegu and the Delta of the Irawadi—to say nothing of our growing influence in Chin-India—affords an opportunity for commerce which we never possessed before; we should, therefore, take the tide "at the flood," while it may lead on to fortune. If the Russians once get hold of Yun-nan, or any of the adjacent provinces to Upper Burma, the Golden Foot will certainly be in a fair way of losing his much-loved inheritance of the house of Alompra. The Chinese inhabitants of Yun-nan in Du Halde's time—and they cannot have changed much since—have a smack of the English character about them—are endued with wit and courage, and addicted to arms or agriculture. In the second city, Ta-li-fu, are made tables and other ornaments of that most beautiful marble, "dug out of the mountain *Tyen-sung*; and which is naturally variegated with so many different colours, that one would think the mountains, flowers, trees, and rivers represented thereon were drawn by a skilful painter." In Du Halde's time, Ta-li-fu—built like the capital, on a lake—was very populous; but now, from the recent disturbances caused by the Panthays (Mahomedans), and various local causes, we may safely conclude that the population has seriously diminished, and is inconsiderable. In the fifth city, Chin-kyang-fu, the inhabitants are described as making cotton carpets, "which are much esteemed." The country where the sixth city, King-tong-su, stands, is full of very high mountains, said to contain silver mines. The land produces abundant rice, and the valleys are well watered with brooks and rivers. On the west of this city, the Jesuits found an iron suspension bridge, or bridge "supported by iron chains," the crossing of which must have been a severe trial for the nervous. The sight of the precipices, the agitation of the bridge, while many passengers were on it at once, never failed to terrify those who had not passed over it before.

III.

The tenth city, Ku-tsing-fu, would suit a large class of British lawyers admirably. It is situated in a fruitful country. The inhabitants are very laborious, and improve every inch of land; but they are so "litigious," that they spend "the best part of their effects at law." A good many years ago, the writer of this paper met a friend in London, with a very long and dejected visage. He seemed to be preparing for some journey or voyage. "Where are you going ? " was asked. "To New Zealand,—the lawyers have driven me out of the country," was the reply. But our ruined friend would have gone from the frying-pan into the fire, had he decided on emigrating to such a city as Ku-tsing-fu, in Yun-nan.

The twelfth city, Ko-king-su, is situated in a country producing musk and pine-apples. Most beautiful carpets were made here. Gold is said to be in the mountains, bordering on the country of the *Si-fan*, or territories of the *Lamas*.

The inhabitants of the fourteenth city, Li-kyang-tu-su, and the territory belonging to it, are said to be descended from the ancient colonies of the Chinese, who settled here. The city is surrounded by mountains (separating it from the dominions of the *Lamas*), wherein, doubtless, are gold mines. The whole country is described as well watered and fertile, yielding amber and pine-apples.

The fifteenth city, Ywen-kyang-su, stands on a pretty large river, called *Ho-li-kyang* ("Kyang" river). The country is mountainous, and its plains are watered by several rivers. It furnishes abundance of silk, ebony, and beautiful peacocks.

The sixteenth city, Mong-wha-su, is in a country which furnishes a greater quantity of musk than any other in the whole Empire.

The seventeenth, Yung-chang-fu, is described as a pretty large and populous city, and is situated among mountains, near an extremity of the province, in the neighbourhood of a rather savage people. This would appear to be a country well adapted to hinder the spread of civilisation, which, on the other hand, a steady commercial intercourse would do much to advance. The country furnishes gold, honey, wax, amber, and plenty of good silk.

Yungning-tu-fu is at the end of the province. There is a fine lake on the east side of this eighteenth city, "with four littles islets in it, which appear above water in pretty eminences." The dominions of the *Lamas* nearly skirt this city. Here, as well as in Tibet, the tails of a particular "sort of cows" are utilised to an amazing extent. Stuffs are made of them which are proof against rain; they even form the material for excellent carpets; and "the Chinese officers employ them also in adorning their standards and helmets"

The last, or twenty-first city, San-ta-fu, stands on the borders of the kingdom of Ava, and is described by Du Halde as "properly a fortress to defend the frontiers" The whole country is mountainous; the valleys are well watered with rivers; and the soil is consequently fertile.

We trust that the commercial advantages of Yun-nan have now been sufficiently noted; but, before going to Sze-chuen, it may be remarked that the fifteenth or adjoining province of Quey-chew is a very important one. True, many of its mountains are considered to be inaccessible; but it contained in Du Halde's time numerous forts, and military places; and he tells us that the Chinese emperors, in order to people this province, often sent colonies hither, and even "Governors with their whole families." The mountains afford mines of gold, silver, and mercury; there is also copper to be found. They have no manufactures for silks in this province, but stuffs are made of a certain fibre, resembling hemp, "very fit for summer wear." Here are numbers of cows, hogs, and wild fowl, and—a most important item of knowledge for the enterprising Briton who may hereafter settle in south-west China—"the best horses" in the Empire. The province just mentioned is situated between those of *Hû-quang*, *Sze-chuen*, *Yun-nan*, and *Quang-si*. Let us now turn for a little to Sze-chuen, to which province Sir George Balfour—ever alive to the interests of commerce—was good enough to introduce us.

Sze-chuen, in extent or plenty, is not inferior to any of the other provinces. It is bounded on the north by that of *Shen-si*; on the east by *Hû-quang*; on the south by *Hû-quang* and *Yun-nan*: and on the west by the kingdom of *Tibet*, "and certain neighbouring people." In Du Halde's time, it was divided into ten districts, comprising ten cities of the first rank, and many of the second and third, besides a great number of fortified towns and smaller forts. The great river *Yang-tse-kyang* (Child of the Ocean) runs through the province, which is described as very rich, not only on account of the vast quantity of silk produced, but also in iron, tin, and lead. Here are also amber, sugar-canes, excellent loadstones, and *Lapis Armenus*, the stone of "a very beautiful blue." The horses used to be very much esteemed on account of their being "little, very pretty, and exceedingly swift." Here are also stags, deer, partridges, parrots, "and a sort of hen with wool like that of sheep, instead of feathers." These strange fowl are "very small, have short feet, and are highly esteemed by the Chinese ladies, who keep them for their amusement."* The best rhubarb comes from Sze-chuen. *Fû-lin* is another most efficacious root, which might, with the valuable *Fen-se*, be introduced to British physicians. Chinese physicians are fond of prescribing certain barks and roots in almost *all cases*; from which we may perhaps safely affirm that the medical quacks of our own country have not even the merit of originality about them, but have borrowed from the Chinese. Sze-chuen is far from the sea, and it is difficult to bring salt hither; but wells are dug in the mountains from which they get salt water, which being "evaporated by fire," leaves a salt behind, but not so good as that of the sea.

The first city of this province is styled Ching-tu-fu, the capital, formerly one of the finest cities in the Empire, but was ruined, with the whole province, in 1646, by the civil wars preceding the change in the dynasty. It retains little or nothing of its former splendour, but in Du Halde's time the city was very populous, and of great trade. Now, here is a most important matter for consideration. The territory of *Ching-tu-fu* is the only one that is plain in all the province; it is watered by canals, cut from the *Ta-kyang*, which there is very gentle; but when that river passes out of Sze-chuen into *Hû-quang*, it becomes very dangerous, "as well on account of the rapidity of its stream, as its being encumbered with rocks, which the country is full of."

The situation of the second city, between two small rivers, renders it agreeable and of pretty good trade. The

* Vol. i. p. 111.

Jesuits found the houses to be well built, and the country depending on it as it were "covered with mountains," but still affording no disagreeable prospect, "especially those that are cultivated and covered with forests."

IV.

Shun-king-fu, the third city, stands on a fair river. The country around yields abundance of silk, and oranges of all sorts, also various roots.

The situation of the fourth city, on the banks of the Yang-tse-kyang, renders it, says Du Halde, "a place of great trade as well as note; and opens a communication with several other cities of the province, besides the capital." The country though mountainous, is described as very fertile, wanting nothing for the pleasures or conveniences of life.

Here are, as in India, "Bambû" canes in abundance, which the Chinese put to many more uses than the Hindus.

The fifth city, Chong-king-fu, is described as one of the handsomest and most trading cities in the province. Standing at the confluence of two remarkable rivers, its commerce is facilitated with the whole province of Sze-chuen. One of those rivers is called *Kin-sha-kyang*, or "the river of Golden Sand," which on its way from the province of Yun-nan collects all the waters of the mountains on the side of Tartary; the other, which rises still further beyond the borders of China, is properly the *Ta-kyang*, though it goes by various names according to the place through which it passes. It is also styled the Yangtso-kyang. Chong-king-fu is built on a mountain, and would seem to resemble portions of Torquay in Devonshire, "where the houses seem to rise one above another, in form of an amphitheatre."

The air of the country is considered healthful and temperate. The lands being of vast extent, intermingled with plains and mountains, would seem altogether to form no unseemly temple for Commerce to dwell in, under the auspices of British enterprise. The rivers are filled with good fish and tortoises, the latter being much esteemed.

As the sixth city, Quey-chew-fu, on the great Yang-tse-kyang, appears on entering the province, in Du Halde's time there was, and probably is now, a custom-house for receiving the duties on goods brought thither. The trade of this city rendered it very rich. Although a mountainous country, the industry of the husbandmen has made it very fertile, there not being an inch of land uncultivated. Du Halde quaintly says :—"In the most northerly parts, the mountains, which are very rugged and difficult of ascent, are inhabited by a very clownish sort of people," quite unlike the Chinese commonalty.

The situation of the seventh city, Ma-hu-fu, on the Kin-sha-kyang, in a small territory, but well watered, and very fruitful, is said to procure it the advantages of trade.

Long-ngan-fu, the eighth city of Sze-chuen, was considered in Du Halde's time to be the key of the province. It commanded several forts which were formerly used to defend the country from Tartar invasion. The key could hardly be in a better position than among steep mountains and fertile valleys.

The ninth city, Thun-i-fu, lies on the borders of the province of *Quey-chew*, defending the entrance of it on that side. The country is mountainous, well watered, and fertile.

We now come to the tenth, or last principal city, Tong-chwen-fu, which is styled a military place. It used to be the Chelsea Hospital of China, the inhabitants being old soldiers, who from father to son had been bred up to arms. But, besides their pay, they had lands assigned to them near the cities they inhabited (the other two military cities were *U-mong-tû-fû* and *Chin-hyung-tû-fû*). These troops, as is customary at the present day, were disbanded in time of peace, but to make them amends, they were distributed into all the frontier garrisons of the Empire.

Among the other less important cities in the province of Sze-chuen, is Tong-chwen-chew, whose district is very fruitful, being watered by several rivers. The air is healthy, and the mountains and plains are well cultivated. The country produces abundance of sugar-canes, from which exceedingly good sugar is made. Du Halde also remarks that "very populous boroughs are seen in great number."

There is also Kya-ting-chew, in a territory watered by many rivers, furnishing plenty of rice and musk; and Ya-chew, a city lying nearest Tibet, commanding several forts, and built on the borders of the province. "Forts, or places of war," are stated to be numerous in Sze-chuen; but as our mission, if we went there, would be the peaceful one of commerce, we need hardly trouble ourselves about them at present.

Having now, we trust, said enough to give the British merchant an idea of the commercial importance of Sze-chuen (chiefly from Du Halde), we shall repeat that General Sir George Balfour, who did good service in the China War of 1840–41–42, who has given much attention to Chinese affairs, and who now sits in the House of Commons, very recently evinced a preference for the route from Assam (Sudiya) to Sze-chuen. We then join a part of China singularly free from troubles, a dense population, and great resources in minerals, and very much in want of the tea which Assam can supply. Sir George studied the route from India to China in 1840 to 1846, with the famous Gutzlaff, and having also the advantage of the information of a Chinese officer who had been twenty years in Yun-nan, he came to the conclusion that of all the provinces Sze-chuen was the one of greatest importance. He considered the population of Sze-chuen infinitely greater than that of Yun-nan, but the grand climax of his argument consists in Sze-chuen being close to Sudiya in Assam. Regarding Yun-nan, he thinks that we are worse off for information about that province than for all other parts of China. We trust that the information which has now been culled from the old pages of Du Halde, will do much to supply the deficiency of knowledge regarding Yun-nan. The Russians —fast making way in Central Asia—are already alive to our neighbourhood to the province of Sze-chuen, and there can be no doubt anticipate our entrance into it. If we, therefore, fail to do something in this quarter, the Russians will certainly checkmate us in the political (and, of course, in the commercial) game which the two greatest empires in the world are now playing in Asia. China and Burma, beyond a doubt, have yet to play mighty parts in the history of British commerce. Let us do our utmost to see that we play ours fearlessly and well! Sir George Balfour remarks that the events of the last twenty-five years have not improved Yun-nan. We have already alluded to the once famous city of Ta-li-fu, for many years capital of the Mahomedan provinces of western China. Intelligence from Rangoon in May last informed us that, about January (1873), the city of Ta-li-fu had been taken by a Chinese army, that the Sultan Soliman, who reigned over those countries had poisoned himself, and that the population of the place, without excepting women and children, had been massacred by the conquerors. Thirty thousand persons were reported to have been slaughtered. Such a wholesale massacre had rarely been heard of, even in China. At first we doubted the authenticity of the intelligence, but, after strict inquiry, we are afraid that it is quite true. The Chinese would rather have the Cross than Islam, which they hope to see speedily wither away. Inquiry as to Mahomedans in Sze-chuen, from one of the highest authorities on such matters in this country, produced the following information:—That the province of Sze-chuen is purely Chinese. If there were any Mahomedans within at any time, they were drawn off into the neighbouring province of Yun-nan, when the Mahomedans got the ascendancy there. Our informant had no doubt that the Chinese had captured Talifoo (another spelling of the word), and massacred the inhabitants. If they reconquer the province entirely, it may be for our good, supposing that they will reopen the trade. As the Chinese at present show a disposition to be friendly with us, why should Great Britain not meet them half-way in the pursuit of commerce in the two provinces of Sze-chuen and Yun-nan? With regard to the safety of our Indian Empire, in 1868, we ought not to have allowed the Russians to advance beyond Samarcand. Be this as it may, for the sake of British commerce in the East, let us not remain inactive, and destroy the splendid trade prospects in view with regard to Upper Burma and south-west China!

NOTES.

NOTE I.

The Anglo-Burmese Treaty of 1867; and some of its effects at the present time.

Arms.

1. The grand difficulty in a peaceful settlement of the present unsatisfactory condition of affairs in Upper Burma will, doubtless, consist in making a new treaty.

It is, in a great measure, our own fault that such a state of things should have arisen; but it can even now be at least partially rectified by decision of character and competent statesmanship. On account of the threatening aspect of affairs in Eastern Asia, even if it had never been in contemplation to make a new treaty, the eighth Article of that of 1867 demands serious attention.

It is therein stated that the Burmese Government "shall be allowed permission to purchase arms, ammunition, and war materials generally in British territory, subject only to the consent and approval of the Chief Commissioner of British Burma and Agent to the Governor-General." But it is known to few that the Chief Commissioner, in a separate article, agreed that "as long as we were at peace with Burma, arms, under the treaty, would not be refused." The Government ratified the treaty, and took no notice of this extra or separate article. The king (Mengdon, Theebau's father), then asked for arms, as we were at peace. They were *refused*; seeming very like repudiation, or a breach of faith on our part. Or, it might be said, as to the Treaty of 1867, that we first ratified it, saying not a word about the arms, and then repudiated the arrangement. Had I known these facts—derived from the highest authority—at the time I wrote the conclusion of my work on *Our Burmese Wars, and Relations with Burma*,* ever wishing to write history honestly, I should certainly have mentioned them. However, a detailed history of Burma during the last twenty years remains to be written.

In a telegram from Rangoon (dated 23rd of May 1880), I find, among the principal points in the "treaty submitted by the Burmese Embassy and rejected by us," that of "the Burmese to be allowed to import arms and munitions of war, subject to the approval of the Chief Commissioner, *who must not refuse his consent if friendly relations prevail*."† Here we have the formerly, by us, unnoticed clause or article of the Treaty of 1867 brought up again, at a time when it would be extremely dangerous to allow our aiding the Golden Foot—especially a slippery one like the present—with arms at all. Probably, with the usual Burmese cunning, the diplomatist who brought forward this desired point in a new treaty, wished to see how we would

* See pp. 384-385.

† See *Daily News*, May 24th, 1880.

again treat the all-important question of arms. I have already said* that it would have been better had there been no mention of arms in the Treaty of 1867, leaving the matter entirely to the Chief Commissioner's good-will and discretion, without any written expression to this effect. And, perhaps, I should have added: But if it were absolutely necessary that the question of arms should be brought into the treaty, then it would have been better to have had the emphatic declaration that no purchase, by the King or his agents, of arms, ammunition, and war materials generally would be allowed in British territory, for use in Upper Burma, or to the northward, on any pretext whatever. The prohibition would be absolutely essential in the event of hostilities between Russia and China.

Royal Monopolies.

It will take the Burmese a long time—especially the Golden Foot—to master the principles of Free Trade. But it should be kept in mind that the loss of Pegu and all his ports, partly, if not wholly, caused the monopolizing sentiments of the King. It is simply a matter of, "You have taken nearly all, and I shall keep the rest entirely to myself." In 1855, the King said to the Chief Commissioner: "If a treaty is made, there must be 'mutual advantage,'" foreshadowing the question of "reciprocity" so much discussed of late. As remarked elsewhere,† after 1862, other obstacles to Free Trade arose, the principle of

* *Our Burmese Wars, &c.*, p. 385. † *Ibid.*, p. 380.

which was that nearly every article of produce in Upper Burma was a Royal monoply. Even in 1866, the King would not reduce his frontier duties (although we had abolished ours), nor forego any one of his monopolies. By the Treaty of 1867, true enough, the subjects of the two Governments were allowed "free trade in the import and export of gold and silver bullion between the two countries." * But the principle must be greatly extended for the sake of "mutual advantage" to Upper and Lower Burma. In the treaty of the present year (1880), put forward by the Burmese Embassy, the clause "the petroleum, teak, and rubies monopolies to be continued," is simply a repetition of the first article of the Treaty of 1867, which commences with: "Save and except earth oil, timber, and precious stones, which are hereby reserved as Royal monopolies," &c. With the abolition of all Royal monopolies in Upper Burma, and the probability of a rapidly increasing trade with south-western China, at no very distant period, notwithstanding the vast difference in population, the trade of British Burma will rival that of British India.

Eastern and Western Karennee.

No treaty concluded with Upper Burma would be safe or complete without the acknowledgment of the independence, under our supervision, of eastern, as well as western, Karennee. As stated in my larger work,† the whole of the Karennee country may be considered by us of great political, as well as strategical importance In the event of a

* *Our Burmese Wars, &c.*, p. 384. *Ibid.*, p. 412.

long war between Russia and China, now or hereafter, such positions held by us would be invaluable for the conduct or base of operations, if such were necessary, by the British troops in various portions of Eastern Asia. [On the other hand, although the possession of both Karennees would be convenient, we have no actual right to Eastern.]

The Resident at Mandalay.

After the absence of a British Resident from the capital for so long a period, it is absolutely necessary that one should be appointed without delay, if we would regain the prestige we have (in the opinion of some unavoidably) lost in the country by the withdrawal of that important functionary last year. In the event of King Theebau coming to his senses, and evincing a conciliatory disposition, it might be desirable not only to have a strongly-armed guard for the Resident at Mandalay, but also a small British force, with artillery, near or on the river. Such an arrangement might be entered in any new treaty; and such would be especially valuable as an advanced post at a time when it is impossible to say how long peace may reign in any part of Eastern Asia. The establishment of a Resident by the British Government is provided for by the fifth article of the Treaty of 1867, and has again been recently mentioned by the Burmese Embassy. As, doubtless, the Indian Government have thought, Residencies at Rangoon or Calcutta would be utterly useless. What we want is, if we are not to have the strong hold on Upper Burma which British occupation alone could give, some security for the future good-conduct of the King and the safety and prosperity of his subjects; and, as our next-door neighbour, so much depending on the actions of the Golden Foot with reference to peace and prosperity in Lower, or British, Burma, some effectual guarantee that the extraordinary massacres and vagaries of the past year or two shall not again occur without the severest displeasure, followed by the prompt action, of the British Government.* [With reference to my remark, suggesting a small British force, with artillery, near Mandalay, or on the river, a great authority has written to me that it would be a most pernicious measure, unless we meant to annex.]

Digest of the newly-proposed Treaty.

In order to give full information regarding this important treaty, the re-publication of the following, from the *Daily News*, of the 9th July 1880, will be of good service. The able correspondent at Rangoon, writing towards the middle of June, remarks:—

"I have already sent you the most salient points of the treaty which the Naingangya Woondouk proposed to our Government for adoption. The following is a digest of the entire thing:—

"'1. Sets forth that perpetual friendship is to subsist between the contracting nations. 2. The two Governments are to refrain from any action which might injure each other's interests. 3. Residencies are to be established in

* In addition to our always having ready a sufficiency of troops in Pegu for any emergency, the British Burma ports—especially Maulmain, Bassein, and Akyab—should all be well fortified. We have not yet given sufficient attention to harbour defences.

Mandalay and Rangoon, or Calcutta, as may be arranged, with power to the Burmese to send a Consul to London. 4. Each Resident is to decide law-suits between subjects of his own country according to their own laws. 5. Criminals are to be tried by the judges and according to the laws of the country where the offence has been committed. 6. Extradition clause referring specially to theft, embezzlement, and murder, to be in force. 7. Political offenders against the Burmese Government taking refuge in the British Residency at Mandalay to be delivered up to the Burmese authorities, and *vice versâ*. 8. British subjects are to be allowed full liberty to work mines others than those for precious stones in Burmese territory. 9. Vessels and traders are to be perfectly free to come and go to every part of both countries. 10. They shall be subject, however, to the laws of the country in which they trade. 11. Traders are not to be hindered in carrying on business in either country. 12. Suitable ground for a Residency is to be granted by either Government. 13. Customs authorities may open packages in transit in order to satisfy themselves that the contents are according to declaration. Transit duty shall be one per cent. either way. 14. Most favoured nation clause. 15. *Petroleum, teak, and precious stones* are reserved by the Burmese Government, and may only be worked subject to such royalty as may be determined on. Other goods will be subject to the following duties in Burmese territory:—Opium and spirits, 30 per cent.; provisions, 5 per cent., except paddy and rice, which will be free; all other goods 10 per cent. 16. A tonnage duty to be levied at the rate of 8 annas per ton on all vessels below 150 tons, and 1 anna per ton above that capacity. 17. Vessels are to load and discharge under the orders of the chief authority of the port. 18. The Burmese Government are to be allowed to import arms, ammunition, ships of war, &c., subject to the approval of the Chief Commissioner, who is not to withhold his permission so long as friendly terms are maintained between the two Governments, as provided in Clause 8 of the Treaty of 1867, concluded by Colonel Fytche. 19. The provisions of former treaties are to hold good, except where they are superseded or contradicted by the foregoing.'

"You will see, therefore, that the great Shoe Question is ignored altogether, or, rather, is retained by Clause XIX. The next most objectionable point is that which renews Fytche's treaty, whereby the Burmese were enabled to import as many arms as they liked, and that is a serious matter now-a-days, when Gatling guns are so easily worked, and Martinis make an enemy, that can fire at all, formidable enough for the best troops. The reservations of petroleum, teak, and precious stones really shut up the most valuable products of the country. Finally, the demand that political offenders shall be given up from the British Residency, is a direct charge of illegal action against the late Mr. Shaw for refusing to deliver up the Nyoung Yan and Nyoung Oke Princes."

I shall here remark that when the Burmese Government asked our Government that the dacoits (as the astute Burmans were pleased to term the rebels), who escaped into British territory after a fight, should be arrested, the Government replied that the affair appeared to be a political rising. The Burmese Government again wrote, forwarding some captives' statements that certain of our officials assisted and encouraged the insurgents, "but our Government denied the charge." Utter imbecility was shown by King Theebau during the whole of this rebellion. When the Burmese Government wrote to our Government that a dacoity had been committed near the frontier, and that the offenders had escaped into our territory, they demanded their delivery. The Rangoon Government very properly replied that it was not our custom to deliver up *political offenders*. The Foreign Minister at Mandalay had acknowledged the receipt of a letter regarding the detention of the British steamer at Sillaymyo, and had promised an inquiry and redress.

NOTE II.

French View of Burma.

Early in the year, the Paris *Nouvelle Revûe*, contained an article by M. Voisson on Burma and Tonquin. It was written with something like a better knowledge of our intentions than we have ourselves:—"When the moment arrives, says the author of this article, England intends to place Nyoung Yan on the throne, and thus establish English supremacy in the land. Far from blaming this policy, M. Voisson finds that it is worthy of being followed, and advises France to adopt it in Tonquin. He is of opinion that, as in the interests of commerce and humanity

England is endeavouring to establish her supremacy in Burma, France should also definitively consolidate hers in Tonquin."*

NOTE III.

Pegu Jars.—Nga-pee.

In addition to the manufactures in Pegu alluded to in these pages, the following may be given:—At Jwan-te are made large water or oil jars, glazed outside with a mixture of galena and rice-water, some standing four feet high, commonly known as "Pegu jars," which are used throughout Burma. Again, in a leading "Review," having been accused of saying nothing about Nga-pee—the very smell of which, in a putrid state, was terrible in the last war—the following information, it is to be hoped, will supply the omission:—"Nga-pee is made principally in the Ru-gyee township. It is of two kinds, one called Nga-pee-goung, and the other Toung-tha-nga-pee. Nga-pee-goung again consists of the ordinary Nga-pee-goung, such as is made here, and of Nga-tha-louk Nga-pee, made from the Nga-tha-louk or Hilsa (Clupea palasah). In making the ordinary Nga-pee-goung, the fish are scaled—if large, by hand; if small, by means of a bamboo, with the end made into a kind of stiff brush, and worked amongst a mass thrown together, almost alive, into a wooden mortar, cleaned, and the heads of the large ones cut off."

* Correspondent of the *Standard*, Paris, January 28th, 1880.

They are then well rubbed with salt, and carefully packed into a bamboo basket, and weights placed on the top. Here they are left for a night, the liquid draining away through the basket. Next morning they are taken out, rubbed with salt, and spread out on a mat, and the next day they are put away with alternate layers of salt in large jars, and left in a cool place. In a month the liquid which has come to the top has evaporated, and left a layer of salt, and they are ready for sale. Sometimes the supernatant liquid gets full of maggots before completely drying up; in this case it is taken off and more salt added. It is a great object both to the makers and to the cooks to keep the fish whole. They are eaten roasted, fried, or in curries. In making Toung-tha Nga-pee, which must not be confounded with Bhala-Khyan vel Tsien-tsa (because it can be eaten uncooked) vel Nga-pee-hgnyeng (Arakan), vel Gwai (Tavoy and Mergui), the fish are scaled, and in large fish the head is removed, and the body cut up. They are soaked in brine for a night, taken out and exposed to the sun on a mat till they begin to turn putrid, and then brayed in a mortar with salt and packed away in any receptacle, and kept for two or three months, by which time the paste is fit for sale. This is made into a kind of sauce with other ingredients, and is used as a condiment."

NOTE IV.

Effect of Opium in Burma.—Opium Traffic and Revenue.

In a report issued (end of 1880), it is stated "that the subject of the traffic in opium, and of the effect of the use of the drug upon the people of Burma, engaged the serious attention of the Chief Commissioner during the year, and in May a memorandum on the question by Mr. Aitchison, with the reports of Commissioners and district officers, and the opinions of a large number of persons, native and European, was submitted for the consideration of the Government of India. One point raised was the extent to which the consumption of opium was promoted by the establishment of shops for the sale of the drug, and Commissioners were called on to report on the various shops in their divisions, and to offer recommendations, with reasons for their maintenance or abolition. When all these reports have been received, the number of shops to be kept open for the future will be regulated. The officer of the Prome district says:—

"These shops are centres from which opium is distributed all over the district. The police are powerless to stop, or, in fact, to check the evil. There is reason to believe that the opium license-holders have their agents scattered freely everywhere. These men buy the opium at the shops in large quantities, at a comparatively cheap rate, and take it with them to their villages. To confirmed opium consumers the drug is sold in its crude state; to novices, or to those altogether ignorant of the taste of opium, a preparation called koon-bone is sold or given away. Koon-bone is sliced betel-leaf, steeped in a decoction of opium, and is chewed. It is made up in small packets which are sold at a pice or two a packet, or more frequently, perhaps, given away gratis, especially if the victim be a lad twelve or fourteen years old. Pure opium would probably at first inspire disgust in one so young. His tastes are, therefore, consulted, and he is invited to take the drug in a milder form. Thus he is allured to evil courses, which soon develop into evil habits, the sequel to which is disgrace and ruin.

"The Chief Commissioner admits that if the practices here described are prevalent, a reform of the law is urgently demanded, but he says it is difficult to believe that such deliberate and systematic demoralisation of youth can be carried on to any considerable extent."

On Monday, June 27th, 1881, the opium traffic in British Burma was alluded to in the House of Commons. "The Marquis of Hartington informed Sir W. Lawson that the principal recommendations of the Chief Commissioner of British Burma (Mr. Aitchison), with respect to the opium traffic had been carried out. The number of opium shops had been reduced from sixty-eight to twenty seven; and the rates at which opium was supplied to the farmer, licensed vendor, and medical practitioner have been raised."

Again, on the 4th July, opium came before the House with reference to British Burma.

"The Marquis of Hartington, in answer to Mr. O'Donnell, said it appeared that the recent increase in the revenue of British Burma was greatly due to the increased consumption of opium, and that, the subject having been brought under the notice of the Government, measures were taken to check the consumption, which would involve a sacrifice of revenue to the extent of £50,000 a year. The increased consumption of spirits in Burma and Bengal was attributed in a great measure to the general increase of prosperity, and to some extent to the adoption of the out-stilled liquor system, whereby a weaker spirit was provided. It was believed that there had been no increase of drunkenness in consequence of the adoption of that system."—*Standard*, July 5, 1881.

NOTE V.

Relative Cost of the Afghan and Burmese Wars.

The difficulty in estimating the cost of a war was commented on by the "Iron Duke" (see "Despatches"), and the great commanders before him. The more you face it, the more you get into the mire, where you are stuck fast, o'erclouded by numerous probable, unforeseen expenses. Even when the war is done, not unfrequently there is no satisfactory statement of the cost forthcoming. A large portion of the account is a mere conjecture; and so the best financiers often become sorely puzzled at the result. Of course, it should be less so than ever in an age like the present. Looking over a Parliamentary paper of twenty-two years ago, it is interesting at the present time to scan the "Return of the Total Charge, so far as the same can be estimated, of the Afghan War, the First and Second China Wars, and the Persian War." And next we have, "the estimated cost of the late Rebellion up to the end of the financial year, 1859–60," amounting to the enormous sum of £28,724,814, exclusive of probable excess in compensation for property. It was not practicable from the accounts to form an accurate estimate of the cost of the First Afghan War; but in another return it came out to be, from May 1838 to May 1842, nearly nine millions sterling. With regard to the China wars, the chief expenses of the First were defrayed by Her Majesty's Government; of the Second, no estimate could be rendered; while of the Persian War extraordinary expenses, estimated at £2,195,728, one moiety was chargeable to India. The cost of the Persian is an approximation to that of the Second Burmese War—considering the grand results, the least expensive war in our Eastern history. With reference to the First Afghan War, it may also be stated that the information is highly unsatisfactory. It runs thus:—"The charges of the Afghan War enter into the accounts of many years subsequent to its termination"; and a very large proportion of the expenses was not separated from the ordinary military charges. Notwithstanding the low statement of cost above noted, in the unpublished return, some judges consider that it may have been nearly £20,000,000; about the cost of the recent, or Second Afghan War, which has cost more than the First and Second Burmese Wars put together. At this rate, then, the relative cost of the Afghan and Burmese Wars may be set down at, say, forty millions *versus* eighteen; while the revenues of British Burma have, over and over again, paid all expenses of the conquest. It may satisfy to give a few details. One of the most expensive wars in our Indian history—the First Burmese War—has now been eclipsed by the Second Afghan War—the relative cost being £15,000,000 and £18,000,000 or £20,000,000. The Second Burmese War may be fairly put down at £3,000,000; but, as to the grand result, in comparison with Afghanistan—or putting beside it Burma, with a brighter future before it than any other country in Asia—

"Look here upon this picture, and on this."

The Parliamentary paper, published in the middle of January 1881, from information called for by Lord Hartington, who desired that "the most complete statement as to the expenditure incurred in the Afghan War" should be laid before Parliament, gives the total of an estimate, including the cost of the occupation of Candahar, to the end of March, of a little over eighteen millions sterling! We may safely say about £19,000,000. At a later period the author wrote, with reference to the relative cost, repeating much of what is above stated, but introducing another view of the question:—When we come to think that the last Afghan War, without the slightest prospect of a return, has cost us about £19,000,000 sterling, or considerably more than double the expense of the disastrous Afghan campaigns of from 1838 to 1842 (if we take the lower or unpublished estimate), and four millions more than the extravagant First Burmese War of 1824–26—which gave us the fertile provinces of Arakan and Tenasserim—and about six times the cost of the Second Burmese War, *which was not a million more than half the deficit in the late Afghan estimate*, and which gave us Pegu, " a princess among the provinces," with the other two forming British Burma, with its great commercial port of Rangoon, the future Liverpool or Glasgow of Eastern Asia, which possessions, chiefly through commercial prosperity, have been making many rich, and furnishing during many years millions to the Indian Imperial Exchequer—surely British and Indian statesmen, and, above all, mercantile men, should give unceasing attention to the growing prosperity of Burma. There is no sham in that quarter of the British possessions in Asia. Our success has been, and is, an earnest, living reality!

NOTE VI.

Manufacture of Paper from the Bamboo.

About the middle of last year (1880) the author of this little work had the honour to receive two pamphlets from Mr. Thomas Routledge; the first (1875) on *Bamboo Considered as a Paper-making Material*, actually printed on paper made by its author from bamboo; and the next (1879) on *Bamboo and its Treatment*. It was pleasing for a writer to receive such an acknowledgment of his being ever anxious to aid in developing the resources of Burma; and when the time came, in the present year, for the reading of Sir Arthur Phayre's paper, and it was known that Mr. Routledge would have something valuable to say on the subject of the manufacture of paper from the bamboo, the theme became one of especial interest. About the same time appeared the prospectus of the Allahabad and N.W.P. Paper Mills Company, Limited, when it was thought that "the Government and the Central Government Printing Press at Allahabad would be large consumers of the paper locally produced, thus saving the cost of carriage from Calcutta." To produce whiteness in the paper, through a good bleaching process, has hitherto been the grand difficulty in India. This the Company resolves to do; and Mr. Routledge, in the specimens exhibited at the Society of Arts—to say nothing of his pamphlet—would appear to have nearly conquered the difficulty already. For if good white paper can be made from the bamboo or other materials by him at home, why the same should not be done in India, with a little careful supervision, it is difficult to say. Energy and practical skill will overcome every difficulty, and of these attributes Mr. Routledge has a share possessed by few workers in this rapid, go-ahead age. On the present occasion (13th May) he said "he was very glad to have an opportunity of adding a few remarks to the very interesting and instructive paper, especially as being greatly desirous of utilising some of the present waste products of Burma. For nearly thirty years he had devoted his attention to the utilisation of raw fibres for paper-making, and during the last six or seven years had devoted himself especially to the bamboo omnipresent in Burma as a valuable paper-making material. There were numerous other fibrous plants indigenous to that country, which might be cultivated with advantage, but the bamboo received his special attention, because it grew in almost inexhaustible abundance, in many districts occupying many hundreds of square miles, to the exclusion of all other vegetation, and the facility of its treatment was unexampled. All the other fibres, such as the aloe, the penguin, the plantain (*musa textilis*), &c., required a large amount of manipulation, and, hitherto, no suitable machinery had been devised for the purpose. This created a difficulty in utilising them, because the country being sparsely populated, the labour requisite for treating these fibres, which were chiefly suitable for textiles, could not be obtained. A paper-maker was compelled, from the exigencies of his trade, to be content with the refuse of these fibres, and he feared that the expense of producing them as textiles would, for some years to come, be prohibitive. The bamboo, on the contrary, threw up long shoots every year, almost perennially —for sixty or seventy years at least when once established. All you had to do was to cut them down, pass them into one of those streams with which the country abounded, float them down to the port, crush them, and convert them into rough 'stock' (a sample of which he produced), and there was the material that paper-makers were so much in want of. These bamboos cost nothing but the collection, and though the population was sparse, he believed the difficulty could be got over. Of course the population could not live in the impenetrable jungle, but as it became cleared, the population would follow, provided there were occupation for them. In a small pamphlet, published some time ago, he drew a parallel between the bamboo and asparagus, the main difference beiug that you could only cut asparagus for five or six weeks, while the bamboo season lasted several months. He believed it would ultimately form a good textile material. The Burmese made rope of it: the houses they lived in, the masts, and spars of their vessels, and nearly everything else was formed of bamboo. An important Blue Book had lately been issued by the Government of India, written by Mr. Liotard, of the Agricultural Department, giving a history of the materials suitable for paper-making in India. As he had said, Burma was exceedingly rich in other fibres, as hemp, flax, jute, and the hibiscus tribe; but all these, like the aloe, required to be cultivated, to be cut and dried, then steeped or retted, and then hand-manipulation was needful to prepare them for the market; whereas the bamboo required nothing at all. The process the bamboo underwent was simply to crush the raw stem and boil it, and reduce it to a tow-like condition, when it could be compressed like jute or cotton, and it would then come into the ordinary freightage of those articles—about forty-five cubic feet to the ton. This was done by a process he had patented in India. The bamboo, when dried and in its natural condition, was very hard and intractable, and, with any system of simple crushing, could not be brought into a suitable bulk for freightage, which, after all, was a most important point, as effecting the cost of any raw material, A ton of produce, whatever it might be, should not occupy more than about forty cubic feet as dead weight; but the bamboo, crushed to the utmost possible extent, would occupy ninety-six cubic feet, and if merely crushed in the ordinary way, even under a pressure of two or three tons to the square inch, would occupy 125 cubic feet, and, therefore, it could not come to this country as a raw material without some previous treatment. Treated as he proposed, its cost here would be about the same as the very cheapest material in the market. He was glad to say that he had received the very warmest support from the Indian Government, and he was pleased to have this public opportunity of expressing his acknowledgments to the Chief Commissioner, Mr. Bernard; Dr. Brandis, the Inspector-General of Forests; and Mr. Ribbentrop and Major Seaton, the Forest Conservators, with whom he had been in communication. There were at first some cavillers, but on the whole they were now coming round to his views. He had now a special concession from the Indian Government in Burma, having chosen that province on account of its very favourable climatic conditions, particularly the large amount of rainfall on the coast, which was as much as 160 to 200 inches per annum. In some parts there, rain or showers fell nine months out of the twelve, which was very favourable to the rapid growth of the bamboo. Towards the north there was not so much rain. The soil was a rich loam, and in Arakan there was an abundance of streams, which enabled you to float the stuff down to the port. (He produced samples of the crushed bamboo, 'paper-stock,' 'half-stuff,' and also paper made entirely of bamboo.) Sir Arthur Phayre had referred to the enormous increase in the shipments of rice from Burma, and he might mention that the first shipment, of 3,000 tons was made by his friend Mr. Begbie, in 1855. In 1856, the shipments were 50,000 tons; and by 1860, 80,000 tons; while, last year, they exceeded 800,000 tons. He had tried rice-straw for paper, but it was too costly, and not good enough. For the cultivation of rice in Arakan they had been compelled to introduce labour from Chittagong; but where things would grow to give a profit, labour would follow. In the southernmost parts of the province, he was informed there was an abundance of Chinese labour, and he had no doubt that if sufficient inducement were offered to those industrious people, they would make their way into other districts. Jute, again, showed the same wonderful development as rice. In 1861, the imports did not exceed 27,000 tons; but last year they exceeded 400,000 tons. Esparto had developed just in the same way. In November 1856, a paper was read in that room by Dr. Royle; and the Society's *Journal*, containing the paper, was printed on esparto paper, which he (Mr. Routledge) had then first introduced. In fact, in 1860, he was the only paper-maker using it, whereas now 200,000 tons a year were used. It was now getting very scarce and dear; it had been almost exhausted in Spain; the same thing was occurring in Algeria; and he feared the result of the French interference in Tunis and Tripoli would be to put a protective duty on it from there. Everything, therefore, pointed to the desirability of developing the resources of India and Burma, so that we might be independent of foreign nations."—Where is the intelligent Englishman who will not back Mr. Routledge in such an opinion?

www.ingramcontent.com/pod-product-compliance
Lightning Source LLC
Chambersburg PA
CBHW020503270326
41926CB00008B/722
* 9 7 8 3 3 3 7 2 3 0 1 8 0 *